AutoRacing/USA

1986 THE YEAR IN REVIEW

Editor: Leslie Ann Taylor

Assistant Editor: Susan J. Peacock

Design and Production: C. W. "Chuck" Queener

Results Editor: Janet L. Detzel

Photo Logistics: Isabel Barney

Advertising Sales: Stevenson & Brown, International, Inc.
    Lakeville, Connecticut

Typography by: Words Unlimited, Inc.
    Newark, Delaware

Printed by: Hunter Publishing Company
    Winston-Salem, North Carolina

Published and Distributed by: Enterprise Publishing, Inc.
725 Market Street
Wilmington, Delaware 19801

Cover and title page photo credit: Bill Stahl

Copyright © Enterprise Publishing, Inc., 1987. All rights reserved. No part of this book may be reproduced in any form or by any electronic or mechanical means, including information storage and retrieval systems, without prior written permission from the publisher. ISBN 0-942103-00-9

CONTENTS

Foreword — Don Garlits	4	
Introduction — Leslie Ann Taylor	6	
Commentary — Peter Lyons	13	
WoO/Copenhagen-Skoal Shootout — Joe Scalzo	16	
USAC/CRA Sprint Cars — Joe Scalzo	22	
USAC/Silver Crown	24	
Midgets	25	
SCCA/Bosch VW Super Vee — Marc Sproule	28	
SCCA/ARS	34	
CART/PPG Indy Car World Series — John Zimmermann	36	
Drag Racing — Dave Densmore	64	
Modifieds — Mike Rowell	92	
Super Modifieds — Mike Rowell	97	
DIRT — Keith Waltz	100	
ASA — Jim Howe	102	
ARCA/Permatex Supercar Series — Ron Drager	110	
All Pro — Keith Waltz	114	
NASCAR/Winston Racing Series — Andy Hall	115	
NASCAR/Charlotte-Daytona Dash — Andy Hall	117	
Commentary — Kay Presto	119	
NASCAR/Busch Grand National — Al Pearce	122	
NASCAR/Winston Cup — Randy Hallman	128	
NASCAR/Winston West — Owen Kearns, Jr.	160	
IROC	166	
Formula One	168	
Formula Atlantic — Steve Nickless	170	
Commentary — Brock Yates	173	
SCCA/Bendix Brakes Trans-Am — Bill Mitchell	176	
SCCA/Volkswagen Cup — Bill Mitchell	197	
SCCA/Escort Endurance — Bill Mitchell	200	
SCCA/Firestone Firehawk — Dave Arnold	203	
IMSA/Barber Saab Pro Series	205	
IMSA/Camel GTP — Bill Oursler	208	
IMSA/Camel Lights — Bill Oursler	228	
IMSA/Camel GTO — John Phillips, III	230	
IMSA/Camel GTU — John Phillips, III	236	
IMSA/Kelly AC — J.J. O'Malley	241	
IMSA/Champion Spark Plug Challenge	245	
Off-Road — Tom Blattler	250	
Pikes Peak	254	
SCCA/Pro-Rally — Su Kemper	257	
Track Profiles/1986	261	
Result Charts	264	
Index	270	

AutoRacing/USA 3

Foreword

by Don Garlits

Nineteen-eighty-six will be a year long remembered by my family and myself. It was the year of the introduction of my Super Shops Streamliner which became the first Top Fuel dragster to exceed 270 MPH (272.56) in the quarter mile at Gainesville, Florida, during the NHRA Gatornationals.

Later on in the season at Englishtown, New Jersey, the Super Shops Streamliner gave me the scare of my life — the highest and longest wheelstand ever. I did, however, walk away unhurt due to the fine safety rules of the National Hot Rod Association and, of course, the Grace of God!!

I am very proud to be included in *AutoRacing/USA* and am pleased to see the excellent coverage *AutoRacing/USA* has given to the exciting sport of drag racing.

I hope that all of my fans enjoyed themselves in 1986 at the races.

I feel confident you will enjoy reading Volume IV of *AutoRacing/USA*.

Don Garlits

Photo by Leslie Lovett

These Volkswagens finished first, first, first, and first, respectively.

Maybe we shouldn't be repeating ourselves, but the 1986 racing season was a very successful one for Volkswagen.

Randy Pobst, for example, became the SCCA's first ever Solo Olympics triple-crown winner. He took the G Stock Class in a Jetta, Pro Solo Stock 5 in a Jetta, and Improved Touring Class B in yet another Volkswagen.

At the SCCA National Championship Runoffs, Thomas Van Camp finished first in Showroom Stock C. In a GTI. As a matter of fact, the top five finishers drove GTIs. And the divisional winners at the event, Charlie Hexom, Jarold Boettcher, Peter Hylton, Clint Kimel, Rich Norgarden, and G. Ed Gerkey (representing the Northern Pacific, Midwest, Central, Southeast, Northeast, and Southwest, respectively), drove to victory in a GTI, a GTI, a GTI, a GTI, a GTI, and a GTI, respectively.

Paul Hacker won the IMSA Champion Spark Plug Challenge series (in a Golf) in another Volkswagen-dominated division (Pro Stock). Walter Boyce and co-driver Jimmy Brandt took the Group A title in the SCCA PRO Rally series in a modified GTI. A mid-season entry for the new Scirocco 16V produced two SCCA Escort Endurance series Showroom Stock B victories for drivers Alistair Oag, Peter Schwartzott, and brothers Phil and Bill Pate.

Whew.

If you're a fan of performance driving, we suggest you see your Volkswagen dealer first. If you want to see anybody else's cars, you can always see them second, or third, or fourth. As we often did during the racing season. ©1987 Volkswagen

VW Sport

INTRODUCTION

by Leslie Ann Taylor

THERE IS A SAYING, "THE EXCEPTION PROVES THE RULE." NOW FRANKLY, I'VE NEVER BEEN COMPLETELY CLEAR ON JUST WHAT THIS MEANS. VAGUENESS NOT WITHSTANDING HOWEVER, I THINK THIS PHRASE IS APPLICABLE TO A NEW COLORING ON THE COMPLEXION of today's auto racing.

Reviewing the season through the words of the writers contributing to AUTORACING/USA, it was difficult not to notice the repeated references to the youth of — not just competitors — but winners. Nineteen-year-old Tom Kendall won *two* IMSA Championships — in the same year. Seventeen-year-old Rob Gordon won Off-Road's prestigious Frontier 500. Larry Pearson, who at 33 couldn't be considered dewy-eyed fresh, is nonetheless the youngest driver to win NASCAR's Grand National Championship since the series took to the road. Michael Andretti has had the audacity (and a March) to outdrive his (Lola encased) father on more than one occasion. Al Unser, Jr., at 23, is not only a contender in any given CART race, but the 1986 IROC Champion. Wally Dallenbach, Jr., at the tender age of 22, just captured his *second* SCCA Trans-Am Championship. And on the NHRA Top Fuel scene, young Darrell Gwynn has all *but* beaten Don Garlits on several occasions. . . and there's that exception mentioned earlier.

Garlits, at 54, isn't over the hill but, after all, he did come out of retirement to race again. He not only out-raced the "kids," he also out-teched the new breed while once again winning the NHRA Top Fuel Championship. So it is that we are quite proud to have the exceptional Don "Big Daddy" Garlits provide the foreword of Volume IV of AUTORACING/USA.

There were other trends in 1986 which couldn't be overlooked. On the surface, it would seem that auto racing has never been healthier. The attendance figures keep growing; the manufacturers are in the ring slugging it out to the racers' benefit and the fans' delight; purses keep expanding; cars are safer to race and to crash; talent continues appearing. However, if you care for a carefully considered dose of reality, spend a few moments reading Brock Yates' Commentary. There are few who see the show of auto racing more clearly.

In terms of clarity, seldom is the racing fan provided such clear insight into the mind of a Champion as Randy Hallman provides the readers of AUTORACING/USA. His conversations with Winston Cup Champion Dale Earnhardt explain much of what motivates this two-time Champion.

Have you ever wondered about the motivation of a driver who, having suffered terrible, crippling injuries, climbs back into a race car? Kay Presto, a long-time observer and reporter of the motor sports scene, has seen so many men and women implement the seemingly impossible decision to race again, she finally could no longer contain her curiosity. She asked the question, "What is it that brings injured drivers back to racing?" The report of her search for an answer and the answers themselves are contained in her Commentary and are intriguing reading.

Auto racing joined the other major sports in 1986 in a less than pleasing arena. It, too, was tainted by the dung of the illegal drug business. I suppose it could be considered inevitable. Big money, which auto racing demands and provides, is inexorably entwined with illegal drug trafficking which to some is synonymous with easy money. All levels of the sport have been infected to some degree. The one encouraging aspect to this discouraging tale is the public, vehement, unanimous stand taken against the use of drugs by the stars — and thus the spokesmen — of our sport.

On the positive side, auto racing's arena itself expanded in 1986. If you enjoy the stockers and believe that competition raises the standard of excellence, than you were pleased to learn that there may be a challenger to NASCAR's dominance in that area. The American Speed Association, All Pro and the American-Canadian Tour have joined forces to create the Stock Car Connection. What the trio of sanctioning bodies have connected with is a set of common rules which will be applied to a high-paying, televised six-race schedule for '87.

There was also growth on the open-wheel scene. The American Racing Series, a younger sibling to Indy cars, survived its first season and is set for another go. In addition, the first entry-level series with turbo-powered, technically sophisticated formula cars appeared in the form of the Barber Saab Pro Series. For a racer who aspires to Indy or Monaco, there is now a logical progression of steps in terms of a car which matches developing skills.

In days gone by, a driver whose goal was Indy started in Midgets and progressed to Sprint cars. If all the pieces came together, the driver graduated from Sprinters to Champ cars. After the rear-engine revolution, however, those Sprint car drivers living the nomad's life so they could one day drive Indy were left hanging. Their skills no longer applied to their ultimate goal but they had been racing too long to quit. They were trapped. Then along came Ted Johnson and his World of Outlaws.

Today, sprint car racing is no longer a stepping-stone series. In the guise of the World of Outlaws, it is an end unto itself. The series has it all: cars which are visually exciting, sounding like barely contained thunder; fan loyalty which approaches adulation; incredible, blood-curdling racing. In 1986, with purses totaling $2.75 million, seven drivers earned over $100,000. Series Champion Steve Kinser banked $340,760 in winnings. That's major league money. Joe Scalzo's report of the '86 WoO season provides the details behind the stats with his usual verve and style.

Being involved in racing can be frustrating both as participant and fan. If you're having one of those days, give yourself a break and take a moment to read Pete Lyons Commentary. His tale of the trials and tribulations of motorsports journalism would have improved even Kevin Cogan's mood the day after the Indy 500.

For all racing's gains in 1986, there were several losses which could only be said to be debilitating. TrueSports' Jim Trueman and BMW's Jim Patterson both had a tremendous influence on not only the sport of auto racing, but also the people who were lucky enough to know them. It is a rotten coincidence that both died of cancer during 1986. Alec Ulmann, the man who gave you Sebring, and Lindsey Hopkins, a man who fielded so many Indy cars both died during '86, victims of age. Thank you gentlemen, for your contributions to and love of our sport.

You'll notice a new look to AUTORACING/USA, symbolic, it could be said, of its growth. Nineteen-eighty-six was a year of change for us.

After having provided the unceasing flow of funds needed to change a dream to reality our publisher, Rob McFarlin, had to bow out. Before leaving, he made a prodigious effort to guarantee the continuation of AUTORACING/USA. His efforts culminated in the introduction of Enterprise Publishing to AUTORACING/USA. He's a pretty good matchmaker. Thank you Rob, for all your trust and your work. And to the folks at Enterprise, Ted Nicholas Peterson and Margaret Buchanan, thank you for your enthusiasm and faith in our labors.

So folks, here it is — 1986 in review. The highs and lows, the funny moments and the tragic, they're all here to remember. Enjoy.

THE ROAD WARRIORS.

© 1987 ESPN, Inc. Programming subject to change.

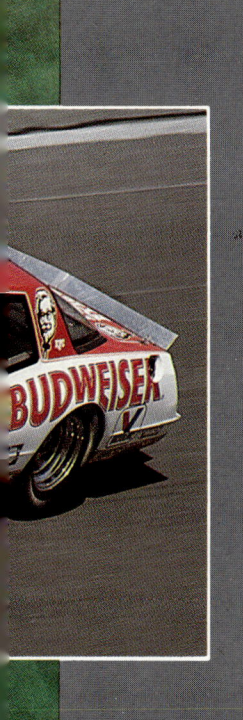

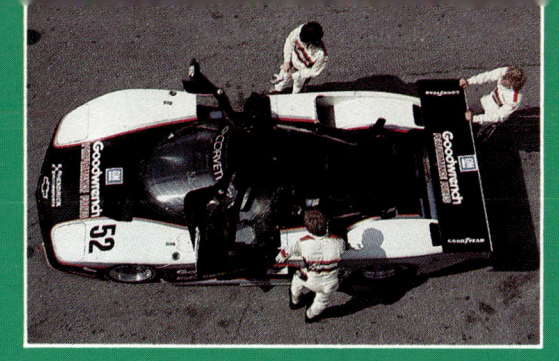

GET READY FOR TELEVISION'S MOST EXTENSIVE AUTO RACING COVERAGE. ONLY ON ESPN.®

<u>1987 AUTO RACING SCHEDULE</u>

3/1	IMSA Grand Prix of Miami
3/28	NASCAR Grand Nationals
3/29	NASCAR TranSouth 500
3/29	F1 Brazilian Grand Prix
4/5	NASCAR First Union 400
4/11	NASCAR Grand Nationals
4/12	NASCAR Valleydale Meats 500
5/2	Indianapolis Motor Speedway Opening Ceremonies
5/2	ARCA 500K
5/3	NASCAR Winston 500
5/3	F1 San Marino Grand Prix
5/17	F1 Belgium Grand Prix
5/25	IMSA GT Series
5/31	CART Milwaukee 200
6/14	CART Portland 200
6/14	F1 Canadian Grand Prix
7/5	F1 French Grand Prix
7/12	F1 British Grand Prix
7/26	F1 German Grand Prix
8/9	NASCAR Winston Cup
8/9	F1 Hungary Grand Prix
8/16	NASCAR Champion Spark Plug 400
8/21	NASCAR Grand Nationals
8/22	NASCAR Busch 500
9/5	NASCAR Southern 500
9/6	American Racing Series: Mid-Ohio Sports Car Course
9/6	F1 Italian Grand Prix
10/3	NASCAR Grand Nationals
10/4	NASCAR Holly Farms 400
10/11	American Racing Series
10/11	CART Laguna Seca 300
10/18	F1 Mexican Grand Prix
11/21	NASCAR Grand Nationals
11/22	NASCAR Atlanta Journal 500

<u>PLUS</u>: Coverage of NHRA, IHRA, Off Road and Rally Racing.

ESPN™
THE TOTAL SPORTS NETWORK®

"THANKS TO YOU, MY LIFE'S A WRECK."

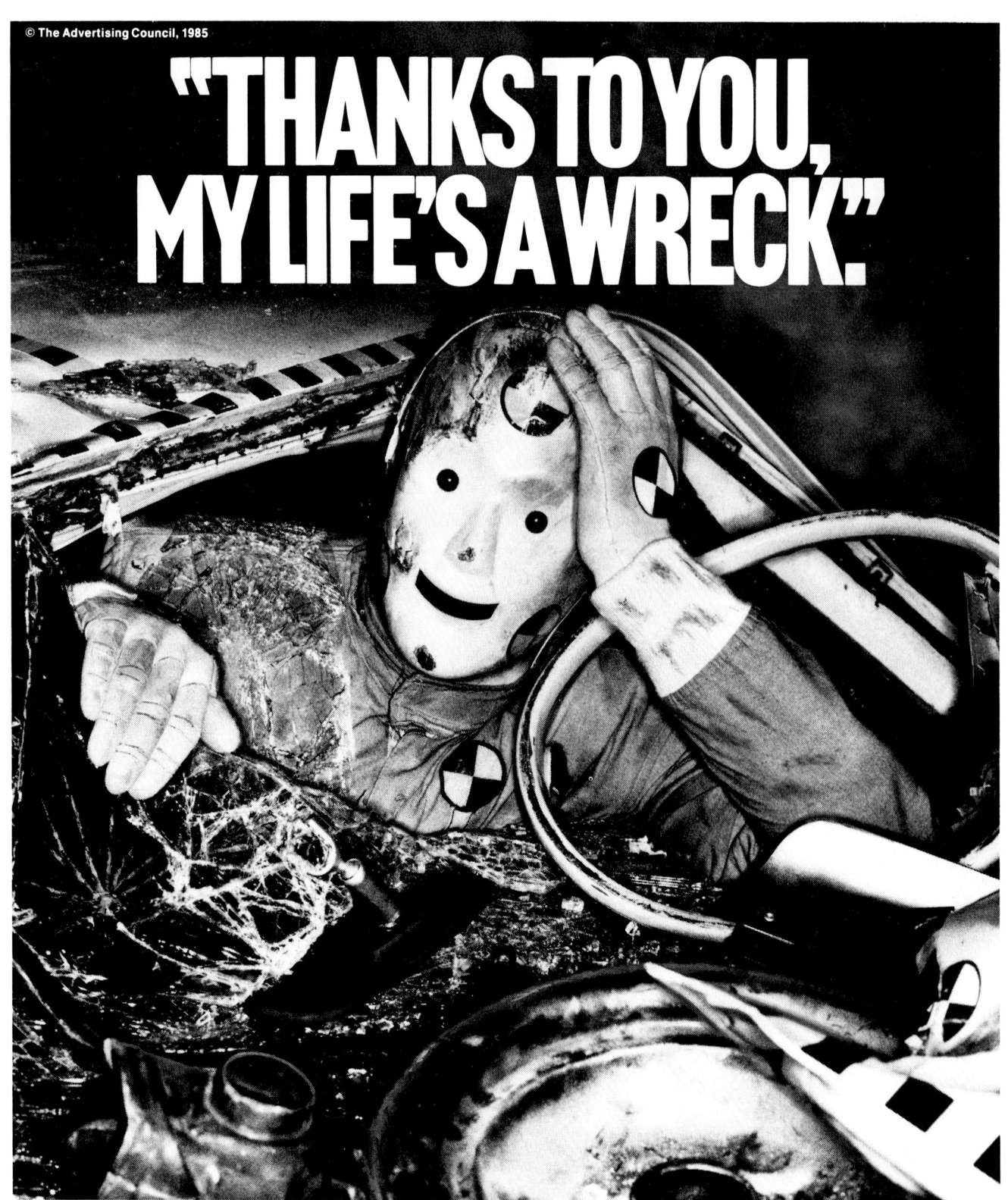

"And it's all because you don't take a couple of seconds to buckle your safety belt. Listen, it doesn't take a genius to figure out that safety belts save lives. So stop destroying my life. Buckle up. Please."

YOU COULD LEARN A LOT FROM A DUMMY. BUCKLE YOUR SAFETY BELT.

A Public Service Message — Ad Council — U.S. Department of Transportation

© The Advertising Council, 1985

THE BEST SEAT IN THE HOUSE.

LEARN TO RACE AT THESE GREAT TRACKS.

Brainerd
Bridgehampton
Firebird (Phoenix)
Hallett
Indianapolis
   Raceway Park
Lime Rock
Mid-Ohio

Moroso
Pocono
Road America
Savannah
Sebring
Summit Point
Waterford Hills
Willow Springs

If you really want to learn to drive a race car, there's only one place to do it—The Skip Barber Racing School.

Our textbooks are state-of-the-art Formula cars, and the emphasis is on driving.

Maybe that's why so many leading CART, IMSA and SCCA professional drivers are Skip Barber graduates.

Call or write for a free brochure. We have a seat waiting for you.

Skip Barber Racing School
Route 7/Bldg. B
Canaan, Conn. 06018
203/824-0771

A HANDFUL OF PROFESSIONAL RACE DRIVERS WILL COMPETE IN CARS POWERED BY THE 1987 SAAB TURBO ENGINE.
THOUSANDS OF DRIVERS WILL GET TO GO TO WORK IN THEM.

Last year, Skip Barber created the Barber-Saab Pro Racing Series as a stepping-stone for talented drivers on their way to Formula 1 or CART competition.

All of the race cars in this series are powered by Saab's 16-valve turbocharged engine. It's the same engine as the one we sell in the Saab 900 Turbo and 9000 Turbo.

Even if you aren't on your way to becoming a top professional driver, you can share the driving excitement of the Saab Turbo. Test drive one soon.

SAAB
The most intelligent cars ever built.

Commentary:
High-tech's Hidden Traumas
by Pete Lyons

"CHILLED BY THE ARCTIC CURRENT CLOSE OFFSHORE, A DEEP CLOAK OF MARINE AIR BRUSHES A WATERCOLOR MIST LOW ABOVE THE TRACK. PERCHED ON ITS HILLTOP ISLAND FROM MONTEREY BAY, LAGUNA SECA IS OFTEN DRY AND HOT IN OCTOBER, BUT TODAY THE sea has overpowered the sun and it is cool here. Racing-jacket cool. The gray daylight dims the colors of the jackets and the tents and the banners, and dulls even the brightest cars. The foreboding sobriety of the scene seems appropriate. Motor racing can look like a game, a happy festival, but the core of the thing is deadly cold, and it is time now for serious work."

With that paragraph done, I thought I was really rolling at last. I wrote it early on Sunday at the 1986 Laguna CART race. I'm not a morning person, nor do I much care for writing in pressboxes, but this time the deadline made me do it.

Deadlines seem to be integral to the word biz. Indeed, I believe few writers have the self-discipline to function without them. I certainly don't. But deadlines seem to have become particularly deadly recently. This time I was reporting the race for *AutoWeek*, the new-look 1986 *AutoWeek* that comes out earlier than ever before. The streamlined publishing schedule has been made possible by portable computers that run word-processing and telecommunications programs (and by the red-eyed dedication of the all-night human staff, of course). Hooray for the readers (and the staff). But consider the plight of the poor race reporters. The previous year we had until mid-morning Monday to hammer our stories out, but with the new schedule, if the Composition Systems typesetting mainframe (a.k.a. "Gort") at Headquarters in Detroit has not started digesting them by Sunday midnight. . .well, Questions Will Be Asked In The House, as the English say.

Note, please, that is midnight in Michigan. From the lefterly time zones the story must be modem-ing its precarious way east by about the hour a civilized reporter is supposed to be supping. So at Laguna I felt it imperative to report as much as I could of the race before it happened. Thus it was that at a thoroughly cheerless hour I found myself slumped over a white-painted plank countertop, coffee and crullers conveniently to hand; not cruising the paddock as I'd have preferred to be doing, but trading blank stares with the glowing, empty screen of my Datavue 25.

At least I had this trusty little portable computer on my side. I was an early and ardent convert to these electronic marvels, because they make the creative process so much faster and more flexible than even the most advanced typewriter. In fact, I, for one, can no longer use a regular typewriter. It'd be like today's race driver trying to express his art in a car with rickety wood-spoke wheels, no front brakes, and a slippery, leather-covered seat. The damned thing simply couldn't do what he's come to expect of a car. No, a good computer can turn a chore to joy. And, not the least of it, owning one makes a reporter feel right in step with the high-tech world of modern auto racing.

Of course, you can get yourself all dressed up electronically and still have no place to go. There I was that chilly morning, set to write, but with not the faintest idea what to write about. Someday there will be a software program — we all dream of it — where you just plug in car numbers and lap times and the story writes itself. Until then we still have to exert a modicum of mental toil.

Dum-di-dum-dum. Cold in here. And so's the coffee, Uhmmm. . .Sure is gray and gloomy out there. Cloud deck hanging down like that. . .say. Maybe there's something I can do with how gray this day is.

It took me, oh, maybe an hour to get my little opening paragraph shaped up, but finally it seemed right. What I had in mind was the Indy-car season coming down to a scant three races with six drivers still in contention for the national Championship, and that more then ever it was now time for hard-core, serious motor racing with no frivolity. My fancy was how the mood in the paddock must therefore match the subdued gray of the sky... I glanced out.

The sky was sparkling blue. The sun had burned the clouds away, and all the banners and buntings billowed brightly in its beams. There wasn't a stitch of heavy clothing visible in the entire raceway. It was a thoroughly festive scene.

Rats.

Obviously, my precious little introductory paragraph found no part in my eventual *AutoWeek* story, which of course, I wound up writing in its entirety *after* the race, and which missed deadline by at least an hour. Closer to two. Mine was not a popular name at Headquarters that long night.

In hindsight, now I suspect that without the trick, high-tech gadgetry, I'd have so dreaded the task before me that I'd have put it off, tackled it finally in a mood of desperate, fearful urgency, and gotten it done nicely by deadline. And instead of wasting my

Commentary: High-tech's Hidden Traumas

morning in the gloomy pressbox, I'd have spent it happily wandering around the racetrack.

I guess I'm not the first to discover that the advent of these magic boxes has been a mixed blessing. Some years ago, in my first flush of computer enthusiasm, a daily newsman warned me of his organization's experience: "Sure, writing is easier on the screen, but that just means you write more. You don't finish any sooner." In the words of the ancient sage, the work expands to fit the time...

And what if you can't get your exquisite creation back out of the computer? It's rare with modern machinery, but it still happens. There you are: It's 29 minutes past deadline, but your story is finally done. . .and the program crashes. Or a diskette takes a dump. Or the power goes off. In the days of typewriters we at least had a piece of paper in our hand, but let's see you pick up an electron.

Or what if the system itself is fine, but you can't get the phone hookup to work? I have reason to fear this. The telecommunications side, to me, is still the blackest art in the business. And it seems to get blacker as I go north.

Do phones operate differently in Canada? Earlier this past season, another *AutoWeek* writer had trouble getting his story back to the magazine from the Toronto CART race. For some reason, the electronic link refused to link, and finally, in sheer desperation, he resorted to dictating it. Boy, does Headquarters hate that. Well, of course I laughed when I heard about it, but I had sympathy, for I'd had to do the same thing the previous year at Montreal. But that was because I hadn't been carrying the right hardware.

The next time I set sail for Sanair with a sack full of stuff, all the connectors in the Radio Shack catalog, odd little gadgets that absolutely guaranteed I could hook up any single phone line with any other. And it was true. I could. I did. And I still couldn't establish a link. Deadline had long since come and gone.

I had one more ace up my crafty sleeve. At home in California was my wife, Lorna, whose own high-tech business has required her to learn all about telecommunications. She was already asleep, but this was a desperate hour. "Honey? Help!"

There *is* something different about Canadian phones, I'm sure of it. No amount of transcontinental advice had any effect. At about 2:00 AM I began dictating.

For some reason, trouble seemed to dog me at Sanair. There's a lot about Quebec and the *Quebecois* I admire, but I'm quite pleased to have that particular race off the schedule for 1987. In '85 I learned not to start writing in the official press room, because somebody'd soon try to lock it up. "Oui, Monsieur, ze race is finish, go home." So this year I set up in the infield auxiliary press "room," which was a barren, unappealing 60-foot house trailer, but where I'd been promised I could stay as long as I wished. Aye, there was the rub. I wasn't five kilobytes into my story before King Kong clambered onto the roof and began stomping around in lead boots, wrenching things off with yanks that shook the entire structure and hammer-blows that would have shattered windows had there been any. Then the electricity went off. Believe me, when your screen goes dead, so does your heart. Sure, I understood: Ze race is finish, time to go home. So I tried to. Lugging two shouldersful of gear, thinking nervously about the Deadline, I hiked all the way across the paddock and down through the tunnel to the outside, where I'd been required to park my rental car. And at the far end of the tunnel I discovered the gate had already been locked.

I've known enthusiasts who've clambered over fences to get *into* a race track, but I'm the only journalist I know who's had to climb one to get out.

This wasn't the only race from which I've had to dictate my report. I used to cover Formula One for the British weekly, *Autosport*, and although this was long before computers, even then I was always alert to Better Ways of Doing It. We normally used air freight in those days, but after Watkins Glen one year, it occurred to me that, rather than scramble to get my typescript to a major airport to put it on a plane to London, I could much more easily and conveniently hand it to a local Western Union office. "Sure thing," said the agent, "we'll transmit it by wire. Be there in minutes." What he didn't tell me was that long messages like mine weren't handled with the urgency of short telegrams. Transmission would indeed take just minutes — once it began. It might begin, oh, Wednesday. But in all innocence, I drove home and went to sleep.

The call came at about 4:00 AM. "Peter! *Autosport* here. Where's your report?" I watched the clock as, phrase by slow phrase, I read them the carbon copy: two hours, 35 minutes.

In Europe, everyone uses a private and personal form of telegram called Telex. Ah, Telex. What a peculiar beast. Terminals are available to the public in many places, including track press rooms, and you can run them yourself, which saves time and money and, hopefully, mistakes. But there is a certain acquired knack in typing on a Telex, or at least there was when last I had to. I found I had to scrupulously avoid watching what I was writing, because there was a lag between my keystroke and the appearance of the character on the paper. I could get four or five keystrokes ahead of the machine, and if I glanced at my story just then, EVERY THI VERYTHING EVERYTHIN WOU ING WOULD LD GET ALLALL SCRAMBLED UP! UP!

Also, Telex offers no lower-case letters, and no underlines, and no way to back up and correct a typo, so you have to trust your editor to mark his copy appropriately before he hands it to the typesetting department. And Telex keyboards in many parts of Europe — I can vouch for Sweden and Germany — transpose the "Y" and the "Z." When you're a tzpist, zour copz can look like a real yoo!

All this, coupled I daresay with my usual pitiless assault on the deadline structure, is why my story about the German Grand Prix of 1975 (I'm sure you remember it well) came out discussing events at the famous "Schwalschenschwanny" corner on the Nurburgring. In German, of course, we call that "*Schwalbenschwanz;*" almost as illegible, but at least more meaningful (swallow's tail).

I've often thought I should write a book about my adventures covering international auto racing. I'd call it, "The Ride of the Schwalschenschwanny."

Truly amazing: No matter how advanced technology gets, it's still so susceptible to random foibles. I remember how excited I was one summer in Europe when I discovered the technology of the telecopier. The Plessey company of England kindly loaned me a machine, which I hauled all the way out to Austria for a trial. There in my little hotel room near the Oesterreichring I pounded out my Grand Prix story on my little typewriter, and then fed the first sheet into the telecopier, turned it on, picked up the phone, made the long-distance call — and noticed that the Austrian telephone handset was too long to fit the two receptor cups on the English-made machine.

But even the good, old-fashioned, mechanical typewriter can play a person false. I used to have a lightweight portable called a Contessa, and she wrote much history under my pounding fingertips, until one sunny Monday morning at an outdoor table at a fine hotel in Monte Carlo she gasped her last. "Sproinggg," she gasped, and gasped no more. Faithless Contessa. I finished that story by hand. Do you have any idea of the cramp that builds up in a writing hand that's not used to it but can't take a break because of The Deadline?

Hell, no technology is foolproof. When it rains you can't take notes with a ballpoint pen, you have to use a pencil. But in my time I've broken the lead in my only pencil, and found I'd forgotten my penknife. Figured it was a good thing, because I was ready to puncture my finger and write in blood.

Come to think of it, I've actually written a (short) note to myself by making impressions in a piece of (soft) wood with a fingernail. I had ten of those, all attached; hard to run out of.

I have another story to illustrate that not even the most human touch is foolproof, though. Ever hear of Stirling Moss? Back when we knew no other way than to physically transport pieces of paper to the magazine office, it was generally considered better to get a cooperative person to hand-carry it, rather than entrust it to air freight. That was the plan at the only Can-Am ever held at Texas World Speedway, which I covered for *Autosport*. Moss, who was on the scene doing promotional work for the series sponsor, was flying back to London that night and kindly agreed to be our courier. It being the last event of the 1969 season, I wanted to do a particularly good story, and I also wanted to get it done early so I could go to the victory banquet.

Well, I did do a particularly good story (I thought), and I did get it done early (by my standards), and on the way to the banquet, I dropped my package off at Stirling's room. I handed it to him, my hand to his hand, personally. I heard him say, "Right, leave it to me!" And I shook his hand in thanks.

It took some weeks for the appropriate copy of *Autosport* to reach me on the road back there in western America, and when it did I was most anxious to see how my story had come out. Quickly I flipped to the "Texas Can-Am" page, and eagerly started reading. But something was wrong. I can remember what I write for years and years, but this didn't seem familiar. Not familiar at all. I glanced back at the byline.

"Edgar J. Beaver," it said. A typical British *nom-de-plume*, meaning, as I eventually discovered, the piece had been written by the staff using information generously contributed at the last possible instant by a colleague at a rival publication. Right: My own story had never arrived. It had been left in Texas. In the Ramada Inn in Bryan, Texas. Room 201. I'd like to think the maid kept it, but I doubt it. And those were the days before I learned to always make a carbon copy.

Ever hear of Stirling Moss? He's the guy who lost my story from the last Can-Am of 1969.

Possibly the single greatest story I've ever written.

Pete Lyons

The 1986 World of Outlaws/Copenhagen-Skoal Shootout Champion Steve Kinser Photo by Dennis Krieger

WoO/Copenhagen-Skoal Shootout

by Joe Scalzo, "Circle Track" Magazine

THE 1986 WORLD OF OUTLAWS (WoO) TOP 10 — STEVE KINSER, BOBBY DAVIS, JR., RON SHUMAN, JIMMY SILLS, MARK KINSER, JAC HAUDENSCHILD, TIM GEE, JEFF SWINDELL, BRAD DOTY, AND BOBBY ALLEN — ARE THE MOST ARDENT SPRINT CAR DRIVERS ALIVE. THEIR 53-race Copenhagen-Skoal tournament lasted nine months and visited 35 dirt tracks. It opened in February in California and Arizona, then swung south into Texas and Oklahoma, went further east to Georgia, and north through Illinois, Iowa, and Indiana. By then it was May, and for the following two months the tour moved east through Pennsylvania, Maryland, and New York, returned to the midwest and Missouri, again dropped south into Texas and Oklahoma, and went north to Iowa and west to Nebraska and Colorado. In July and August it traveled north to South Dakota, Minnesota, Wisconsin, and North Dakota, south to Illinois, Indiana and Iowa, over east to Pennsylvania once more, then west to Ohio, further west to Iowa and Colorado, and finally clear to California for the crucial wrap-up months of September and October (except for one exhausting, last-gasp, return swing across the continent to New York and back for the $142,000 mile track meet on the Syracuse fairgrounds).

Naturally enough, the year was another Steve Kinser year. Other Steve Kinser years have been 1978, 1979, 1980, 1983, 1984, and 1985. For this campaign Kinser won better than $320,000, which was a WoO record. And he won 18 of the 53 races, among them a record-tying fourth Knoxville Nationals and a second Syracuse Nationals. Other wins: two more at Knoxville (Iowa), two at Colorado National Speedway, and at Manzanita (Arizona), Lanier's (Georgia), Granite City (Illinois), I-70 (Missouri), West Fargo (North Dakota), Cedar Lake (Wisconsin), Kokomo (Indiana), Lernerville (Pennsylvania), and Hanford, Chico, and San Jose (all in California).

All his dominance and dollars notwithstanding, Kinser wasn't able to clinch his seventh seasonal point title in nine years until the third-to-last race. This was at San Jose, where he won, and where Bobby Davis, Jr., his tenacious, season-long pursuer who needed to win to remain in contention, finished only third. Bobby Davis, Jr., as WoO insiders say, is a "hammer" driver — he's always got it down. Piloting a sprint car, he has an intense Steve Kinser-Don Branson lean. He also leans forward while walking and even while standing still. As his '86 performance demonstrated, Davis is one of only a few WoO drivers possessing most of the blistering, pulverizing, groove-changing maneuvers and tactics needed to pressure Kinser. But driving so hard for nine months took an increasingly visible toll on Davis. A chain-smoker, he pulled on his cigarettes after each race as if he really *needed* them. And his 23-year-old full head of hair was at times streaked with gray. (Critiquing Davis and other young WoO chauffeurs, one long-time mechanic said all of them still need to learn to do what apparently only Kinser, Sammy Swindell and Doug Wolfgang can: get a sprint car going so fast it goes completely out of control, then bring things back under control again without crashing.)

Good news to Kinser, but a blow to the WoO tourney was that Sammy Swindell was too busy competing in the new American Racing Series (still ambitiously trying to get an Indianapolis career developed) to come to all the races. Swindell missed so many races that he didn't even make it into the top ten point standings. But he made the races he attended hot ones, both for himself *and* Kinser (within the WoO, it's said that the only time Kinser extends himself is when he has Swindell — whom he doesn't like and vice versa — there to inspire and irritate him).

Swindell was especially brilliant on the tour's narrowest and tightest tracks; his red car erupted through traffic with its front wheels moving like flippers in a pin ball game. He won 12 races. But Swindell also experienced a dark July night at Black Hills Speedway he would rather forget. After suffering engine troubles during warm-ups and missing time trials, he and his crew made the engine change in time for Swindell to finish third in the final heat race. The effort, however, caused the replacement engine to,

Steve Kinser, seven-time WoO Champion, won a record-setting $320,000 in '86. Photo by Mary Hodge

WoO/Copenhagen-Skoal Shootout

Ohio's Brad Doty. Photo by Dennis Krieger

Bobby Davis, Jr. with the hammer down. Photo by Mike Arthur

Ron Shuman in the groove at Knoxville. Photo by Dennis Krieger

The intensity of Bobby Davis, Jr.'s season-long pursuit of Steve Kinser never abated yet failed to break Kinser's seeming invincibility. Photo by Dennis Krieger

Ron Shuman, third in points, puts a Bobby Allen tee-shirt to the tire test. Photo by Dennis Krieger

18 AutoRacing/USA

At Black Hills Speedway, Jeff Swindell added a new dimension to the meaning of "brotherly love." Photo by Dennis Krieger

itself, expire. Turning for aid to his younger brother, Jeff, Sammy borrowed Jeff's backup car and won the B Feature. But in the main event the brothers got together in an accident, leaving Sammy bewildered and out of engines and Jeff with two broken cars.

With just about everything known to man in their respective sprint car racing repertoires, Kinser, Sammy Swindell, and Doug Wolfgang are the sort of stars the WoO desperately needs more of. (Wolfgang, still doggedly campaigning as an independent in Pennsylvania, attended even fewer races than Swindell did. But he still won four times, making himself, with Kinser and Swindell, the only driver to capture at least one WoO feature every season since the association was born in 1978.) Unhappily, the WoO's real stars during '86 weren't its drivers but its cars: wedge-nosed, be-winged and with aluminum-block V8 engines which sound ravishingly crisp and in some cases cost $19,000. The emphasis on horsepower isn't surprising, since many of the WoO's most influential car owners, mechanics and builders are hot rodders, recent defectors from the sport of drag racing. Hot rodders love high-tech, speed tricks and, of course, horsepower.

Jac Haudenschild, "whose choirboy face masks an irrepressible will to do audacious things in a Sprint car." Photo by Bob Mays

Jimmy Sills. Photo by Dennis Krieger

Mark Kinser of the Indiana Kinser clan. Photo by Dennis Krieger

AutoRacing/USA 19

WoO/Copenhagen-Skoal Shootout

Jeff Swindell (#91) in Casey Luna's Ford-powered Sprinter goes under Tim Gee at Baylands. Photo by Mike Arthur

A contemplative Bobby Allen. Photo by Dennis Krieger

Brad Doty (#18) goes below Sammy Swindell at Texas' Devils Bowl. Photo by Al Steinberg

Sammy Swindell, perhaps one of Steve Kinser's greatest motivating factors. Photo by Mike Arthur

Doug Wolfgang (#29) and Steve Kinser (#11) set up for a turn at Middletown, New York. Photo by Howard Hodge

Sammy Swindell (#1), Steve Kinser (#11), Jac Haudenschild (#1st), and Bobby Davis, Jr. (#6) comprise the front row of parade lap at Cedar Lake Speedway. Photo by Phil Dullinger

20 AutoRacing/USA

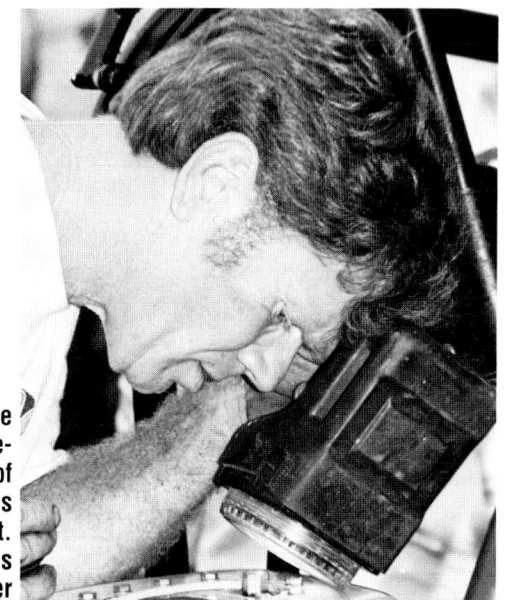

Horsepower is what contemporary aluminum engine sprinters have at least 700 of. Reluctant to limit horsepower — even after cars developed so much of it that they could barely stay on track — the WoO, back in 1982, did something else. It mandated the addition of ugly overhead wings to anchor the cars flat. Wings anchored the cars so well that they got faster; safety, for once, had elicited speed.

Wings haven't as some critics moan, "taken the driver out" of sprint car racing. WoO drivers, in fact, probably are undervalued. Knowing that their overpowered cars have such built-in safety equipment that in a violent tumble they stand no worse chance of serious injury than a stock car driver with a roof over his head, present-day drivers are free to race at an incredible pitch. They take big chances. Schooled in the art of traffic driving, they take most of their big chances in traffic, and that's where the main spectacle of a WoO race lies. Wings, however, have taken the race track out of racing. Winged cars, which can travel just as fast on the top, bottom or middle of a hard-packed dirt track made all 35 WoO tracks look pretty much the same.

Karl Kinser, the behind-the-scenes genius of Steve Kinser's winning effort. Photo by Dennis Krieger

At Baylands, Doug Powell tests the WoO Sprinter's built-in safety features and proves that today's WoO drivers "in a violent tumble...stand no worse chance of serious injury than a stock car driver with a roof over his head." Photo by Mike Arthur

Sammy Swindell (center) put his WoO efforts on a back burner, but when he did come to the races he managed to raise the temperature of the competition, at the very least. Photo by Mike Arthur

The Champion's crown is no protection from the mud-slinging of racing. Steve Kinser's helmet shows the effects of open-wheel dirt competition. Photo by Dennis Krieger

AutoRacing/USA 21

USAC/CRA Sprint Cars

by Joe Scalzo, "Circle Track" Magazine

IN THE MIDWEST THE U.S. AUTO CLUB (USAC) CROWNED STEVE BUTLER THE CHAMPION OF ITS BRIEF, 11-RACE, SEVEN-TRACK, CRESTLINER VAN SERIES. OUT ON THE PACIFIC COAST, THE INCREASINGLY POWERFUL CALIFORNIA RACING ASSOCIATION (CRA) SANCtioned better than 40 non-wing races, most of them at the Los Angeles facility of Ascot Park, and made the 25-year-old Brad Noffsinger its Champion.

The CRA calls itself the oldest sprint car club going. It's also one of the most interesting, partly because of its captivating teams. Three of 1986's were Noffsinger's Jack Gardner team, comprised of all the fathers, sons, brothers, uncles, wives, and mothers of the enormous Gardner clan, whose living and dead members raced at Legion Ascot, were chief mechanics in the Indianapolis 500 and who, as now, insisted on building as well as maintaining their own race cars; the Wirth-Davis team, a combination of a loose-limbed ex-motorcycle racer (Eddie Wirth), and a vigilant, workaholic former drag racer (Steve Davis); and the vaunted Bruce Bromme team, holder of most major win records within the CRA. The racing roots of the Brommes go clear back to grandfather Lou Bromme, who campaigned Indy cars in the thirties, forties and fifties. This year the Brommes went an amazing ten months and 40 races without a victory. First they tried driver Mike Sweeney, then Jeff Heywood, and then John Redican. Almost as a gamble, they finally went to the almost-legendary 45-year-old Bubby Jones, once one of their greatest adversaries. Jones won them their first race in November. And then he got the Brommes a second one in the big season-ending Don Peabody Classic.

Meanwhile, because it's accepted in modern racing that lightweight sprint cars with 700 horespower crash more violently without wings than they do with them, the CRA (and USAC, which has capitulated to wings for 1987) came under fire from WoO people for continuing to promote non-wing racing. Being anti-wing is like being anti-safety and being anti-safety is like being pro-war. Yet the controversial wings don't necessarily seem to be the only or even the best safety weapon available. Another way to make cars safer might be a radical reduction of horsepower (if sprint racing didn't have 700 horsepower engines, it wouldn't need wings and gargantuan tires to harness it). Perhaps what some brave sanctioning body really needs to do is admit that the WoO is unique and quit trying to ape everything it does — like embracing wings, for example. What a hip treat it might be if some association switched to narrow tires and small engines — the coming V6's from Detroit and Dearborn, say — and then carefully manicured its dirt track surfaces to promote and reestablish broadsliding, rim-riding and other exhilarating, almost-forgotten sprint car glories. A man named Jake Bozony was reported attempting to do something like that in Minnesota.

At the wheel of the Jack Gardner Racing Team's Skoal Bandit, Brad Noffsinger dominated the 1986 CRA action, culminating in the series' Championship. Photo by Phil Dullinger

The 1985 runner-up, Steve Butler drove his Phil Poor-owned racer to the 1986 USAC Crestliner Van Series Championship. Photo by Larry Van Sickle

Bobby Kinser, patriarch of the Racing Kinsers, has won over 400 Sprint car races and 26 track Championships in well over 20 years of racing. Photo by Larry Van Sickle

At the wheel of the Genesee Beer wagon, 1985 USAC Sprint Champion Rick Hood navigates the Terre Haute track. Photo by Larry Van Sickle

Eddie Wirth (#77) chases fellow CRA pilot Mike Sweeney around Ascot Park's dirt oval. Photo by Phil Dullinger

Many-time USAC Sprint car Champion Sheldon Kinser (#2) passes Tray House on the high side at Terre Haute. Photo by John Mahoney

Hot lapping Terre Haute, USAC'S winningest Sprint car driver Rich Vogler. Photo by John Mahoney

Warren Mockler (#7) provided additional scope to that now-cliche, "Up close and personal" — fortunately to the misfortune of no one. Photo by Dennis Krieger

AutoRacing/USA 23

USAC/Valvoline Silver Crown

USAC's 1986 Valvoline Silver Crown Champion, Jack Hewitt, in action at the Hoosier 100. Photo by Larry Van Sickle

At the wheel of his Champ Dirt Car, Hewitt won all six of the races he entered in USAC's eight race series. Photo by Dennis Krieger

Once upon a time, there were Champ Cars. And then this simple classification evolved into Champ Cars and Champ Dirt Cars. Finally, one day the Champ Cars became Indy Cars and the Champ Dirt Cars were the only Champ Cars around, just like in the beginning except oh, so very different. Just ask Damon Fortune, the man behind #39. Photo by Larry Van Sickle

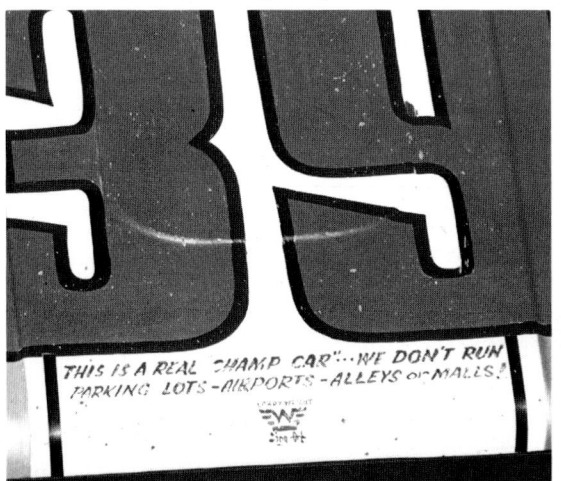

Champ Hewitt (#63) and Gary Bettenhausen duel at the only pavement race in the predominantly dirt series. Photo by John Mahoney

24 AutoRacing/USA

USAC/Jolly Rancher Midgets

The 1986 USAC Jolly Rancher Midget Champion Rich Vogler at Indiana's Winchester Speedway on his way to one of his six '86 wins. Photo by Larry Van Sickle

Mel Kenyon, second in points to Vogler, won two races during the '86 season. Photo by Larry Van Sickle

USAC/Jolly Rancher Midgets

Jack Calabrase, the 1986 WWAR Midget Champion. Photo by Larry Van Sickle

Bob Ciconni (#59) and Steve Knepper (#55) bang wheels during the 1986 Hut 100 Midget Race at Terre Haute. Photo by Larry Van Sickle

Mike Gregg (#98), the many-time Champion of the Rocky Mountain Midget Racing Association, leads the USAC pack through Turn One at Terre Haute. Photo by Larry Van Sickle

Johnny Parsons, Jr., won the season-opener at Memorial Coliseum in Indiana. Photo by Larry Van Sickle

Racing can be a dirty business, especially during hot laps at Terre Haute. Photo by Larry Van Sickle

Warren Mockler, winner of the Turkey Night Midget event at Ascot Park (California) is a triple threat in USAC competition, driving both a Champ Dirt car and a Sprint car as well as a Midget. Photo by Larry Van Sickle

Mack McLellan, winner of the 1986 USAC Regional Midget Championship held in Indianapolis' Speedrome, in action. Photo by Larry Van Sickle

Eric Moore (#79) points the way through Turn One at the Indianapolis Speedrome. Photo by Larry Van Sickle

AutoRacing/USA 27

SCCA/Bosch VW Super Vee
by Marc Sproule

ONE OF THESE YEARS SOMEBODY IS GOING TO COME ALONG AND CHANGE THE TRADITION. UNTIL THEN WE'LL JUST KEEP SEEING THE CHAMPIONSHIP OF THE BOSCH VOLKSWAGEN SUPER VEE SERIES BEING DECIDED IN THE FINAL RACE OF THE SEASON.

For the fourth time in as many seasons, the series title was decided at the season closer, held at the St. Petersburg, Florida street circuit. And this time, the outcome remained undecided until the moment the final checkered was displayed. Separated by only nine points going into the fray, the warriors engaged in this determinative battle were Mike Groff, Didier Theys and Steve Bren.

Theys made the most of the weekend, however, as he qualified on the pole, broke away from the field on two occasions and led every lap. He really didn't have much choice in the matter, though, as Groff held on to finish fourth in the finale. Had Theys not won the race, the crown would have been Groff's.

Bren's challenge for the crown ended early in the race as he smacked a wall in his haste to make up for a disadvantageous seventh qualifying spot. Time spent in the pits to repair the resultant suspenion damage put paid to Bren's run at the title.

Theys' race at St. Petersburg fairly well characterizes the season for the 30-year-old driver from Nivelles, Belgium. Not until the final flag was he able to relax, even though he was the fastest qualifier and a dominant leader until two full course yellows allowed the pack to catch up with him. With less than ten miles left in the season the green came out for the final time and Theys was able to hang on to a half-second margin of victory over series newcomer, Paul Radisich. The 20 points for the win gave Theys the crown by two points over Groff, 155-153.

Theys clearly had the best season of the over 90 drivers who took part in this year's series. He entered 12 of the 13 races, scoring points in each of the 10 he finished. He won five and had six pole positions. In the two races in which he had DNF's he fell out from either first or second place.

As in 1985 when he made eight appearances in the series — including an impressive win at Watkins Glen — Theys was at the wheel of a French-built Martini chassis. His Championship was the first by a driver in a chassis other than a Ralt since 1978 when Bill Alsup won in in an Argo. Ralt chassis picked up the other victories not garnered by Theys and only one other chassis, an Anson in the hands of rookie Johnny O'Connell, was represented in the final top ten in the points.

Groff was the leading Ralt points scorer as he moved up one notch in the standings from his 1985 results. The 25-year-old Southern Californian led the points race after the first five races, with his first win on an oval coming at Milwaukee in the third race. His only two DNF's of the year happened at the midpoint of the season. In the last six races, Groff had nothing less than a top-ten finish, including a somewhat controversial win at Phoenix. (The controversy came from the starter letting the race go too many laps. This was compounded by a scoring question that was answered in Groff's favor, to the chagrin of '85 Series Champ Ken Johnson who ended up second after a fine drive in his first appearance of the year.)

Didier Theys. Photo by Craig Fischer

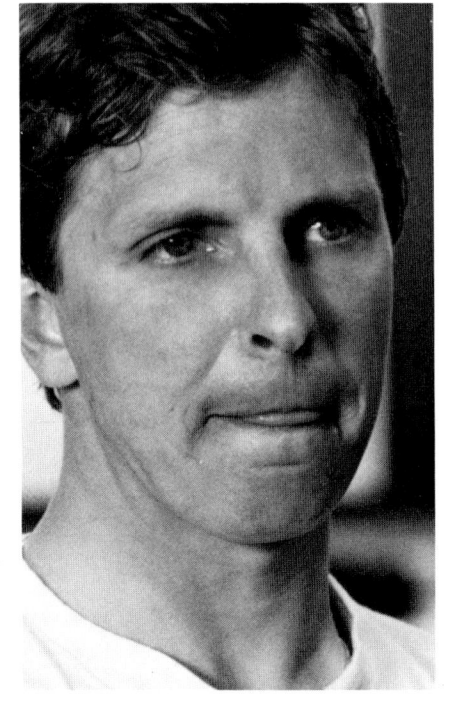

For Steve Bren, the '86 SV series had to be somewhat frustrating, in spite of scoring four pole positions — second only to Theys in that category. Although he won three races, he had another two get away from him. At Milwaukee a late yellow allowed the field to catch up to him. On the restart he got passed by Groff and lost by 0.2-second, the closest margin of victory of the year. At Detroit he was disqualified from the lead for "numerous track infractions." The points from those races would have given him the series crown.

Fourth in the standings went to the series' leading rookie, 1985 SCCA National Formula Ford Champion Scott Atchison. Entered in all 13 races, the 24-year-old Bakersfield, Californian finished in all but two and was in the top 10 in all those finishes. His first and only win came at Detroit after Steve Bren's disqualification. He had two second-place finishes, both of them coming on road circuits.

The Martini racer of 1986 SCCA/Bosch Super Vee Champion Didier Theys. Photo by Al Steinberg

SCCA/Bosch VW Super Vee

Didier Theys ensconced and awaiting the word to go. Photo by Craig Fischer

Steve Bren posted four '86 pole positions and three wins. Photo by Gene Rosintoski

Mike Groff, the leading Ralt driver and, but for two points, series Champion. Photo by Peter Gloede

Cary Bren filled the final spot in the top five. Entering the last 10 races of the season, he posted two DNF's and then had an eight-race string of top-10 finishes. One second and three thirds added to his points total.

The final five places in the top 10 went to Dave Kudrave, Gary Rubio, Thomas Knapp, Dennis Vitolo, and Johnny O'Connell.

Kudrave's record included six top-five finishes and he turned the fastest race lap in the first Road America race. Knapp had the distinction of being the only driver to win two races at the same track as he inherited and kept the lead at both meetings at Road America. O'Connell distinguished himself by having five top-five finishes in the six races he completed. Running a low-budget program in all of the races, O'Connell also had a second at Indianapolis Raceway Park and a third at Milwaukee.

Numerous foreign drivers entered races but only Paul Radisich, from New Zealand, had a top three result. Radisich, experienced in Formula 3 and Atlantic cars, entered the last two races. He finished a fine fifth at Miami after mechanical problems in qualifying forced him to start in the 32nd spot. At St. Petersburg he qualified and finished in the second spot, an impressive performance for the series newcomer.

SCCA/Bosch VW Super Vee

Former Super Vee Champions Ken Johnson ('85) and Bertil Roos ('73) both entered races at the end of the season. As mentioned before, Johnson lost an appeal on the Phoenix race ending up second on the sheet, had a seventh at Miami and a third at the finale.

Roos, who runs a driving school at Pocono and probably has more experience than the top five point getters combined, ran Theys' '85 Martini in the last two races. He placed 11th and 10th respectively in those races.

As we wrote last year there was some concern that the then newly-announced American Racing Series might have an effect on the health of the '86 Super Vee series. As it turned out, there needn't have been much concern. All of the SV races, except the ovals at Indianapolis Raceway Park and Milwaukee, had at least two dozen cars entered. Average subscription for the grids over the 13-race schedule was over 30 cars.

Costs to run a top-flight effort — somewhere between $250,000 to $400,000 per season — are admittedly high. It still appears, however, that with the continuing support of Bosch and Volkswagen, this series will remain the most sensible venue for a young driver trying to make it into the Indy Car ranks.

The series' top rookie, Scott Atchison (#7) leads Ted Prappas (#98) and Fabrizio Barbazza (#12) through a turn at Long Beach. Photo by Craig Fischer

Thomas Knapp conveys a winner's joy at Road America. Photo by Al Steinberg

Davy Jones fills the mirrors of Didier Theys at Long Beach. Photo by Anne Peyton

At the head of the pack, Jeff Andretti (#84) followed by Steve Bren (#43), Mike Groff (#5) and Didier Theys (#30). Photo by Craig Fischer

SCCA/American Racing Series

On his way to the '86 ARS Championship, Italian Fabrizio Barbazza captured three pole positions, five victories, $163,400 in winnings, and a seat in the ARS March Buick for the '87 Indianapolis 500. Barbazza competed in nine events of the ten-race series. Photo by Ron McQueeney

The Arciero Racing Wildcat of the 1986 SCCA American Racing Series Champion Fabrizio Barbazza. Photo by Ron McQueeney

Series runner-up Jeff Andretti garnered three pole positions, one win and completed the most laps in his US Can/STP/Ralph Sanchez Wildcat. Photo by Al Steinberg

34 AutoRacing/USA

A graduate of USAC's dirt tracks and a contender in Super Vee competition, Mike Groff won two ARS races — one oval and one road course event — to finish third in points. Photo by Ken Brown/Competition Photographers

Fifth in the ARS points battle, Juan Manuel Fangio, III, (#10) copes with Jeff Andretti (#85) at Mid-Ohio. Photo by Gene Rosintoski

The power plant for the Wildcat (a modified March Formula 3000 chassis) is the 4.2-liter Buick V6 engine. Photo by Ken Brown/ Competition Photographers

Steve Millen drove his True-Sports Wildcat to victory in the season-opener at Phoenix but found himself without a ride after the death of Jim Trueman. A subsequent seat in the ARS "house car" resulted in a win at Mid-Ohio and an ultimate fourth place standing in the points. Photo by Craig Fischer

AutoRacing/USA 35

CART/PPG Indy Car World Series

by John Zimmermann
Motorsports Editor, "AutoWeek"

THE 1986 CART/PPG INDY CAR WORLD SERIES FACED A FORMIDABLE TASK. IT HAD TO SOMEHOW TOP THE '85 SEASON, A SEASON AWASH WITH THE EMOTIONS THAT AL UNSER'S THIRD NATIONAL CHAMPIONSHIP — WON BY A SINGLE POINT OVER HIS SON, AL JR. — generated. The '86 season proved equal to the challenge. Once again, throughout the campaign, mere handfuls of points separated the half dozen serious threats sitting at the Championship table. Once again, father and son — this time the Andrettis — fought hard at the front of the fields and at the top of the standings. But this time only the son stayed in the title fight to the end.

Again the quest for the crown went down to the final race on the schedule. Again the Champion-to-be would not win the race itself. (Ironically, that went to the son denied the title last year.) Again, the son would lose the Championship. But there the similarities stopped.

Bobby Rahal went to Miami for the season finale prepared to do whatever was required to secure his first Indy Car National Championship. When challenger Michael Andretti ran quickly early on, Rahal hustled to stay ahead of him, and had the Budweiser/TrueSports March closing on runaway leader Roberto Guerrero from second place when Michael pulled off, the STP/Kraco March's transmission drained by an oil leak. After that, the PPG Cup his, Bobby backed off and drove carefully to the finish, helping his crew win the season-long pit crew competition by staying out despite being physically overcome by the relief of his accomplishment. It was a wholly appropriate posthumous honor for team founder Jim Trueman, just as Bobby's record-setting victory at Indianapolis had been fitting final tribute.

While earning the right to wear #1 in '87, Rahal won six races, the first PPG Cup contestant to do so since Rick Mears in 1981, and became the first Indy winner to collect both the season's biggest race and the national title since Johnny Rutherford swept through 1980 with the Chaparral.

But the studious Ohioan did not sweep through 1986. He and Steve Horne's crew worked hard for every break they got, all of TrueSports forced additionally to cope with the ultimate loss of friend, mentor and backer as Trueman finally succumbed to cancer.

As usual, Bobby's season opened dismally. Despite the buoyancy new daughter Michaela brought to his and wife Debi's life, the season's opening pair of races brought only pointless retirements. But then he won the year's third — and most important — race, Indianapolis. The euphoria of the biggest win of his career was, however, genuinely flattened within a fortnight by Trueman's death.

By the Meadowlands, where Bobby was punted out of the lead by Danny Sullivan, the edge had begun to return. At the series' well-played Toronto debut, not even an unusual stop-and-wait penalty for an alleged pace car infraction could keep him from victory. After becoming the latest Indy winner unable to win the Triple Crown 500's, Bobby settled in, logging three wins in succession at Mid-Ohio, Sanair and Michigan. In the midst of this hot streak, the Championship also began to sizzle, with five drivers separated by only five points at the top of the standings!

With six 1986 wins to accompany his two pole positions, the presence of Bobby Rahal in victory circle became a familiar sight. Photo by Werner Fritz

Bobby's sixth win came at Laguna Seca, where he won for the third year in a row. However, young Michael ran third there and then won at Phoenix, so that heading into Miami he trailed Rahal by only three points.

Michael Andretti's season ran in streaks, which meant that several good showings ended prematurely with engine failure. He was, nonetheless, still able to manage an effort sufficiently consistent to carry three wins and only a three-point deficit into the season's decisive race. Maurice Kraines' complete reorganization of his Kraco team around its hungry driver proved the right move. The signing of Barry Green as Crew Chief and Adrian Newey, the designer of the March 86C chassis the team would use, as engineer resulted in Michael completing more laps and more miles than anyone

The Budweiser TrueSports March 86C Cosworth of the 1986 CART/PPG Indy Car World Series Champion, Bobby Rahal. Photo by Werner Fritz

AutoRacing/USA 37

CART/PPG Indy Car World Series

The 1986 CART/Vandervell Rookie of the Year Dominic Dobson drove the Leader Card Racing entry in the series road races, scoring three points in 1986. Photo by Marc Sproule

Danny Sullivan made the points battle a three-way fray until late in the season. Photo by Craig Fischer

except Al Unser, Jr. Further, he led more laps than everyone else, a third more than even Rahal could manage. During the season, 23-year-old Michael firmly established his own identity as a racing driver. Though most assuredly an Andretti, he is no longer "only" Mario's son any more than Al, Jr. is "just" Al Unser's kid.

Al-the-younger's last lap victory in the season finale brought the number of 1986 race winners to eight — including two first time victors. And with three races to go, nine men still held mathematical hope for the Championship, although the number of contenders narrowed first to four and finally to two.

As the season opened its seven-month, 17-race road show with the Dana 200 in the desert on the southwest side of Phoenix, defending PPG Cup Champion Al Unser found himself performing a familiar role — test driver for a brand new car. The Penske PC-15, team designer Alan Jenkins' first complete Indy Car, carried the all-new turbocharged four-cam Chevrolet racing engine that has been produced by Paul Morgan and Mario Illien. The combination qualified a strong seventh, but electrical problems struck as the field rolled off for the start and took Unser immediately out of contention.

Once the race was underway, Michael set about reinforcing his position as a serious threat for the Crown. He'd only just lost the pole to his dad by seven-hundredths-of-a-second, but Mario's eldest son and his blue-and-yellow Kraco March handily led 78 of the 164 race laps they ran before its engine failed. "I won the Phoenix 150," he said of the newly lengthened 200-mile distance. With Michael shrouded by the smoke of defeat in the pits, it was rim-riding Kevin Cogan who staked claim to his first Indy Car triumph.

The blond Californian and his 7-Eleven March had been the match of anyone on the testy tri-oval mile all weekend — anyone but Michael, that is. In the race he escaped an early third turn near-miss with Josele Garza to take a well-deserved and long overdue trip to victory circle, kicking off his relationship with Pat Patrick's team in fine style.

A week later everyone re-assembled on the Long Beach tidelands for the third Indy Car chapter in the Toyota Grand Prix of Long Beach's 12-year history. It was here, as proclaimed by Little Al, that the younger generation took over. Sons of Champion fathers took all three spots on the victory rostrum as Michael rang up his first win, just edging his old pal Al with former teammate Geoff Brabham running third right behind them. The race was sparked by tense combat for the lead in the late laps between Andretti and Unser, which remained unresolved until Michael slipped under the checkered a third-of-a-second before Al.

From Long Beach everyone headed east to Indianapolis, where this year, in addition to record speeds all around, the longest month of the year got even longer. In qualifying, Rick Mears stunned participants and onlookers alike by turning the expansive two-and-a-half mile oval in just under 42 seconds, an

38 AutoRacing/USA

Under the capable leadership of Barry Green, the team of Kraco's Maury Kraines evolved from an "also ran" to an "almost Champion." Photo by Bruce Schulman

Chuck Sprague, the Crew Chief on Sullivan's Miller American Special. Photo by Marc Sproule

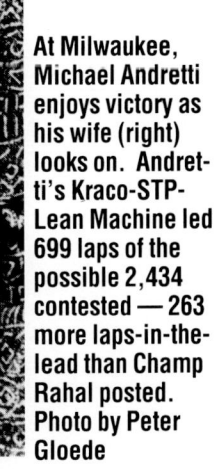

At Milwaukee, Michael Andretti enjoys victory as his wife (right) looks on. Andretti's Kraco-STP-Lean Machine led 699 laps of the possible 2,434 contested — 263 more laps-in-the-lead than Champ Rahal posted. Photo by Peter Gloede

AutoRacing/USA 39

CART/PPG Indy Car World Series

Third in the series through the two poles and two wins posted in his Penske Racing Miller American Special March 86C Cosworth, Danny Sullivan also attempted to race the Miller American Special PC-15 Chevrolet. Photo by Bill Stahl

Series runner-up Michael Andretti scored three poles and three wins in Maury Kraines' Cosworth-powered Kraco-STP-Lean Machine March 86C.
Photo by Rich Chenet

As the field, with Roberto Guerrero on the pole, took the green at Tamiami, the Championship was up for grabs.
Photo by Bill Stahl

CART/PPG Indy Car World Series

The Lola T8600 may not have been a natural winner, but under the direction of Dennis Swan, Crew Chief for Al Unser, Jr., it was a strong contender. The Domino's Pizza entry finished 2,188 laps of a possible 2,434 — a record no one else even approached. Photo by Marc Sproule

astounding one-lap record of 217.581 MPH, with an accompanying four lap mark of 216.828. The *average* for the entire field — an astonishing 210.358 MPH — was well over Tom Sneva's record polewinning speed of just two years ago, and the slowest car in the race would have won the pole in 1982.

But all the speed didn't really help when it came time to run the actual race. The greatest spectacle in racing — this year set for a first-ever live broadcast by ABC-TV — nearly began on time under ominous gray skies, but then the rain started and didn't really let up, turning the infield into a no-man's land of puddles and mud. A second try was made again the next day — with no better luck — and after much discussion and deliberation behind closed doors it was decided to run the race the following Saturday. The day turned out to be picture perfect, but a precious week had been eaten out of the season to follow.

The race itself proved well worthy of the wait. The events of the 70th Indy 500 produced a magnificent show for all, providing true heroics in Victory Lane as winner Rahal's ailing car owner, Jim Trueman, was able finally to savor the kind of success for which he'd worked so long and hard. Likewise for Bobby. What could be the cap on a career for some drivers became just the first link of a Championship chain, since for the first time in his career, Rahal had won a race before mid-season.

The late stages of the contest condensed to a three car tussle

The words of Unser, Jr. (left) are received with less than glee by Johnny Rutherford (center) and Geoff Brabham (right). Photo by Peter Gloede

42 AutoRacing/USA

Driving for Patrick Racing, Kevin Cogan blossomed during 1986, winning the season-opener at Phoenix and, but for a yellow flag with the attendant restart, the Indy 500. Photo by Ken Brown

between old hand Mears, with two Indy wins to supplement his three CART Championships, Rahal and Cogan. The Phoenix winner had brought his top-of-the-groove methods to the Speedway, and with 10 laps to go, held a three-second advantage on the other two. But Kevin's dream began to erode when a wheel failure sent Arie Luyendyk's Lola spinning out of the fourth turn with just seven laps left. The yellow caution period lasted five laps so that when the pace car turned out its lights and headed for the pits, just two tours of the big speedbowl remained with which to decide whose face would go on the Borg-Warner Trophy.

As the field gathered for the restart, Rahal bolted for the impending green earlier than Cogan, and by the time the two cars reached the strip of bricks at start-finish, Bobby's red Budweiser March edged ahead of Kevin's blue-and-white machine. Mears, his Pennzoil March a handful in the turbulence of traffic all day, could only watch and hope for the best.

Clean air ahead of him, Rahal ignored his flashing low-fuel light and surged to a pair of the fastest laps in race history — the final tour at an incredible 209.152 — leaving a devastated Cogan wondering why he wasn't the one rolling into Victory Lane. Instead, Rahal uncorked one of the most emotional scenes the old brickyard had ever see, dedicating his day of days to waning friend Trueman.

Less than a week later the rest of the season got underway as

Once a transporter is emptied of cars and equipment, it becomes a convenient office for the team's engineer. Patrick Racing's Tony Cicale takes advantage of the relative privacy and quiet to calculate and contemplate. Photo by Marc Sproule

Bob Sprow, Crew Chief for Andretti, worked in the midst of a difficult situation with authority and dignity. Photo by Marc Sproule

The two wins posted by Mario Andretti (Portland and Pocono) had to have been especially fulfilling. But the 15 losses had to be a source of frustration for this consummate professional. Photo by Peter Gloede

Roberto Guerrero, in Cotter Racing's True Value March 86C, contends every race but the worst of luck has prevented him from becoming a contender. Photo by Bruce Schulman

AutoRacing/USA 43

Facing the controlled pandemonium of Indy's Victory Circle, Bobby Rahal made a moving moment even more poignant. He said, "This one is for Jim Trueman. I think everybody knows I love him, and this is the one thing I can give him. If anything can repay him for all the things he's done for me over the years, maybe this can."
Photo by Bill Stahl

At Michigan, Rick Mears shattered the closed course record with a pole qualifying speed of 223.401 MPH, a record which stood only a few months until he again took to Michigan's banks. Photo by Bill Stahl

44 AutoRacing/USA

Although Rick Mears contested half the '86 events in Penske Racing's Pennzoil Z-7 Special March 86C Cosworth, the other half were devoted to developing the PC-15 and/or the Chevrolet engine. At Mid-Ohio, the Pennzoil Special was the Chevy-powered March 86C. Photo by Bruce Schulman

CART/PPG Indy Car World Series

the assemblage rolled into Milwaukee for the traditional post-Indy 200-miler. Here young Andretti put his stamp on the proceedings and drove to a handy one lap victory over oval-master Tom Sneva. Newey had Michael's Kracomobile working so well it seemed he might be in another class altogether. Mears ran third for the second time in eight days. The Miller American 200 win installed Michael atop the PPG Cup standings for a 10-week run.

From Wisconsin the teams loaded up and headed west along the Oregon Trail to Portland. Under flawless Father's Day skies Michael's command of the G.I. Joe's 200 looked to be stretching both win streak and point lead — until he ran short of fuel in sight of the checkered. Coasting ever-so-agonizingly toward the line, he could only watch his dad — who's been victimized by similar fate may times — steal the win by a nearly immeasurable 0.07-second, about four inches after 200 miles! It rewrote the record book as the closest finish in Indy Car history.

After the race, the rigs were quickly loaded up again and pointed east, headed for New Jersey's Meadowlands. There, in the shadow of the Big Apple where he had once wheeled a taxicab, Danny Sullivan put a cabbie's move on Rahal with 25 laps to go, shoving the leader out of the way and streaking off to win the Chase Grand Prix. Rahal struggled on to third place with his misaligned chassis, losing second place to Emerson

Galles Racing's Roberto Moreno (here leading Tom Sneva and Rick Mears) showed fine form in his Valvoline Spirit II Lola T8600 Cosworth and was ready to win the re-run at Road America until clipped from behind by Jacques Villeneuve. Photo by Craig Fischer.

A graduate of the road racing ranks, engineer Lee Dykstra worked his magic for Cotter Racing. Photo by Marc Sproule

Crew Chief for Cotter Racing, Phil Casey. Photo by Craig Fischer

46 AutoRacing/USA

Fittipaldi's March in the race's closing moments. Michael, starting from the pole, departed after only 22 laps, a thick plume of white smoke marking his surrender of yet another race lead.

The next weekend, as the nation celebrated Miss Liberty's rejuvenation, the Indy Car teams set up their traveling show along the runways of Cleveland's Burke-Lakefront Airport. Here Sullivan ran his victory string to two with a dominant drive, winning the Budweiser Cleveland Grand Prix by two-thirds of a lap from Michael, with Mario third. Rahal retired just past mid-distance when his engine quit.

After a welcome weekend off, everyone showed up on the grounds of Toronto's Canadian National Exhibition for the first

Tom Sneva had a difficult year, best personified by the Indy 500. There, he began well, qualifying seventh, only to have his efforts go to the dogs with his pace lap crash. Photo by Peter Gloede

Driving the Alex Foods Racing Vermont American March 86C Cosworth, Johnny Rutherford's win at the Michigan 500 was a crowd pleaser. Photo by Bruce Schulman

Geoff Brabham, a driver whose reserve belies his competitve fierceness, coped with the development of a new engine in his Honda-powered Galles Racing Valvoline Spirit Lola T8600. Photo by Peter Gloede

Peter Parrot, Crew Chief for Rick Mears. Photo by Marc Sproule

AutoRacing/USA 47

CART/PPG Indy Car World Series

Rick Mears (left to right), Michael Andretti and the Al Unsers Senior and Junior share a moment of camaraderie before embarking upon 112 laps of competition at Tamiami. Photo by Bill Stahl

Jim Trueman (white hat), Bobby Rahal (center) and Crew Chief Steve Horne confer during Indy's Month of May. Photo by Bruce Schulman

CART/PPG Indy Car World Series

At the wheel of his Schaefer-Machinists' March 85C Cosworth, Garza leads Sneva and Moreno at Long Beach. Photo by Craig Fischer

Brazilian Raul Boesel qualified and ran second for a while at Tamiami as his efforts with Dick Simon's tightly budgeted Duracell Lolas began to draw the kind of recognition his abundant talent deserves. His season total of miles completed trailed only Al, Jr's. and Michael Andretti's. Photo by Marc Sproule

Boesel (#22) goes below Tom Sneva at Pocono. Photo by Ken Brown/Competition Photographers

Molson Indy-Toronto. The race was perhaps the best organized of the year, as not only was the circuit well-conceived and perfectly executed, but its operation was also among the best. Despite all this, the race almost turned into a comic farce as a pace car mix-up nearly stole Rahal's second win of the year. Instead he drove fiercely back from a novel stop-and-wait penalty to sweep into the lead with a dozen laps to go, dumping Sullivan's win streak into second place.

By the time the Michigan 500 rolled around, the teams had run seven races in 10 weeks, at venues from coast to coast, and were pretty nearly worn down by it all. The races showed it, attrition consuming fully 75% of the field by the end.

In qualifying for this second jewel of the Triple Crown, Rick Mears had pushed the frontiers of speed further back than anyone had expected, making the freshly repaved MIS tri-oval the world's fastest speedway with a lap at 223.401 MPH! When the checkered waved, however, it was Johnny Rutherford who saw it first, the Texan and his Vermont American March running with the leaders all day and outlasting them all to record the fifth 500-mile win of his storied career. Josele Garza was reeling Rutherford in at the end, but couldn't get his Machinists' Union March close enough in time and accepted a joyous second place ahead of Pancho Carter in Rick Galles' Coors Light Silver Bullet.

Two weeks later the Andretti family held a happy homecoming at the Pocono 500 as Michael took a record-setting pole, Mario drove his Newman-Haas Lola to a full lap victory in the race to take over the points lead from Michael, and second son Jeff collected the supporting American Racing Series event. Running second to Mario in the 500 was Cogan (therefore winning Domino's Pizza's Triple Crown Award for scoring the most points in the three 500-milers) while Pancho Carter once more took third, this time ahead of A.J. Foyt who scored his best result of the season with fourth place.

The Andrettis: Michael (left), Mario (center) and Jeff (right). Photo by Marc Sproule

50 AutoRacing/USA

Josele Garza took a second at the Michigan 500 and showed he's on the verge of becoming a race winner, even though his season with the Machinists' Union was curtailed by his brutal Mid-Ohio crash. Photo by Marc Sproule

Johnny Parsons started eight races in his Machinists' Union Racing March 86C Cosworth. His best finish was a seventh at Sanair. Photo by Ken Brown/Competition Photographers

Despite fracturing his shoulder at Cleveland and breaking his arm at Pocono — missing a total of six races — Ed Pimm had a promising season with Bob Fernly's closely knit little Skoal-backed team. Photo by Mark Sproule

Rick Galles of Galles Racing. Photo by Marc Sproule

Al Unser, Jr. in for fuel at Long Beach. Photo by Craig Fischer

AutoRacing/USA 51

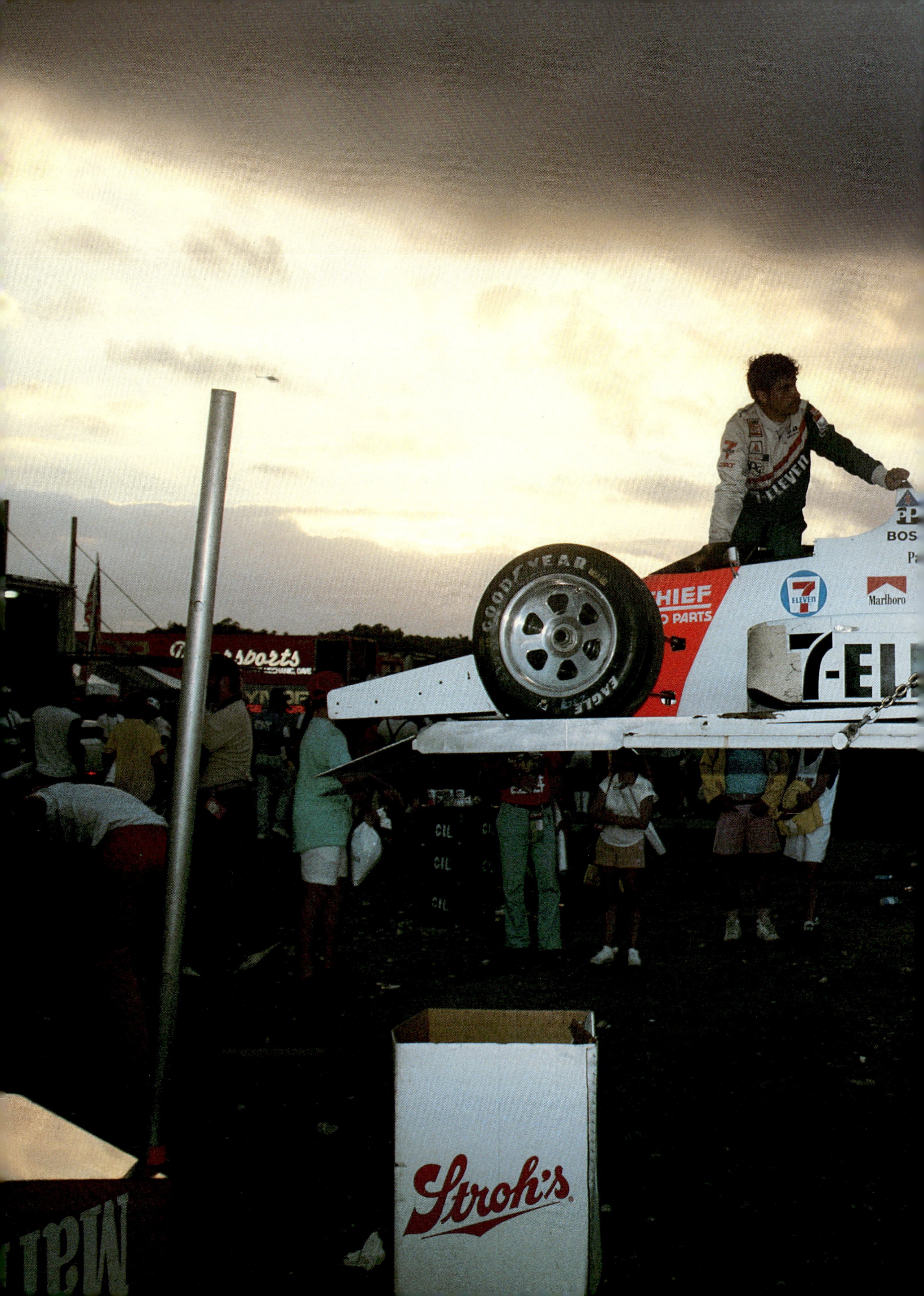

GOODYEAR
EAGLE
7-ELEVEN
Marlboro
Stroh's

It's time to move on. The 7-Eleven March 86C Cosworth of Kevin Cogan makes it back into the truck almost before the day ends. Photo by Bruce Schulman

CART/PPG Indy Car World Series

The Galles Racing Honda CART engine. Photo by Craig Fischer

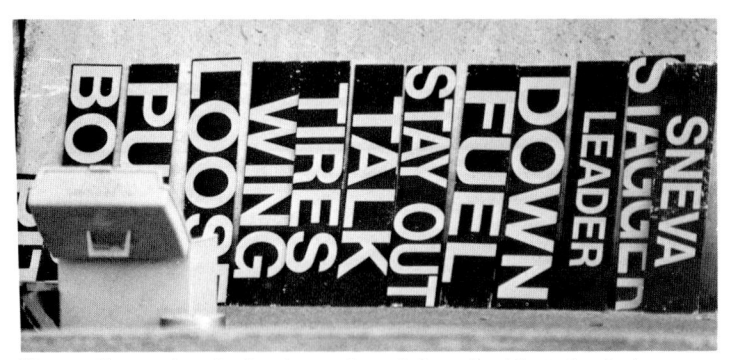

Ah yes, the modern technology of...pit boards. Photo by Craig Fischer

As Michael Andretti approaches his pit at Phoenix, he almost gets rude with Johnny Parsons. Photo by Steve Swope

Labor Day weekend took the series to Mid-Ohio for the Escort Radar Warning 200. Under blazing blue skies Rahal outdueled Sullivan and Guerrero for his third win of the year, Sullivan falling prey to fuel pickup difficulties and the Columbian's late charge cut short by the yellow flag for Josele Garza's devastating crash into the front straight bridge. Happily the talented young Mexican escaped with only a broken leg and a severe shaking, one more testimony to the strength which CART's regulations require of the modern Indy Car.

The next weekend everyone assembled in the eastern townships of Quebec for what would be their final visit to the seven-eighths-mile Sanair Superspeedway in Ste. Pie de Bagot. The hectic little tri-oval's 225-lap farewell program produced another win for Rahal, and another bout with confused officiating.

This time the victim was Al Unser, Jr., hit with a stop-and-wait penalty for "beating" the pace car onto the track during a mid-race yellow. Doug Shierson's driver eventually finished second to Rahal, rightly feeling he'd been robbed of a chance for the win. The race was also notable in that it produced the first pole position for both the new Chevrolet Indy V8 and the Penske PC-15, as Mears, out of the Championship, shouldered development duties for the new engine. In the race Rick was slowed by poor handling and eventually quit when a connecting rod failed. Rahal drove hard, credited with leading the last 137 laps, and moved into a tie for the points lead with the junior Unser. Sullivan sat a single point behind, while just five points out of the lead were both Andrettis. The Championship battle had never been tighter.

From Quebec's eastern townships it was into Wisconsin's fabulous Kettle Moraine country for an unseasonable late mid-September date for the Race For Life 200 at Elkhart Lake's Road America. Consequently, the weekend was drenched with nearly constant rain, and even though Rahal put his TrueSports March on the pole in nearly dry conditions, few held out any hope of a dry race. No one, however, was ready for what really transpired.

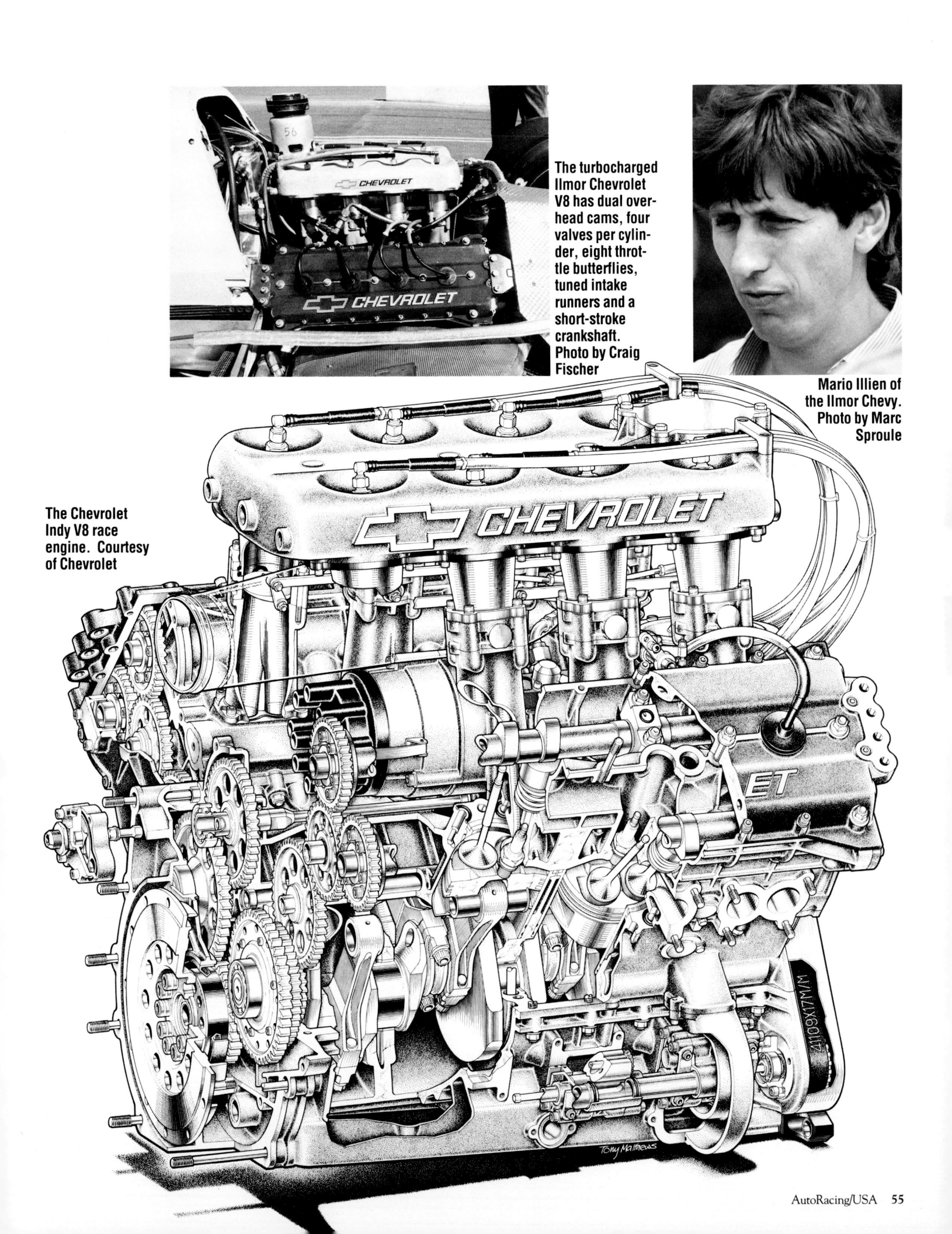

The turbocharged Ilmor Chevrolet V8 has dual overhead cams, four valves per cylinder, eight throttle butterflies, tuned intake runners and a short-stroke crankshaft. Photo by Craig Fischer

Mario Illien of the Ilmor Chevy. Photo by Marc Sproule

The Chevrolet Indy V8 race engine. Courtesy of Chevrolet

AutoRacing/USA 55

Emerson Fittipaldi's understated approach to learning the art of Indy car racing has earned him the position of being a respected contender. Photo by Werner Fritz

Fittipaldi paired his '85 oval win with a road course victory when he successfully tamed the torrents besieging Road America with his Patrick Racing Marlboro March 86C Cosworth. Photo by Ron McQueeney

BUDWEISER NAT'L CHAMPIONS

This year, Budweiser Racing Teams swept the National Championships in Indy car racing, Hydroplane boat racing and Funny Car Drag racing.

The Budweiser Indy car, driven by Bobby Rahal, won the 1986 Indy 500 *and* the 1986 CART PPG Championship.

Miss Budweiser, piloted by Jim Kropfeld, is the winningest entrant in the Unlimited Hydroplane circuit winning her *eighth* National Championship and her second World Championship in '86.

The Budweiser King, with Kenny Bernstein at the wheel, captured the 1986 Funny Car Championship for the second year in a row.

We salute our championship teams for carrying on Budweiser's winning tradition and the racing fans who cheered them on...

THIS BUD'S FOR YOU.

Budweiser

BUDWEISER®•KING OF BEERS®•ANHEUSER-BUSCH, INC.•ST. LOUIS

CART/PPG Indy Car World Series

Provimi Racing's Aat Groenvelt first chose a Lola T8600 for driver Arie Luyendyk but then switched to a March 86C to bear the MCI-Race for Life colors. Photo by Al Steinberg

The skies opened just as the green flag waved, the deluge creating instant puddling at the apexes of several corners and along the back straight. It was in one of these that Al, Jr., looking to gain some positions from the cautious approach of others, spun heavily into the inside guardrail out of the kink at station 11, and the race was red-flagged. Junior suffered a slightly separated shoulder in the crash, and after lengthy appraisals of the conditions and discussions of the upcoming schedule, the decision was made to postpone the race two weeks and run the Pepsi-Cola 250 at Michigan as scheduled in the interim.

Uncommon late September humidity helped to keep lap speeds from approaching those of early August, but Mears gave the Chevy engine — this time in a March chassis — its second pole position with a lap at 219.445. The race featured the kind of howling, multi-pack dicing from which MIS's two-mile high banks are famous, and ended with Rahal besting young Andretti in the pits to carry a three-second advantage across the line. The win, Rahal's fifth, lifted him into a nine-point lead over Michael as the two pulled out some breathing room on Al, Jr., Sullivan and Mario, all of whom failed to finish.

Rick Mears still utilizing two wheels to wander the pits and paddock, enjoys a moment with Mario Andretti and Bobby Rahal. Photo by R.L. Montgomery

Back to Elkhart Lake for the rescheduled race, any hope for blue skies was abandoned, but at least the rain was not as devastatingly heavy as before. After the 50 four-mile laps had been completed, the first man under the checkered was Emerson Fittipaldi, who used every bit of his experience to bring his Marlboro March home a couple of car lengths ahead of Michael, who narrowed Rahal's points advantage to only two with three races to go. Notable in third place was Rick Mears, who recorded the new Ilmor-Chevy engine's first point-scoring finish, while Roberto Guerrero and Rahal filled up the top five.

Next on the schedule came a cross-country haul to the Pacific Ocean environs of lovely Laguna Seca for the Champion Spark Plug 300K. There, although the elder Andretti set a new track record to claim the pole, Rahal dominated the race, leading all but a dozen laps along the way to his sixth victory ahead of Sullivan, Michael and Mario. Bobby's win cut the list of Championship contenders to just that foursome.

Returning to Phoenix for the Circle K Fiesta Bowl 200, Rahal won the pole, but could not hold off Michael, who led 166 of the 200 laps to take nearly a full lap victory over Sullivan, with

A grand total of $25,000 went to the Steve Horne-led Budweiser TrueSports Racing crew as winners of the Dana Pit Crew Award. Photo by Bruce Schulman

Gilmore-Copenhagen teammates A.J. Foyt (#14) and Sprint car magician Sammy Swindell. Photo by Ken Brown/Competition Photographers

Jacques Villeneuve was limited to racing the road courses in Hemelgarn Racing's Living Well Fitness March 86C Cosworth. Photo by Peter Gloede

Danny Sullivan obliging a fan at Pocono. Photo by Ken Brown/Competition Photographers

The 1985 CART Champ, Al Unser, Sr. made only five starts in 1986, mainly in a test driver's mode for Penske Racing. Photo by Marc Sproule

AutoRacing/USA 59

CART/PPG Indy Car World Series

Al Unser, Jr., fourth in points, finally scored a win with his Shierson Racing Domino's Pizza Lola T8600 Cosworth at the last race of the season. Photo by Gene Rosintoski

The wonders of modern technology. First they chilled the fuel and now they warm the tires. Photo by Steve Swope

Fifth in points, Mario Andretti — although hampered, some would say, by his mount — managed to put his Newman-Hass Lola T8600 Cosworth on three poles and in two victory circles. Photo by Paul Webb

CART/PPG Indy Car World Series

Roberto Guerrero attempts to drive his way out of a mighty impact with the Michigan wall. Photos by Bob Brodbeck

62 AutoRacing/USA

Just as the '86 season of Indy 500 Rookie of the Year Randy Lanier came to an abrupt end at Michigan, so his racing effort in toto ended suddenly when he was arrested for alleged drug trafficking. Photos by Bob Brodbeck

Steve Horne (left) and Bobby Rahal, the torch-bearers of Jim Trueman and all for which he stood. Photo by Peter Gloede

Rahal third and Mario fourth. The result eliminated both the Penske and Newman-Haas drivers from the hunt for the PPG Cup, and sent the other pair down to Miami separated by just three points to decide the crown.

Undaunted by the Championship duel swirling about him at the Nissan Indy Challenge, Roberto Guerrero gave his best effort of the year, taking a new record pole position and streaking off to lead every lap of the race — except the one that counted. As Roberto sat helplessly out of fuel in his faltering True Value March, Little Al — up from 19th on the grid — sped exultantly by to pick up his first win of the year and edge Mario by a single marker for fourth place in the points.

Filling out the top 10 point scorers were: Cogan, who had his best season yet and collected his first win along the way; Fittipaldi, who showed that he has comfortably adapted to all the varied aspects of Indy Car racing; Mears, who despite failing to win a race for the first time in nine seasons clearly showed his recovery from those dreadful Sanair injuries is complete; Guerrero, who ran on the pace everywhere once engineer Lee Dykstra joined Dan Cotter's team, but who still suffered from appalling on-track luck; and Sneva, who used consistency to score points during his second straight winless season.

Joining Chevrolet in the ranks of new engines was a Honda V8 which John Judd developed for Geoff Brabham to use with Galles Racing. The engine produced good power and excellent response, which Brabham put to good use, but suffered from a severe shortage of replacement parts and consequently was only a part-time player in Brabham's season.

With its road course radial tire program proceeding trouble-free, Goodyear introduced its superspeedway radials with no problem at Pocono, ran them later on the high banks of Michigan International, and as the season closed, was preparing to debut them at Indianapolis in 1987.

Also preparing for an entry into Indy Car racing were Ferrari and Porsche, the legendary Italian and German car builders both wanting to tackle the premier racing series in the country of their largest markets, as well as try for that all-important victory at Indy.

The 1986 CART/PPG Indy Car World Series proved worthy of its heritage, offering crisp competition at every venue that only enriched the experience for all involved, whether participant or fan. More of the same seems in store for 1987.

To the victor and runners-up goes the privilege of spraying the champagne — a driver's revenge on the media. Celebrating at Road America, Rick Mears (left), Emerson Fittipaldi (center) and Michael Andretti. Photo by Peter Gloede

Drag Racing

by Dave Densmore

FOR THOSE WHO HAVE FOLLOWED WITH KEEN INTEREST THE CAREER OF ONE DONALD GLEN GARLITS, A SEMI-BIOGRAPHICAL MOVIE PRESENTLY IN DEVELOPMENT MAY PROVE TO BE A DISAPPOINTMENT. FOR, IF THE TRUTH BE KNOWN, THERE SEEMS TO BE NO way in which it could do justice to the reality of one of the most eccentric and exceptional individuals in sport. In the case of "Big Daddy" Don Garlits, the 54-year-old patriarch of Top Fuel drag racing, truth is indeed stranger than fiction.

Nevertheless, the movie, which has become something of a Garlits obsession since the release of the Shirley Muldowney film, "Heart Like A Wheel," may have a direct bearing on the venerable one's bid to become the first driver to reach 280 miles per hour in a quarter mile. That's because Garlits and Crew Chief Herb Parks are committed to the construction of 12 cars for use in filming and that is almost certain to delay development of the Super Shops streamliner in which the sport's best known personality will pursue an unprecedented third Winston World Championship in 1987.

The car, to be built — as usual — from an original Garlits' design, is said by Parks to make the '86 model "Swamp Rat" look like a Model T Ford. That would be remarkable considering the fact that the car Garlits debuted in the second race of 1986 was so revolutionary there wasn't a production tire available for it.

With the surprising indulgence of the usually hard-line National Hot Rod Association (NHRA), the only sanctioning body to contest a series for Top Fuel dragsters in '85 and '86, Garlits first used industrial engine belts as substitutes. Despite claims that they had been tested to 300 MPH in Garlits' Ocala, Florida shop, the belts proved exceedingly ineffective. For one thing, they tended to separate from the wheels at high speed and, even when they were molded to the wheel frames and secured with studs, they were poor alternatives to Goodyear rubber. Finally, in cooperation with the Akron tire giant, Garlits was able to adapt an aircraft tire to fit the 13-inch rims on the "bullet nose" machine designated "Swamp Rat #30" by its builder.

In its first race — the NHRA Gatornationals at Gainesville, Florida — the new design carried its creator to a convincing victory that included the sport's first 270 MPH quarter mile. That performance was something of a surprise in that Garlits had announced before the first round that he would not push the car to its limits until he had a chance to develop an acceptable solution to the tire problem.

That plan went by the board, however, when former National Football League quarterback Dan Pastorini, in his first full season on the pro tour, pressed the issue. Pastorini, who had beaten a comeback-ing Muldowney in round one and veteran Chris Karamesines in round two, stayed with Garlits till half track

That was something "The Old Man" had not anticipated. His response was to put the hammer down — and hold on. The result was a best of the event 5.409-second time at an incredible 272.56 MPH. That performance propelled the Auto Racing All American to the first of five '86 victories although both his reign and his design would become subject to challenge by year's end.

The 1986 NHRA Winston World Top Fuel Champion Don Garlits. Photo by Leslie Lovett

Garlits' confident prediction that his "bullet nose" design and canopied driver's compartment would become the standard before season's end proved somewhat premature — especially after 25-year-old Darrell Gwynn raised the performance ante in a dragster of conventional configuration.

Gwynn, the 1982 World Champion in the Top Alcohol Dragster category, had won the season-opening Winternationals at Pomona, California, but quickly lost the momentum when his family-run-and-financed team exhausted its resources in a series of mechanical failures. On the verge of having to park his racer, the Miami, Florida, pro got a boost from an unexpected source when Dale Armstrong, Crew Chief to reigning World Funny Car Champion Kenny Bernstein, offered to help the Gwynns sort out their engine woes.

At the NHRA Grandnational at

64 AutoRacing/USA

During the Summernationals, it seemed Garlits was about to become a memory when, "Like a drawbridge, the car rose until, balanced only on the rear wheels, it appeared on the verge of falling over backward. Instead, it executed a pirouette worthy of Baryshnikov and came back to earth, engine still lit, tires smoking, pointed directly at the starting line."

Photos by Leslie Lovett

Photos by Jon Graves

Drag Racing

Montreal, the first race in which Armstrong served as the team's unofficial consultant, Gwynn qualified number one and beat Dick LaHaie of Lansing, Michigan, for the title. Two weeks later, at the Budweiser Summernationals at Englishtown, New Jersey, Gwynn stunned everyone by pushing his privateer to 272.39 MPH without benefit of the aerodynamics which formed the cornerstone of Garlits' "new breed" concept.

In response, Garlits first argued the legitimacy of the speed, then put his streamliner ahead of the pack at 5.343 seconds, at the time the quickest clocking in history. However, his hope of winning world record certification of that time (by completing an NHRA-required back-up within one percent) evaporated on the final qualifying day when, running alongside Gwynn, he was involved in what could have been a catastrophic incident.

As the 25-foot-long missile left the starting line, the rear-mounted, 3,000-horsepower engine snatched the front wheels smoothly off the concrete "launch pad," an occurrence not uncommon under optimum conditions. This time, however, gravity failed to do its job. By the time Garlits realized that the nose was not coming down, it was too late.

Like a drawbridge, the car rose until, balanced only on the rear wheels, it appeared on the verge of falling over backward. Instead, it executed a pirouette worthy of Baryshnikov and came back to earth, engine still lit, tires smoking, pointed directly at the starting line.

Garlits regained control and brought the car to a stop but its weekend was over and Gwynn duplicated his final round victory

**"Big Daddy" lights off the 1986 version of the "Swamp Rat."
Photo by Leslie Lovett**

Darrell Gwynn, Garlits' nemesis, participates in all phases of his team's operation. Photo by Leslie Lovett

66 AutoRacing/USA

Dick LaHaie checks out one of his Goodyears with Crew Chief (and daughter) Kim LaHaie. Photo by Leslie Lovett

Gwynn embarks on one of his 278 MPH runs. Photo by Leslie Lovett

Two wins during '86 helped LaHaie nail down the third spot in the NHRA points battle. Photo by Leslie Lovett

Drag Racing

At mid-season, '84 Champ Joe Amato (hat on) debuted a new, covered front-end dragster with dismal results. It soon vanished not to be seen again. Photo by Leslie Lovett

by beating the father-daughter team of Dick and Kim LaHaie, who won twice and were runners-up on four other occasions during the season.

Gwynn would not win again until the season-ending Winston World Finals even though he qualified his dragster number one in five of the last seven races and twice shattered the existing world records for both time and speed.

He set the record for the second — and final — time during the inaugural Chief Auto Parts Nationals at Ennis, Texas, a race which proved to be a microcosm of the season as a whole.

Gwynn, who left the race with records of 5.261 seconds and 278.55 MPH, waited in line for two hours on Thursday to assure that his would be the first Top Fuel dragster down the Texas Motorplex quarter mile, the sport's first all-concrete racecourse.

He was rewarded with a time of 5.280 seconds at 278.29 MPH — remarkable considering that the previous records were 5.34, 272 MPH. Gwynn broke the 5.30 barrier two more times before qualifying was complete and, when he dipped to 5.272 at 276.83 MPH in the semifinals (despite an engine change), Garlits' bid to become the first driver to repeat as Top Fuel World Champion appeared jeopardized.

Still, while Gwynn was realizing the full potential of the track's concrete construction, Garlits methodically was assuring another showdown with his young antagonist. Nonetheless, when Garlits slowed to 5.466 seconds in his semifinal victory, it appeared that the youngster might finally win a head-to-head meeting of genuine significance. It was not to be. After a 90

Gary Ormsby in the Castrol GTX carbon fiber streamliner streaks off the starting line as John Carey blazes his Keenan & Pike entry. Photo by Leslie Lovett

68 AutoRacing/USA

Gary Beck (left) and Joe Amato about to do battle. Photo by Leslie Lovett

In '86, Dan Pastorini arrived as a contender with his win at the NHRA Southern Nationals. Photo by Leslie Lovett

AutoRacing/USA 69

Drag Racing

During a lull in the racing action, former NFL quarterback Pastorini aired out the football for his fans. Photo by Leslie Lovett

As demonstrated by this photo of Gwynn's automotive head, one of the latest dragster and funny car tricks is the supplying of fuel directly behind the intake valve. Photo by Leslie Lovett

Garlits VS Gwynn: the Top Fuel story of the year. Photo by Leslie Lovett

70 AutoRacing/USA

minute rain delay, Gwynn's concentration obviously was shattered. At the first hint of a green light, Garlits hammered the throttle. He beat Gwynn off the line by a .456- to .615-second margin, massive by drag racing standards, and was never pressed.

Although he had to wait until the finale to mathematically clinch his third title, when Garlits left Texas, there was little doubt that the Championship — and the accompanying $75,000 Winston bonus — were his.

The victory was the 34th of Garlits' 30-year career, tying him with Don Prudhomme for second place on the all-time list. Further, it was his 13th in 29 starts since, late in 1984, he abandoned his job as curator of the Don Garlits Museum of Drag Racing to return to the tour on a full-time basis.

Still, there was evidence at season's end that his task in 1987 may be even more difficult. Gwynn signed on as part of Bernstein's well-heeled Budweiser King Team. Pastorini got a boost from Coors. And, in a shakeup that left two-time former World Champion Gary Beck without employment, Larry Minor signed the LaHaies to a contract under which they will race wearing the colors of Minor's sponsor, Miller American.

Furthermore, the International Hot Rod Association's (IHRA) decision to reinstate Pro Dragster in 1987 is certain to stimulate further interest in a hybrid category from which many were prepared to remove life support systems just two years ago.

His past records notwithstanding, Garlits most significant accomplishment may prove to be his contribution to the salvation of the breed. Of course, in essence, it was nothing more than self-preservation — his personal racing history and that of the fuel dragster being irrefutably intertwined.

Garlits aimed to please in 1986. The 270 MPH barrier fell in March at the Gatornationals. Photo by Leslie Lovett

How true...still. Photo by Leslie Lovett

Drag Racing

In the fastest side-by-side Funny Car race ever, NHRA Champ Kenny Bernstein (near lane) beat IHRA Pro Funny Car Champion Mark Oswald (far lane). Bernstein won with an elapsed time of 5.57 seconds to Oswald's 5.61. Photo by Leslie Lovett

Bernstein's Crew Chief Dale Armstrong and his "Terrible Towel" with which he hides his latest invention — or so his competitors think. Photo by Kay Presto

Funny Car

If the drag racing season was only eight races in duration, perhaps neither Kenny Bernstein nor Mark Oswald would enjoy a clear-cut advantage in the race for the Winston World Championship. Unfortunately for everyone else in the Funny Car division, the 1986 Winston Racing Series was comprised of 24 NHRA and IHRA events and, given the time to establish their individual rhythms, Bernstein and Oswald were without peer.

The two-time reigning NHRA Champion and Auto Racing All-American, Bernstein, has never won the season-opening Chief Auto Parts Winternationals. He extended this unfortunate streak with the beginning of the '86 campaign when his Budweiser King Ford Tempo suffered an uncustomary loss of traction in a semifinal heat against eventual winner Tim Grose of Saugus, California.

Remarkably, Oswald has been even less productive. Three times in four years the 33-year-old Cleves, Ohio pro has failed to even make the field in the Paul Candies and Leonard Hughes Pontiac. He, too, extended his streak. In fact, he and Bernstein, true to form, each won only once in the first seven '86 races while Ed McCulloch, Grose and Tom McEwen were winning on the NHRA tour and Grose, Paul Smith and Dale Pulde were victorious in IHRA competition.

It was a false image of Funny Car parity. In the last 17 races of the season, beginning with the June 15 NHRA Springnationals at Columbus, Ohio, Funny Car racing's two dominant drivers combined for 15 victories and as many "poles." When the last piston had been spent, Bernstein was NHRA Champion for the second straight year and Oswald was the IHRA king for the third time in four seasons.

In the dollars battle, however, Oswald was a clear winner. Not only did he claim the $75,000 IHRA Champion's bonus and the second-place money on the NHRA circuit ($15,000), he also claimed the $25,000 Winston Funny Car bonus (awarded the driver who accumulates the most points in both series) and the $25,000 top prize in the Big Bud Shootout bonus race at Indianapolis, Indiana.

Additional subtraction from Bernstein's bottom line occured

Kenny Bernstein checks the nitro/alcohol mix prior to every run he makes in The Budweiser King. Photo by Leslie Lovett

Drag Racing

After his spectacularly bad season debut, Funny Car pilot Ed McCulloch had a streak going with consecutive wins at Gatornationals and Southern Nationals. Photo by Leslie Lovett

IHRA Pro Funny Car series runner-up Paul Smith scored a win at the Pro-Am Nationals. Photo by Teresa Long

when Bernstein found himself immersed in a bidding war to retain the services of his talented — and soon to be wealthy — Crew Chief, Dale Armstrong.

Author of the aerodynamic refinements that enabled Bernstein to become the first Funny Car driver to break the 260 and 270 MPH barriers, Armstrong was offered $1 million for three years to jump from Bernstein's Budweiser King team to that of California potato farmer Larry Minor. Minor's offer, sufficient testimony to Armstrong's perceived expertise, was designed to insure the future of Minor's Miller American team. Waiting for the Armstrong magic were Minor's two Top Fuel dragsters and an Oldsmobile Funny Car in which McCulloch had won two of the season's first three races.

To keep his team intact, it cost Bernstein every dollar he earned in 1986 purses — and some more besides. The end result was a five-year contract with Armstrong reportedly worth $1.5 million. Armstrong, himself a former Funny Car driver forced out by a lack of sponsorship, may be worth every penny. He certainly was afforded the bulk of the credit for Bernstein's five NHRA and three IHRA victories in '86.

Still, although Armstrong-less, Oswald matched the 42-year-old Newport Beach, California pro stride-for-stride, winning five

Young Funny Car pilot Tim Grose, working on a small budget and doing most of the work on his car, stunned the regulars when he knocked off Kenny Bernstein to win the Winternationals. Photo by Kay Presto

Dale Pulde opened the IHRA Pro Funny Car season with a win at the Winter Nationals. Photo by Leslie Lovett

AutoRacing/USA 75

Drag Racing

Ed McCulloch boomed a blower at the first race of the year and had to ride out the ball of fire. Photo by Mickey McGiver

The smoking glove of Ed McCulloch attests to the fact that yes, when the blower goes as it did in McCulloch's car, the driver is in danger. Photo by Leslie Lovett

76 AutoRacing/USA

times in IHRA competition and three times in the NHRA series.

Ironically, of the six times the two met in the finals, NHRA Champ Bernstein won the three contested under IHRA sanction. IHRA Champ Oswald was victorious in the three NHRA confrontations.

Statistics notwithstanding, few would dispute the contention that, of the two, Bernstein, with Armstrong turning the wrenches, today is the most feared driver in the division. A measure of his consistency is the fact that he has qualified his car first or second in 17 consecutive NHRA events dating back to 1985. Moreover, in scaling back his IHRA effort in '86, Bernstein opted for quality instead of quantity. That he reached the final round in each of his five appearances and posted the quickest time on each occasion bespeaks his success.

Down the stretch, Bernstein simply was unbeatable, winning the last three NHRA races: the Chief Auto Parts Nationals at Ennis, Texas; the Fallnationals at Phoenix, Arizona; and, for the second straight year, the Winston World Finals, back at Pomona, California. He was particularly impressive at Indianapolis Raceway Park (site of the Labor Day U.S. Nationals) and at Texas Motorplex, the $6.5 million supertrack built by Funny Car rival, Waco, Texas' Billy Meyer.

At Indy, Bernstein had top speed of the entire event (including the fuel dragsters as well as Funny Cars) at 271.41 MPH. He balanced that with low elapsed time at 5.509 seconds which, until Texas, was the quickest documented clocking in Funny Car history.

At the Chief Nationals, the first race run in Texas since the World Finals moved from Amarillo in 1974, he pushed his carbon fiber-bodied, computer-directed Ford to a time of 5.425 seconds. The only glimmer of hope for the opposition came in the finale when, after winning a second round race against Jerry Jefferson of Choctaw, Oklahoma, Bernstein tripped over the tow strap while exiting his Ford van and took a hard fall. Dazed, he regained his composure — and his senses — in time to beat Oswald in a semifinal showdown that produced the quickest side-by-side clockings in history: 5.563 seconds for Bernstein's Budweiser King; 5.643 seconds for Oswald's Old Milwaukee Beer entry.

In the final, "King Kenny" disposed of Billy Meyer, the 32-year-old veteran who extended to 10 the number of consecutive years in which he has gained at least one final round, the longest such streak in the division. In fact, the 10-time tour winner reached the finals on three separate occasions, thus earning enough points to finish third in the NHRA standings.

Despite the dominance of Bernstein and Oswald, at season's end, the Funny Car situation was more muddled than ever. For one thing, Bernstein announced that, after six years, he was jumping ship — taking his Budweiser sponsorship to Buick. That move opened the door for Candies and Hughes who subsequently announced that they were leaving Pontiac and Old Milwaukee for Ford and Motorcraft.

Furthermore, two of the sport's most prolific winners revealed 1987 comeback plans underwritten by rival tobacco companies. Don Prudhomme, the four-time NHRA World Champion who sat out the '86 campaign, will return next season in a Pontiac sponsored by Skoal smokeless tobacco. Raymond Beadle, a three-time series champion on both the NHRA and IHRA circuits, will be back full time in a Pontiac-based Blue Max Racing entry sponsored by Kodiak.

Tom "The Mongoose" McEwen had his best year ever with two NHRA wins. Photo by Leslie Lovett

Drag Racing

The Chief Auto Parts Thunderbird of 1986 NHRA Pro Stock Champion Bob Glidden. Photo by Leslie Lovett

Pro Stock

Six months before he clinched an unprecedented seventh Winston World driving Championship, Bob Glidden felt anything other then the winningest driver in NHRA drag racing history. The date was April 20 and Glidden, who has won one of every 2.6 races he has entered as a professional, was looking at the mangled mass of metal and fiberglass that, just seconds earlier, was the quickest and fastest carbureted stock car in the sport: the Chief Auto Parts Thunderbird. That he was even capable of pondering cause and effect was a minor miracle considering the punishment absorbed by the blue-and-white T-bird as it tumbled on top of the steel guardrail stretching beyond the quarter-mile finish line at Atlanta Dragway.

The 42-year-old Whiteland, Indiana, veteran, winner of at least one NHRA event title in 13 straight seasons, had just beaten Butch Leal in the semifinals of the Castrol-Nationwise Southern Nationals when the car turned hard left, apparently caught in a wind gust just as the braking parachute was beginning to blossom. As a result, instead of preparing to race Warren Johnson in the Atlanta finals, he was wondering if perhaps he had lost it all — everything for which he and his family had worked in the 14 years since he quit his job as a line mechanic for an Indianapolis Ford dealership.

Nevertheless, even while he was questioning his future, Glidden still was thinking like the Champion he has proven himself to be. His first act after determining that the car was a total loss, was to shed his driving jacket and use it to cover the sophisticated, custom-built manifold atop the car's 500 cubic inch Ford engine. Then, upon assuring wife Etta, his Crew Chief and confidant, that he was uninjured in this, the most serious accident of this 137-race career, he assigned #1-son Billy the job of securing the crash scene until he returned from the obligatory trip to the hospital. "Some NHRA people thought that (gesture) meant we were doing something illegal," Glidden said, "but after all the work we had put into our engine program, I just didn't want to give it all away (to the competition)."

Although, thanks to the efforts of chassis whiz Jerry Haas whose craftsmanship had withstood the ultimate test at Atlanta, Glidden didn't miss a single start, his fortunes did not enjoy a significant upturn over the next two months. The low water mark for the slightly built pro was Englishtown, New Jersey, the site of the NHRA Budweiser Summernationals. There, Glidden broke his own NHRA record for quarter-mile time — and then lost to

The Glidden family won six of 14 NHRA events this year, providing Rusty and Billy Glidden ample opportunity to practice their high fives. Photo by Leslie Lovett

AutoRacing/USA 79

Drag Racing

Bob Glidden (center) compares notes with Tim Hyatt (right) while son Rusty listens. Photo by Leslie Lovett

Indiana neighbor Don Coonce in the semifinals. By failing to reach the winners' circle in the first seven races, Glidden was off to the worst start of his career.

Conversely, Leal and Johnson were enjoying extraordinary success. Between them, they had won five of the first seven races and were separated in the driver standings by only 96 points — less than one round.

Johnson, a 16-time NHRA winner in a series of Oldsmobiles, finally appeared destined to win the World Championship after a series of close calls. But when Glidden drove his Ford to quarter-mile-clockings of 7.446 and 7.443 seconds at Englishtown, Johnson had a premonition that it wouldn't be that simple.

Still, by mid-July, the only title for which Glidden appeared in contention was that of the rival IHRA circuit in which he had won four times in the first seven races. It was Glidden's first legitimate bid for the IHRA Championship since 1976 — a season in which he had finished "only" sixth in NHRA points, the poorest showing of his career. His IHRA bid was enhanced by the fact that Johnson, a two-time former IHRA Pro Stock Champion, and Leal were not participating. Moreover, when defending series Champion Bruce Allen of Arlington, Texas, left the tour in mid-season (with one victory to his credit), Glidden apparently had clear sailing. But it was not to be.

Glidden stumbled down the stretch, winning only once in the last four races. Because of the high premium paid by IHRA for qualifying performance and consistency, he fell back to fourth place in the final standings.

Although the title was won by '82 Champion Rickie Smith of King, North Carolina, there was little doubt as to whose Thunderbird was the most powerful. Glidden, who missed the IHRA opener because of a conflict with the NHRA Gatornationals, finished the season with the IHRA record tucked safely away at an incredible 7.216 seconds. He also was clocked in 7.235 seconds and 7.221 seconds.

The extraordinary difference in his IHRA and NHRA records is testimony to the premise that, "There is no substitute for cubic inches." When NHRA adopted a Pro Stock format in 1982 closely resembling that pioneered by IHRA, it felt compelled to impose a limit on engine displacement, setting it at 500 cubic inches. IHRA's more liberal rules have invited "bigger is better" construction which, in '86, produced the sport's first 700 inch motor. In fact, it was the reality of having to maintain two separate research-and-development programs that ultimately forced car owners David Reher and Buddy Morrison to pull the Allen-driven Levi Garrett Camaro off the IHRA tour.

Reher and Morrison, who in 1984 and 1985 won both the

Billy Meyer's brand-spanking-new Texas Motorplex. Photo by Leslie Lovett

Drag Racing

Warren Johnson. Photo by Leslie Lovett

NHRA and IHRA World Championships with the late Lee Shepherd at the wheel, admitted that their engine-building business was suffering because of the time they were having to spend on the road. As a result, the yellow-and-white Chevrolet, part of the Rick Hendrick effort, left the last five IHRA events to the Ford's of Glidden, Smith and Roy Hill.

Despite the decision to focus its efforts solely in the NHRA series, the Texas team failed to win a single race for the first time in seven years. After winning 29 times in 80 NHRA races from 1980 through 1985 (and earning runner-up honors on 20 other occasions), Reher-and-Morrison had only a repeat victory in the Mr. Gasket bonus race to show for their '86 effort. Nonetheless, they did reach the finals three times in the last six events, and finished third in points.

Meanwhile, Johnson's NHRA season was coming apart in a

Glidden was unscathed after his crash at the Atlanta Southern Nationals. Photo by Leslie Lovett

82 AutoRacing/USA

Warren Johnson posted three wins in '86, finishing second in NHRA Pro Stock points. Photo by Leslie Lovett

Bruce Allen, third in NHRA Pro Stock points. Photo by Leslie Lovett

Drag Racing

After almost two years recuperation from grievous injuries suffered while racing, Shirley Muldowney returned to the drag strips of America. Photo by Leslie Lovett

Drag Racing

series of early round defeats coupled with Glidden's patented late-season charge. Still, despite Glidden victories in six of the last seven races, Johnson might have won the title but for losses to such relatively obscure Pro Stock drivers as Stan Mizell (in the first round at Brainerd, Minnesota), rookie Mark Pawuk (in the second round at Indianapolis), Don Campanello (in the first round at Reading, Pennsylvania), Darrell Alderman (in the second round at Phoenix), and Don Beverley (in the second round of the season-ending Winston World Finals at Pomona, California).

Although Beverley and Campanello each won once in '86, (their first career victories) and while Alderman won the biggest race on the IHRA circuit — the Winston Spring Nationals at Bristol — neither would be considered a threat to Johnson's GM Goodwrench Oldsmobile. Had Johnson just made it as far as the semifinals in those five races, certainly a reasonable expectation, he would have padded his point total by 1,400 points. Glidden won by only 1,842.

The biggest win for Glidden, of course, came in the 32nd annual U.S. Nationals at Indianapolis, in which he lowered his

Roy Hill, third in IHRA Pro Stock points. Photo by Leslie Lovett

Frank Iaconio's Ford Thunderbird won the first NHRA event of the year but then hit hard times. Photo by Leslie Lovett

Newcomer Don Beverly, aided by an electronic shifter, outdrove the old pros at the NHRA Keystone Nationals to win his first event. Photo by Leslie Lovett

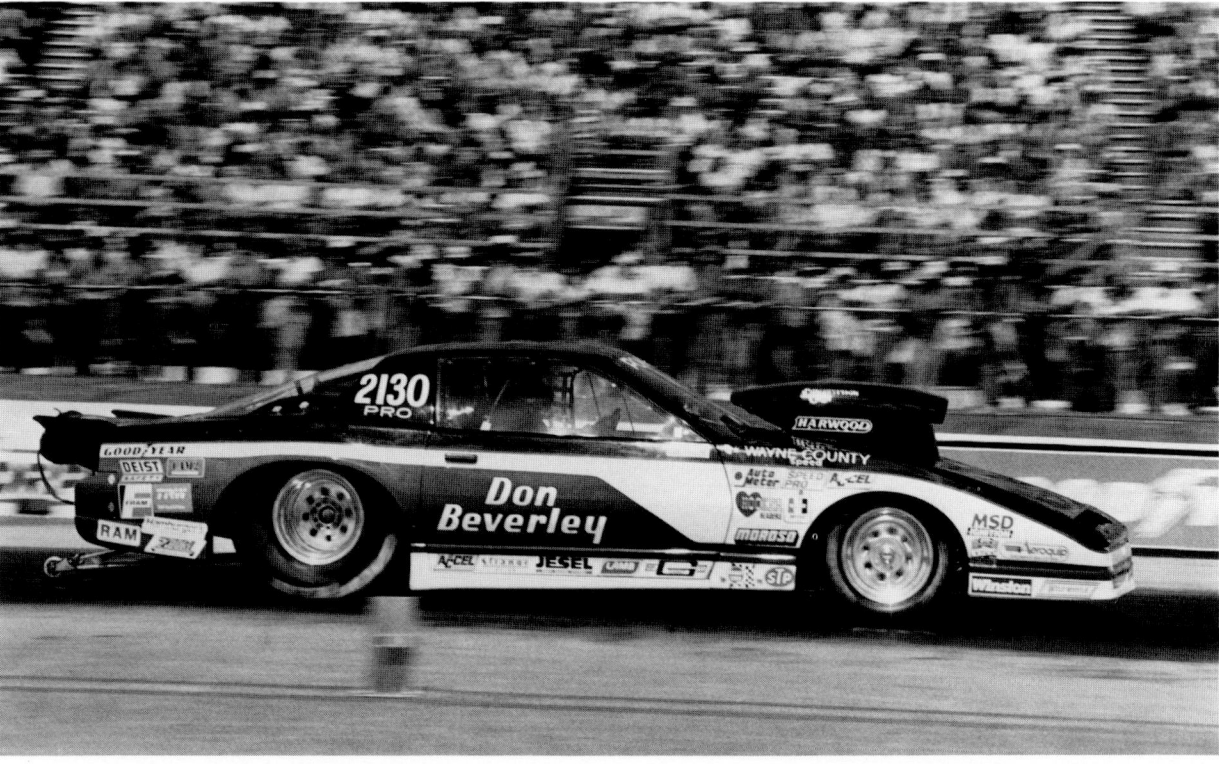

AutoRacing/USA 87

Drag Racing

The 1986 NHRA Winston World Funny Car Champion Kenny Bernstein. Photo by Leslie Lovett

Drag Racing

Butch Leal posted two NHRA '86 wins, finishing fourth in points. Photo by Leslie Lovett

Drag racing's Man of the Year may well be Billy Meyer — not because of his Funny Car efforts but because of the magnificence of his Texas Motorplex. Photo by Leslie Lovett

own NHRA world record from 7.443 to 7.377 seconds and beat Allen for the Championship. It was "Hoosier Bob's" 10th straight Indy final and seventh win in the Labor Day classic.

Johnson, a mechanical engineering and psychology major at the University of Minnesota who now makes his home in Duluth, Georgia, fired one last salvo at Indy in pushing his Firenza to an NHRA record 190.07 MPH. He thereby offset the 200 points awarded Glidden for the elapsed time record.

However, for all intents, the season was already over. Beginning with the July 27 Mile-High Nationals at Denver, Colorado, Glidden won 25 rounds of racing, losing only one. The lone defeat came in the second round at Reading, in which a slower reaction to the starting signal offset his performance advantage over the Reher-Morrison Camaro. Glidden lost in 7.558 seconds; Allen won in 7.576. That miscue denied Glidden a victory in the only NHRA event he has never won.

Nevertheless, at season's end, having once more devastated the competition and having announced a new sponsorship agreement with Motorcraft, there seemed little doubt that even that Championship could not elude him forever.

The NHRA season opens at Pomonoa's Winternationals. Photo by Leslie Lovett

Just moments before this picture was taken, this fan had nothing other than a knife, a cardboard box and some free time. Photo by Leslie Lovett

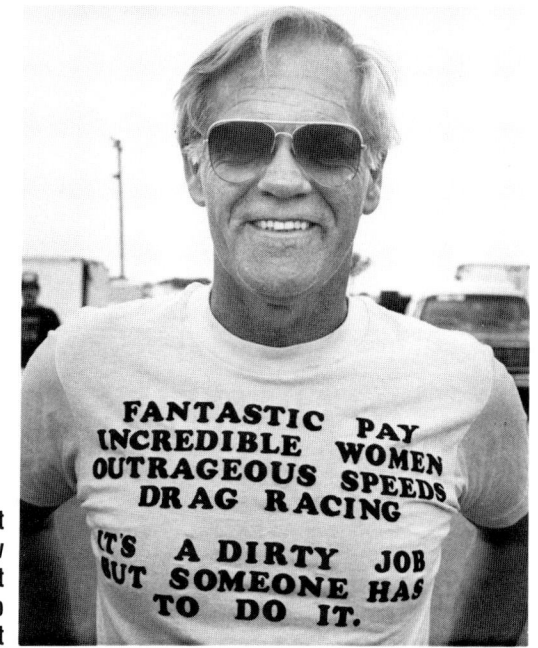

Drag racers tell it like it is. . .or how they wish it would be. Photo by Leslie Lovett

Modifieds

by Mike Rowell

NASCAR MODIFIED RACING HAS BEEN DOMINATED BY THREE GREAT DRIVERS. IN THE LATE '60s, CARL "BUGS" STEVENS WAS NATIONAL CHAMPION AND MASTER OF THE MODIFIEDS. IN '71, '72, '74, '75 AND '76 JERRY COOK WAS CHAMPION. IN '73 AND EVERY YEAR FROM '78 TO '85 the incomparable Richie Evans swept all before him. With Evans untimely death at the close of last season, the question on everyone's mind was who might be the next King of the Modifieds.

Actually there is no National Championship. Instead, there are two points races: the Winston Modified Tour, a 25 race series; and the Northeast Regional Points Race involving points gathered at a myriad of NASCAR sponsored Modified events. Due to tradition established by Richie Evans only a driver who wins both of the points Championships can call himself the National Champion.

For the '86 season NASCAR dropped the 390 CFM carburetor rule in favor of a more liberal 750 CFM carb. Engine builders predicted the six-liter small block V8's would gain 100 horsepower and last 30% to 40% longer. The full implications were not realized, however, until the first Martinsville race. There, Greg Sacks, in the Fiore machine, blistered around the half mile at 101.014 MPH, breaking Evans old mark of 97.513 MPH. At the Thompson Ice Breaker, the top seven qualifiers all went faster than the old mark with the quickest topping 117 MPH on the 5/8-mile oval.

The season began unofficially with four races at Smyrna, Florida in February. Reggie Ruggiero of Forrestvillle, Connecticut, driving the superb Mario Fiore #44, won the first three races and took second in the last. But then Ruggiero switched teams to Perry Greci's #11. Ruggiero won some races later in the season for Greci; and Fiore's #44, with Greg Sacks or Doug Heveron at the wheel, also won some races. However, what some considered a magic combination of car and driver never came together again.

Charging Charlie Jarzombek from Baiting Hollow, Long Island won at Rougemont, North Carolina in the season's first regular race. Though he was to win still more important races, DNF's and bad luck kept him out of the points lead later in the season.

At the beginning of the season, Brian Ross, Mike McLaughlin, and Corky Cookman seemed like good bets to go all the way. But by mid-season the trio had faded, and George Kent had the Tour points lead due to his fast and consistent, if unspectacular driving. He began to falter later in the year despite a big win at the Pocono Race of Champions, finishing third in the Winston Modified Tour. However, great performances by the "Duke of Kent" at Shangri La and Spencer speedways located near his Horseheads, New York home tacked down first place in the Regional Championship.

Jamie Tomaino of New Jersey was fast all year with numerous second places. A win at Martinsville in the last race of the Winston Tour let Tomaino edge out Kent for second spot in the Tour.

Jimmy Spencer had a slow start this year, but he persisted. In 1984, battling for points with Richie Evans, he learned the Championship was a long haul. In the 80-to-100 race season, money runs short, tires become scarce, crews get groggy, and drivers suffer fatigue. Spencer paced himself well this year. Well before the end of the season, he had a commanding lead in Tour points which remained unchallenged. Furthermore, he finished second to Kent in the Regional Championship with 3475 points to Kent's 3495.

Since George Kent won the Regional Championship and Jimmy Spencer of Berwick, Pennsylvania took the Tour title, there was no clear "King of the Modifieds" this year. Nonetheless, both will be back with a vengeance in 1987, attempting to become "Champion" in the Evans' tradition.

Jimmy Spencer. Photo by Howard Hodge

At Thompson (Connecticut) Speedway's Ice Breaker, 1986 Northeast Regional Modifed Champion George Kent. Photo by Howard Hodge

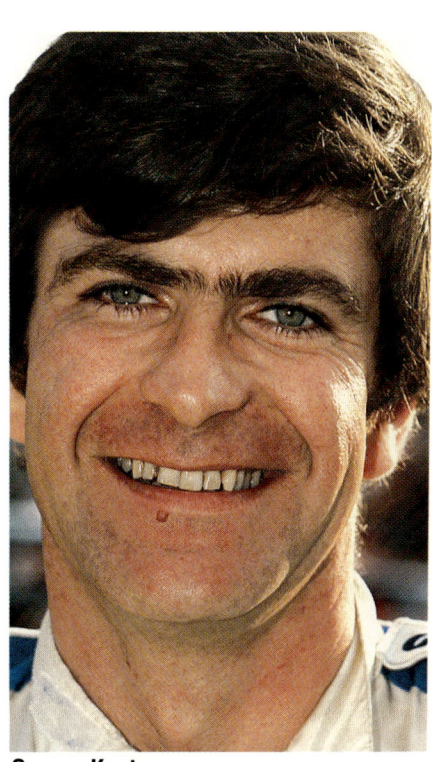

George Kent. Photo by Howard Hodge

The 1986 Winston Modifed Tour Champion Jimmy Spencer in action during the Stafford (Connecticut) Pentax 200. Photo by Howard Hodge

AutoRacing/USA 93

Modifieds

Mike Stefanik (#15) leads Roger Treichler (#41) and George Brunnhoelzl, Jr. (#28) during Oswego (New York) Speedway's Port City 200. Photo by Howard Hodge

As Jeff Fuller (#2x) and Allan McClure (#66) slip by, Bruce D'Allesandro (#10) and Bob Polverari (#70) take to the air after tangling with Carl Pasteryak (#75) and Bob Park (#19). Photo by Howard Hodge

Coordinated, effective pit work by Jimmy Spencer's crew during Thompson Speedway's Winston 300 help put Spencer in victory circle. Photo by Howard Hodge

Brian Ross (#73) and Jamie Tomaino (#99). Photo by Howard Hodge

Reggie Ruggiero shares his victory champagne with his fans at Stafford Motor Speedway. Photo by Howard Hodge

AutoRacing/USA 95

Modifieds

George "The Duke of" Kent (#26) leads Greg Sacks (#44) during Thompson Speedway's Ice Breaker. Photo by Howard Hodge

Passing Joe Mammolito (#31), Reggie Ruggiero could do little wrong in the #44. Photo by Howard Hodge

Mike McLaughlin (#12) is about to pass Charlie Jarzombek (#5) on the high side during the Port City 200 at Oswego Speedway. Photo by Howard Hodge

96 AutoRacing/USA

Super Modifieds
by Mike Rowell

IT WAS BENTLEY WARREN'S YEAR IN SUPER MODIFIED RACING. THE EX-INDY DRIVER FROM MASSACHUSETTS WON THE SEASON CHAMPIONSHIP AT OSWEGO, THE $115,000 OSWEGO CLASSIC; THE SANDUSKY CLASSIC IN SANDUSKY, OHIO; AND THE SEASON finale at Winchester, Indiana. It wasn't an easy year for Warren though, as Ed and Tom Bowley's "Flying Five" was dogged with handling problems throughout much of the season. The machine has seen six tough seasons.

Warren boycotted part of the International Super Modified Association (ISMA) series this year, which may have handed that points race to the boyish-looking, but very fast Steve Gioia. ISMA and Oswego cooperate in scheduling non-conflicting dates. While the ISMA rules allow wings and more radical engines, the same drivers and machines compete in both schedules. This season ISMA featured races in Lancaster, Pennsylvania; Quebec; Kalamazoo, Michigan; Sandusky, Ohio; Star Speedway in Epping, New Hampshire; and Shangri La Speedway in Owego, New York.

Another standout driver was Joe Gosek who finished second in points in both the Oswego and ISMA Championships. Gosek started as a crewman for Steve Gioia, and had never won a Super race until the 1985 season, but this year he won seven, five at Oswego and two in ISMA. Gosek's point totals were held down by several DNF's. Gosek's #00 car is a low buck operation in which Joe, his brother Ed, and Crew Chief Tony Osetek do everything including the engine building. The #00 was always fast. One night Gosek blistered through a 15-lap heat at Oswego at an *average* of 127.9 MPH — faster than some other Supers can do a *single* lap.

Rookie driver Jere O'Neill, who used to shoe Top Fuel dragsters, won two races this year and a reputation as a hard charger. Paul Richardson won his Season Championship at Star Speedway and then blew away all the big-block stroker cars in the ISMA final at Thompson, Connecticut, with his small block Chevy. Kevin Lyons scored his first-ever Super win at the tough high-banked Kalamazoo, Michigan track.

The old pro, Bentley Warren, took most of the marbles this year, but the young chauffers such as Gosek, O'Neill, Richardson, and Lyons are ready to take over.

Although cursed with season long handling problems, Bentley Warren made 1986 a year to remember. Photo by Bill Zmirski

AutoRacing/USA 97

Super Modifieds

Steve Gioia (#9), 1986 ISMA Champion goes inside Bentley Warren. Photo by Howard Hodge

Jere O'Neill (#26) charges ahead of Warren Coniam (#99) and Todd Gibson (#0). Photo by Howard Hodge

Bentley Warren (#5) points the way for Terry Johnson (#20). Photo by Howard Hodge

The Miller American Ford of the 1986 ASA Racing Series Stock Car National Champion Mark Martin. Photo by Phil Dullinger

ASA

Series runner-up Dick Trickle (#99) and third man in the points battle Butch Miller (#52) battle for position during the Winchester 400. Photo by Don Thies

Tom Jones (#0) and Bob Senneker (#84) duel for position during the Molson 300 — a battle from which Senneker ultimately emerged victorious. Photo by Don Thies

104 AutoRacing/USA

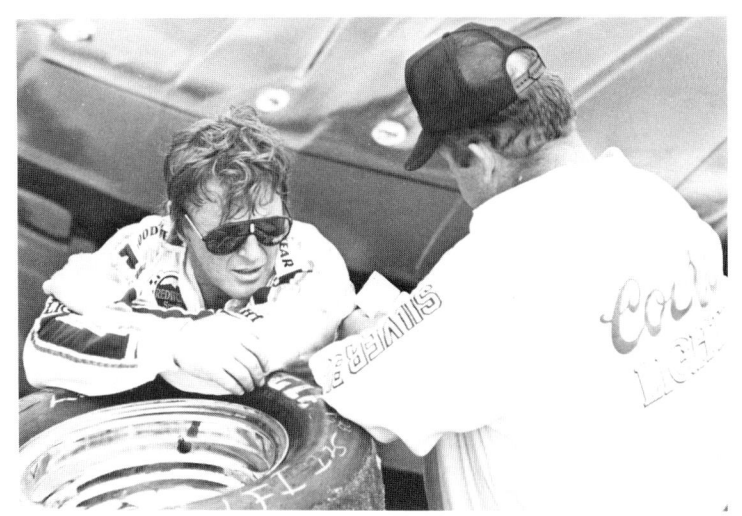

A permanent fixture in the ASA firmament, Dick Trickle discusses tire stagger with his Crew Chief, Vic Getzloff. Photo by Don Thies

ASA Rookie of the Year Kenny Wallace (#36) battles with fellow rookie Jerry Churchill (#25) during the season opener at Queen City. Photo by Don Thies

Mike Eddy (#88) and Ed Cooper (#78) on the banking during the Winchester/ASA 400. Photo by Don Thies

ASA

Howie Lendel, Crew Chief for Bobby Dotter. Photo by Don Thies

The clock ticks down towards the green flag as Dick Trickle and crew change engines. Photo by Don Thies

Greg Mol, Crew Chief for Russ Urlin, gets high on a head. Photo by Don Thies

Kenny Wallace (left) gives sponsor and crewman John Childs his full attention. Photo by Don Thies

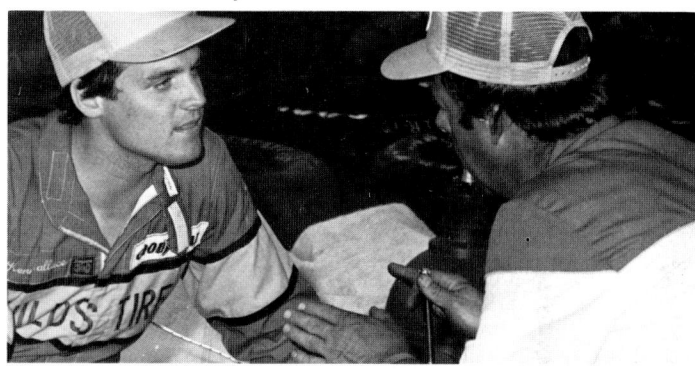

Under the leadership of Jimmy Fennig, Mark Martin's crew goes into action during a pit stop at Nashville's Coors 250. Photo by Don Thies

AutoRacing/USA 107

ASA

ASA drivers Ed Cooper (left) and Bobby Dotter indulge in a little pre-race communication. Photo by Don Thies

The post race mingling of fans and racers in Capital Superspeedway's infield. Photo by Don Thies

Mark Martin, awaiting the call for drivers to their cars. Photo by Don Thies

Ed Cooper wasted no time exiting his car after a losing confrontation with the wall at Cayuga International Speedway. Photo by Don Thies

Gary Balough spreads his joy of victory in the Nashville Miller All American 400 winner's circle. Photo by Don Thies

AutoRacing/USA 109

ARCA/Permatex Supercar Series

by Ron Drager

DAYTON, OHIO DRIVER LEE RAYMOND EXTENDED THE DYNASTY OF THE JIM COYLE-OWNED, RIVERSIDE AUTO PARTS-SPONSORED ORANGE #1 CHEVROLETS, RECORDING THE TEAM'S SECOND CONSECUTIVE ARCA PERMATEX SUPERCAR SERIES CHAMPIONSHIP IN A 17-event season.

The schedule was comprised of seven superspeedway races, six paved short tracks, two one-mile dirt contests, and one race each on a dirt short track and a road course, reinforcing the ARCA Permatex Series' status as the most diversified in existence. One hundred twenty-five drivers competed for the $847,100 in total posted awards in '86, traveling from Pocono in the east to St. Louis in the west; from Daytona in the south to Michigan in the north. And when all was said and done, a familiar sight: Coyle and Raymond again atop the Series standings.

Raymond's 1986 accomplishments — 12 top-five and 13 top-10 finishes, 261 laps led in nine races — further established the team's potency against admittedly stiffer competition than in 1978-79, when Coyle won his first ARCA car owner titles. The feats of Coyle-fielded cars since 1978 speak for themselves: 101 starts, 23 wins, 59 top-five and 79 top-10 finishes, 2015 laps led in 54 races, 32 poles. The only driver or car owner in ARCA's 33-year history to win more Championships than Coyle is the legendary Iggy Katona with six crowns.

Raymond won the season-opening Jiffy Lube 300 at Atlanta International Raceway, out-pitting polesitter Brett Bodine in the USA Network-televised race.

The 23rd annual Daytona ARCA 200 during February's Speedweeks saw Grant Adcox in Victory Lane, which was to become a familiar sight at superspeedway contests in '86. Adcox outran eight cars on the lead lap at the end of the 200-miler, including second-place finisher Ralph Jones' polesitting Ford Thunderbird.

Atlanta also provided the setting for Series veteran Bill Venturini to score his first-ever superspeedway win. Venturini, at the wheel of the Amoco Ultimate-MSW Chevrolet, overtook polesitter David Sosebee 13 laps from the finish, beating Sosebee by one second.

In the ESPN-live-televised Talladega ARCA 500 at Alabama International Motor Speedway (AIMS), Jones stole the early thunder with a lap of 203.536 MPH in his Ford. Jones' lap set an all-time, absolute ARCA speed mark, with Venturini, Raymond, Adcox, Sosebee, and Howard Rose also joining the 200 MPH club in the Talladega Pole Position qualifying. Adcox outdistanced the former speed record holder, Davey Allison, by one second for '86 superspeedway win #2.

ARCA's first road course race since 1960, held at the St. Louis International Raceway modified oval, saw Bob Schacht of Lombard, Illinois put his Engineered Fastener-TRW Pontiac on the pole and increase his career ARCA win total to 11, tops among active drivers.

Bob Brevak hit paydirt in his Race Glaze Buick on the 1/4-mile paved Spartan Speedway in Lansing, Michigan after going winless in 58 previous ARCA starts. Brevak was also the Talladega Pole Position winner and led nine other drivers on the lead lap in the 100-lap event.

The ARCA Permatex Series' 24th annual visit to Flat Rock Speedway in Michigan saw Ed Hage's Oldsmobile Delta 88 V6 set pole time and win the Miller High Life ARCA 125 for the second year in a row as 24 of the 27 110-inch wheelbase stockers crowded the 1/4-mile oval.

Bobby Jacks and Raymond started their racing careers on the tricky 3/8-mile paved Kil Kare Speedway near Dayton, Ohio. Returning to home territory, Raymond's Chevrolet V6 started from the pole only to be taken over by Jacks' V8 Oldsmobile 12 laps from the finish for Jacks' first win of 1986.

Bob Strait weaved his way through traffic on the Cloverleaf Speedway 1/4-mile in Cleveland, Ohio to post the first ARCA win for the Roulo Brothers Racing team. Scott Stovall was polesitter and 13 of the 27 starters were on the lead lap at the finish.

In an invitational, non-championship points event at Pocono International Raceway,

The 1986 ARCA Permatex Supercar Series Champion Lee Raymond. Photo Courtesy of ARCA

Reigning ARCA Champ Lee Raymond (#1) leads Bill Venturini around Atlanta's banking. Photo by Mike Slade

ARCA/Permatex Supercar Series

Bill Venturini (#25) and Ralph Jones (#82), winner of the overall Talladega Pole Position award, lead the start of Daytona International Speedway's ARCA 200. Eventual winner Grant Adcox (#2) lurks in third. Photo by Howard Hodge

Lee Raymond (#1) leads the ARCA/Dayton Enterprises Rookie of the Year Mark Gibson (#90) and Roger Blackstock (#42) around Atlanta. Photo by Mike Slade

112 AutoRacing/USA

Handling the jack, air gun — in fact every aspect of his pit activities — is Bill Venturini's all-female crew. Photo by Mike Slade

Jacks' Oldsmobile nipped three-time Pocono ARCA winner Schacht by less than a car-length at the finish line of the 150-miler.

The Permatex 500 at AIMS spelled another victory for the red-hot Adcox, who inherited the lead from a spinning Venturini (broken oil line) coming up on the white flag lap. Dave Simko was the Talladega Pole Award winner with a 201.464 MPH run.

Rookie Bob Keselowski won the pole and paced eight drivers on the lead lap at the end of the 100-lap event at Chet Mysliwiec's Berlin Raceway 7/16-mile paved oval in Marne, Michigan.

When you think of success on the mile dirt State Fairgrounds tracks at Springfield and DuQuoin, Illinois, Dean Roper comes to mind. The Fair Grove, Missouri driver held off polesitter Lee Raymond and eight other drivers on the lead lap in the Coors-Allen Crowe Memorial 100 at Springfield. Jacks set his fourth consecutive pole at DuQuoin, but at the finish line it was Keselowski racing Roper to the checkered with the veteran Missourian winning by less than a car-length after 200 tough miles.

Toledo Speedway's 125-lapper saw Stovall win his first ARCA event since 1982, when he won the Series Championship. Polesitter Keselowski crashed while leading in the early going. Stovall then outran the field in the Jim Stovall-owned, Fleet Vehicle Auction Chevrolet.

Local hot-shoe Kris Patterson gave promoter Dave Simko's

Grant Adcox (#2), leading a 200 MPH parade around Talladega, set an ARCA record with four superspeedway wins in 1986. Photo Courtesy of ARCA

Chevrolet a good run at Owosso Speedway. But it was a wild last-lap tangle which saw the top three positions change hands with Terry Pearson winning his first-ever ARCA race, '70-'71 Series Champ Ramo Stott in second and white-flag lap leader Raymond third.

Adcox won an ARCA record fourth superspeedway contest in a single season after a late-race battle with polesitter Venturini and a decisive pit stop for new tires in the season finale, the 96 Rock 300 at Atlanta. An ARCA superspeedway-record 70 cars entered the event.

In the year-end awards, Mark Gibson was named the Dayton Enterprises/ARCA Rookie of the Year; Ralph Jones won the overall Talladega Pole Position award; and the late John Litton was memorialized with the President's Award.

AutoRacing/USA 113

All Pro

by Keith Waltz, Associate Editor, "National Speed Sport News"

A COLD CUP OF COFFEE, A QUICK MEAL IN A TRUCK STOP AND THEN ON DOWN THE ROAD TO THE NEXT RACE. FOR NEARLY 20 YEARS THAT WAS THE LIFESTYLE OF STOCK CAR DRIVER GARY BALOUGH.

The Ft. Lauderdale, Florida resident didn't care about points or loyalty to a sanctioning body. His only priorities were getting to the next race and driving into victory lane.

But in 1986 that lifestyle changed and Balough turned his attention to winning the All Pro National Championship.

"We set out at the start of the year to win the Championship," he said. "I had spent so much time the past 20 years chasing different races and going for wins, I just thought it was time to settle down, prepare for a season-long effort and go for the All Pro National Championship.

The All Pro circuit is a series of 20 asphalt short-track late model races conducted throughout the Southeast under the direction of Bob Harmon, who founded the organization in 1981.

With over $1 million in prize money up for grabs, Balough and his Prime Time Racing Team had their eyes on the Championship trophy when the season opened at Florida's Five Flags Speedway in March. By the time Harmon and his traveling band of merry men returned to Five Flags for the season finale in December, the dark-haired driver already had his name on the Championship check.

Balough and his Fredrikson/Prototype/Dillon Chevrolet Camaro were the stars of the series, winning nine of the 20 races, including the prestigious All-American 400 which annually pits the best drivers from the north against the stars of the south at Nashville (Tennessee) Motor Speedway.

Balough posted his nine victories on seven different speedways and two of the triumphs came at the track he calls "home," Hialeah (Florida) Speedway. He also recorded the fastest qualifying time on eight occasions. In all, Balough led 1,646 of the 3,879 laps during the season and by the end of the year had taken a commanding lead on the all-time All Pro victory list with 20. Balough finished the year with a 299-point lead over runner-up and former series Champion Darrell Brown.

Winston Cup driver Rusty Wallace was the other big winner, capturing three All Pro checkered flags on his weekends off from the NASCAR wars. Brown, defending Champion Steve Grissom and veteran Jody Ridley each visited victory lane twice while Alton Jones and Randy Porter won one event each.

Grissom ended up third in points. Despite changing rides in the middle of the season and suffering a severe knee injury Dick Anderson took fourth. Ridley held down fifth spot in the final points tally.

The series hosted an impressive class of rookie drivers who were making their way into major-league racing during 1986. Bill Bigley, Jr. proved to be the cream of the rookie crop, taking Rookie of the Year honors and finishing seventh in points.

Early in the year, Harmon joined forces with Tom Curley and Rex Robbins, the heads of this country's two other major short-track late model sanctioning bodies, to form the Stock Car Connection.

The Stock Car Connection has scheduled a series of six races, the Great American Challenge Series, for 1987. All six events will be televised on The Nashville Network and carry a total purse of $1 million. Many of motorsports' insiders see the Stock Car Connection as the first real threat to NASCAR's domination of the stock car sanctioning world.

If the Stock Car Connection sets out with the determination Gary Balough had going into 1986, it too is likely to achieve its goals.

Gary Balough, the 1986 All Pro National Champion. Photo by Al Steinberg

NASCAR/Winston Racing Series

by Andy Hall

JOE KOSISKI OF OMAHA, NEBRASKA, A 29-YEAR-OLD AUTO PARTS DEALER, BECAME THE FIFTH DIFFERENT DRIVER TO CAPTURE THE NASCAR WINSTON RACING SERIES NATIONAL CHAMPIONSHIP IN THE FIVE YEARS THAT NASCAR HAS HAD A SYSTEM TO DETERMINE A National Champion of weekly short track racing.

In 1986, NASCAR sanctioned 65 weekly short tracks across the nation, with thousands of drivers participating. The system divided the country into five regions, with drivers competing for their Regional Championships under a uniform point system that awards points based on the drivers' best 20 finishes in a 22-week period. At the end of the 22-week season, the best 30 finishes of the five Regional Champions are compared to determine the NASCAR Winston Racing Series National Champion.

Kosiski won 29 races in 66 starts on Midwest dirt tracks to win the Central Region title, and his win total was superior to those of the other four Regional Champions. Pacific Coast Region titlist Doug McCoun of Prunedale, California, who had been the 1985 National Champion, won 19 races on central California dirt tracks, while Bubba Adams of Chesapeake, Virginia, won the Mid-Atlantic Region Championship, taking 17 wins while racing on both dirt and asphalt short tracks.

Dirt track racer Robert Powell of Moncks Corner, South Carolina, won 14 races to take the Southeast Region title, while 12-time winner George Kent of Horseheads, New York, won the Northeast Region while competing on paved tracks in a NASCAR Modified.

Kosiski won $35,000 in point fund awards for his Championship, while the other four Regional Champions received $11,500 each. In addition, the second through 10th place finishers in each region divided $15,000.

Kosiski's weekly schedule included Friday night racing at Lakeside Speedway in Kansas City, Kansas, Saturday night at I-70 National Speedway in Odessa, Missouri, and Sunday night action at Sunset Speedway in Omaha.

While Kosiski led the Central Region all season, he did not clinch the title until the final weekend of the season, when he edged Roger Dolan of Lisbon, Iowa, to take a win at Lakeside Speedway. Kosiski added another win the next night at I-70 to cement the regional and national titles.

Kosiski became the second Central Region Champion to take the national title, joining Tom Hearst of Wilton, Iowa, who was the inaugural Winston Racing Series National Champion in 1982. Southeast Region Champions Mike Alexander of Franklin, Tennessee, (1983) and David Into of Hardeeville, South Carolina, (1984); and Pacific Coast Region Champion McCoun (1985) are the other former National Champions.

NASCAR will expand the Winston Racing Series in 1987 with the addition of the Sunbelt Region, which will include tracks in Florida, Alabama and Texas.

Central Region titlist Joe Kosiski, of Omaha, Nebraska, ended the '86 season as the 1986 NASCAR Winston Racing Series National Champion. Photo by David Allio/Courtesy of NASCAR

NASCAR/Winston Racing Series

Prunedale, California's Doug McCoun, the Pacific Region Champion and 1985 Winston Series Pacific Region and National Champ. Photo by Patty Sands/Motorgraphics

Bubba Adams, of Chesapeake, Virginia, the Mid-Atlantic Region Champion. Photo by David Allio/Courtesy of NASCAR

From Moncks Corner, South Carolina, Robert Powell, the Southeast Region Champion. Photo by David Allio/Courtesy of NASCAR

The Northeast Region Champion, George Kent from Horseheads, New York. Photo by David Allio/Courtesy of NASCAR

Kosiski drove his racer to 58 top-five finishes, including 29 victories. Photo Courtesy of NASCAR

116 AutoRacing/USA

NASCAR/Charlotte-Daytona Dash

by Andy Hall

HUT STRICKLIN OF CALERA, ALABAMA DOMINATED THE 1986 COMPETITION ON HIS WAY TO WINNING THE CHAMPIONSHIP OF THE NASCAR CHARLOTTE-DAYTONA DASH SERIES FOR SUB-COMPACT, FOUR-CYLINDER RACE CARS. HE DROVE TO VICTORY IN NINE OF the series' 17 races.

Stricklin had a large enough lead in the series standings that he only had to start the final event of the season to take the title. However, he didn't quite do that. Instead, he won the Templeton 200 at North Wilkesboro (North Carolina) Speedway to build an even larger lead in the final standings.

The 27-year-old Stricklin, a former standout in NASCAR Winston Racing Series weekly short track racing in Alabama, as well as on the NASCAR Winston All-American Challenge Series, enjoyed a superb Dash Series season in cars owned and prepared by Richard Mash of Taylorsville, North Carolina. Stricklin had been an occasional competitor in the Dash Series for the previous two seasons, but had never had a full-time ride before joining forces with Mash.

Though he maintained a residence in Alabama, Stricklin spent much of 1986 living in Taylorsville, where he helped prepare Mash's Pontiac Sunbird for races. The extensive preparation proved to be the deciding factor in the title chase. In 17 races, Stricklin finished first or second 13 times, failing to finish the other four races.

Championships, however, are nothing new to Mash. He prepared cars for the 1983 series Champion Mike Waltrip, as well as five-time titlist Dean Combs. In addition, he was the mechanical force behind the late Dr. Charles Ogle, who won Rookie of the Year honors in the '85 Dash Series.

Stricklin won two races at South Boston (Virginia) Speedway, and scored single wins at Bristol (Tennessee) International Raceway, Orange County Speedway in Rougemont, North Carolina, Southside Speedway in Richmond, Virginia, Hickory (North Carolina) Speedway, Langley Speedway in Hampton, Virginia, Franklin County Speedway in Callaway, Virginia, and North Wilkesboro. He ended the season with 2730 points, while 18-year-old Rob Moroso of Madison, Connecticut, was second with 2475. Moroso won three races during the year, including two at Hickory and one at Hampton.

Other race winners during the season included two-time series Champion Mike Swain, of Archdale, North Carolina, who won superspeedway races at Daytona International Speedway, Charlotte Motor Speedway and Pocono International Raceway. Series veteran Larry Caudill of North Wilkesboro, North Carolina, captured an event at New Asheville (North Carolina) Speedway, while 18-year-old Jesse Samples, Jr., of Rock Hill, South Carolina, won at Charlotte.

Karen Schulz of Yorktown Heights, New York, a former go-kart racing Champion, finished eighth in the Dash Series standings and was awarded the series Rookie of the Year honors. The 21-year-old Schulz drove on a two-car team with Caudill.

As a capper to his Championship season, Stricklin married his longtime companion, Pam Allison, daughter of Winston Cup driver Donnie Allison.

From Calera, Alabama, Hut Stricklin. Photo Courtesy of NASCAR

NASCAR/Charlotte-Daytona Dash

The Richard Mash Pontiac Sunbird of the 1986 NASCAR Charlotte-Daytona Dash Champion Hut Stricklin. Photo by Mike Slade

The series' runner-up, Rob Moroso from Madison, Connecticut. Photo by Mike Slade

Mike Swain (#21) leads Hut Stricklin (#33) and Denny McClain (#88) in a mini-train. Photo by Mike Slade

Commentary: What Is It That Brings Injured Drivers Back To Racing?

by Kay Presto

IT WAS THE 1975 CALIFORNIA 500 AT ONTARIO MOTOR SPEEDWAY, BUT I DUBBED IT, "THE RACE OF THE WALKING WOUNDED." BETWEEN MY ROUNDS OF REPORTING, I WATCHED WITH INTENSE INTEREST AS FIVE — YES, FIVE — DISABLED DRIVERS WENT THROUGH their paces with USAC so that they might be allowed to drive in the race. Stopwatch ready, the USAC official timed each one as he struggled into his car; he had to be able to enter and leave the car within USAC's allotted time. Some were in leg casts, some in arm casts, and one — Jimmy Caruthers — had just been through extensive radiation for cancer. Despite great pain, they all passed, to race.

Caruthers, defying his body-weakening treatments, drove his Alex Morales mount hard, until a broken valve forced him out on the 54th lap. The following night, to dispel all doubts about his ability to handle a race car, he charged home first in a USAC Midget race at Manzanita Speedway in Phoenix. Six-and-a-half months later, on October 26, 1975, Caruthers passed away, leaving a colorful legacy of racing behind him.

At that California 500, as I watched these men racing intently despite their painful injuries and illness, I wondered, "What is this invisible force that continually draws these drivers back behind the wheel of a race car?" When I read of Caruthers' death, I wondered even further, "Why did he race?" Then I began to search for this elusive, compelling quality, and ask the drivers, "Why?"

Don Garlits feels this mysterious force. In 1970, when the motor of his front-engined dragster exploded, he lost half his foot. Did he quit racing? No. Propped up in his hospital bed, Garlits designed the rear-engined Top Fuel dragster, revolutionizing his sport. In 1986, the 54-year-old Garlits again advanced the technology of drag racing through the introduction of his bullet-nosed "Swamp Rat #30," winning yet another NHRA Top Fuel World Championship along the way.

Most everyone wrote off Shirley Muldowney's drag racing career after her devastating crash during qualifying for the Molson Grandnational in Montreal. But after many operations and extensive therapy, Muldowney not only came back, but, while testing her new car at Phoenix, after her half-pass, ran just .03-second off her best racing time: a 5.59 seconds!

Why did she come back? "The first reason was that I missed it terribly," said the three-time champ. "Also, I happen to be one of the few people who can make a living at something they love. I'm not ready to retire."

In December of 1977, Pancho Carter lay near death in a Phoenix hospital: His Indy Car had hit the Turn Four wall at Phoenix International Raceway and careened down the straight. *If he lived*, the doctors said, he'd never walk again. In April, a scant four months later, Carter entered his first post-crash race, *winning* the 40-lap Sprint car event at Indianapolis Raceway Park. At Winchester two weeks later, he *won again!*

To Carter, who walks with a permanent limp, the "mystery" is nonexistant. "I just wanted to go racing again," he said. "Some doctors aren't used to people getting well in a hurry. And when most people get injured, they're not concerned about getting well fast because they have some kind of disability insurance. Well, I didn't; I had to get back to racing to make a living. And I also enjoy what I'm doing, so there was no reason to stay away."

Danny Ongais suffered critical orthopedic injuries during his terrible Indy crash in 1981. After his recovery, I had two high-speed laps around Riverside International Raceway (and a good lesson in intense G-forces) in the Interscope Racing Porsche with Ongais at the wheel. His driving was fluid, efficient.

In July of 1983, IMSA driver Kathy Rude, the first woman to ever win an IMSA GTO race, hovered near death in a Minneapolis hospital. A severe crash at Brainerd International Raceway had left her body broken, her hold on life a narrow thread, months of painful recovery ahead. Two years later, she was again behind the wheel of a race car, this time competing in the Toyota Pro-Celebrity Race at Long Beach. After the race, she was ecstatic. "I was extremely nervous on the first three laps," she said, "because I was out of practice. Now, I'm looking forward to more racing so I can feel as good at the beginning of the race as I did on the fourth lap."

Why had she returned to racing? Her eyes, whose lids had been burned shut by the flames at Brainerd, sparkled as she answered. "It's important to have goals and challenges that a person strives for in their life and this is the ultimate challenge for me, physically and mentally; I really enjoy that part of it." She had shown no signs of fear. And there was that word, "enjoy," again.

How had she come back so well — this driver who lay in a coma for five weeks, had nine operations and so many blood transfusions that her blood was completely exchanged eight times? "I just concentrated on making my body as normal as

Commentary: What Is It That Brings Injured Drivers Back To Racing?

possible," she replied. "I was looking forward to the chance that, if I did want to race, I'd be fit enough to do so. For me, it was a real accomplishment to get physically and mentally back to the point where I could race again."

Rude credits her family and the racing community for her recovery. She was especially inspired by driver Brian Redman who, himself, had recovered from a broken neck, broken arms and severe burns to race again. "He told me it would take a long time, but they would get me driving again," she said, "and that it would take a lot of practice, so now I'm continually practicing."

By now, I had found several things making up that mysterious lure which returned drivers to the arena in which they'd been so grievously damaged: determination and "loving racing."

In 1984, the Indy Car scene was hit hard, with Rick Mears, Kevin Cogan and Derek Daly suffering severe foot and leg injuries in their car-rending crashes. Yet all three of these drivers have struggled through severe pain, operations, medication, addiction, and lengthy therapy, to return to racing. They, too, showed no signs of fear, only their joy to be back.

Derek Daly was lucky: In his September, 1984 crash at Michigan International Raceway, he could have lost both feet. "Just before it hit," he explained, "I knew I was going to hit that wall pretty hard, so I pulled my legs back as far as I could. If I hadn't done that, my feet probably would have been torn off with the front end of the car. After the crash, I didn't know how bad my left leg was, but I could see it wasn't pointing in the right direction. I had a very warm, glowing feeling in my legs, then I got cold all over; I knew I was going into shock. But, on the stretcher, as they described my injuries, I kept telling myself, 'That's only a couple of races I'll be out.'

"Seven weeks after the accident, I went to Las Vegas to see the race there. I was still in the wheelchair, and still pretty sick and sore, but when I saw those race cars, I knew instantly that my desire to drive was still there, and I'd be ok.

"My doctor felt that I recovered so well because I was originally in such good physical condition. I also kept after him to continually update me on things I could try in physical therapy to get better."

But Daly's toughest battle was getting off the painkillers. "I began to depend on the medication to stop the dizziness and shaking," the Irishman said. "I was no longer taking if for pain. It got so bad that I finally just went 'cold turkey' off everything. It was an extremely rough three weeks."

By the end of November, Daly was driving to his daily physical therapy sessions — a forty-mile one-way trip. Back in Ireland the following March, he again drove a race car. "I tried out my brother's Formula Ford to see what it was like," he said, "and it was the most natural thing I could have done. There was no fear at all. Afterwards, my mother asked, 'How was it mentally?' and I said I never even thought about it."

About his recovery, Daly explained another point. "I think the will to make myself better, to get up and not waste time indoors, helped. Life passes so fast that I had to get out again and fulfill my life's ambitions."

On the first day of practice for the 1984 Pocono 400, Kevin Cogan's March 84C spun across the track on the exit from the corner and crashed nose first into the wall. "It was an explosion of pain," recalled Cogan. The talus bone in his right foot was badly smashed, his left foot was broken, his Achilles tendon severely damaged. "It was toughest right after the accident," remembered Cogan. "Going someplace in a wheelchair for five minutes and getting worn out, I felt like such a weakling." Despite his severe foot injuries, he progressed rapidly, under the care of Dr. Bob Chandler in California. "I used the VIP treatment and got them to push me on," he said. "I had to make a living."

Rick Mear's '84 Sanair Super Speedway crash could have easily ended his career. The triple Champion's Penske-March hit the guardrail at an angle, pulling loose a retaining post. The now unrestrained guardrail sliced through his car like a can-opener. "The guardrail caught behind the pedal," said Mears, "behind my feet, folding them back to my shins and tearing both Achilles tendons off my heels. But I was lucky. Instead of tearing the actual tendons themselves, it ripped a chunk of bone out of the heel, so the healing process was faster since bones heals faster than tendon."

But it wasn't that simple. Dr. Terry Trammell of Indianapolis' Methodist Hospital, using a variety of screws and pins, had to delicately rebuild Mears' injured feet and re-attach both Achilles tendons. Wired up for 15 weeks, Mears also had to have skin, flesh and muscle transplanted from his back to his heels.

When asked what brought him back to race again, Mears stated, "I *love* the sport and the competition. The competition is what makes it fun. There was also a determination which brought me back. I had to prove to myself that it was no problem. . . that I could still do it. . . that I could still run. . . to ease my own mind. After an injury, a person wants to come back to what is normal for themselves, come back even *harder*, and be even better than they were when they left."

Mears wanted to recover even faster. "I got angry at times, because I wanted to heal even more quickly than I did," he said. "I wanted to get back on the road and get going, do better." Was there an invisible force which brought him back to racing? Mears thought for a minute, then answered, "I don't know of any special name for it. I do know that it takes determination, will-power and self-discipline. I think drivers recover faster than other people and come back to racing because of those three factors."

"Not only do drivers recuperate faster than the doctors think they can, they also usually come back stronger than what the doctors expect. And they usually come back with a greater percentage of mobility than the doctors expect. I have more movement in the side mobility of my right foot than I had before. So I'd say it's the determination, will-power and self-discipline that makes it all happen.

"But that's what this sport is all about," he added. "There's an element of danger to it, and that's the way it's always going to be. If it weren't dangerous, and there wasn't anything to it, and it was easy, everyone would be doing it. And I wouldn't have a job."

Another thing that surfaced in my search was the drivers' sense of humour about their mishaps. I found no self-pity. During his recuperation, Daly joked that being in a wheelchair made his Christmas shopping easier that year because he could park in the "Handicapped" zone. Mears laughed as he said, "My feet hurt all the time. I'll probably be able to tell the weather by them the rest of my life."

Still looking for a steady ride, Daly alternates between racing and sportscasting for television. In 1986, Kevin Cogan logged his first CART Indy Car victory. On November 17, 1986, Mears blazed to a new American closed-circuit record at Michigan International Speedway — 233.934 MPH — in his turbocharged Pennzoil March/Chevrolet.

Two of the "miracle-workers" who played a large part in the drivers' recoveries were orthopedic surgeon Dr. Terry Trammell and the director of CART's medical team, Dr. Steve Olvey, a specialist in the critical care of race drivers.

During a quiet moment at Indy, I asked Olvey for his impressions. "I'm not sure anyone really knows the reason these drivers go back to racing," he replied. "But the first thing they ask when they're injured is, 'When can I go back to race?' In the last eight years, I haven't met one injured drivers who chose to retire. They also have an intense desire to live, which puts to rest that old song about drivers having a death wish. They have a very intense desire to survive and to continue doing what they really like to do.

"People have also said that drivers race because they really don't know anything else, they're not trained for other jobs, and so on. That is absolutely untrue. Many of the drivers are college graduates. Some have given up excellent careers to race. And many are financially independent. But they still choose to race.

"It's very apparent to me that they have an intense drive to get back into racing: They want devices which will enable them to drive with a broken hand, or foot or leg. Sometimes it's not technically feasible, but their desire is overwhelming. Our orthopedic surgeons will often tell a driver he'll be out for six to eight weeks; they usually get well in half the time. The doctors often use Pancho Carter as an example of that."

Do the drivers have a higher threshold for pain than others? "They feel the pain just as much as anyone else," said Olvey, "but they're really a dream to take care of, because they are so intent on getting back to the sport that they'll follow any instructions we give them, to the letter. If we say they should get out of bed and walk, or use crutches, or go to the whirlpool, or to therapy, they'll do it without question, even though it causes them a lot of pain and discomfort. There's an intense willingness to go through all that to get well."

Olvey has an additional concept of the mysterious lure of driving a race car. "One thing I can come up with is that medical literature shows that there is a "high' associated with flirting with danger, or being in a dangerous position," he explained. "Tests show that circulating compounds activate in the body which actually give a person a natural 'high' — like runners experience when they run 10 to 15 miles a day. These compounds are classed as endorphins.

"And I can relate to that feeling," he added. "Steve Edwards, the safety director for CART, and I were on one of Wally Dallenbach's famous motorcycle runs through the rugged terrain of the mountains. We hadn't eaten properly and were riding in sleet and hail and driving rain. After six to eighty hours, Steve and I realized that we didn't know where we were: We were lost. But we had no panic, no sense of fear or danger. We felt like a million dollars — perhaps it was that natural 'high.' Finally, we found our way back and made it in before nightfall. When we arrived at camp, we were soaking wet, and cold and probably had borderline hypothermia. But we wouldn't have traded that experience for the world. It was terrific!"

By this time, I had begun to understand this mysterious lure a lot better. But, although I had a lot of definitions and a lot of reasons why race drivers go back to racing after they're hurt, I never did find a name for "it." However, I think one more element should be added — one which was never mentioned, even once by any of these valiant drivers. That element is: *courage*. Incredible *courage*.

Kay Presto

NASCAR/Busch Grand National Series

by Al Pearce, "AutoWeek"

IT MIGHT HAPPEN THAT OVER THE NEXT 15 OR 20 YEARS LARRY PEARSON WINS DOZENS OF RACES, CHAMPIONSHIPS ON END, AND ACCOLADE UPON ACCOLADE. WISH FOR IT, FOR THAT MIGHT BE THE ONLY WAY PEOPLE FORGET THAT THE 33-YEAR-OLD SOUTH Carolinian's first NASCAR Championship was — to put it kindly — a gift.

Even Pearson, son of three-time Winston Cup Champion David Pearson, will agree that his Grand National title (formerly, Late Model Sportsman) didn't exactly come through the front door. But he'll also quickly explain that if the Championship indeed slipped through the back door, *he* certainly didn't leave it open.

This much is indisputable: Five-time Champion Jack Ingram forfeited the Busch Championship when he lost his temper at Asheville (North Carolina) Speedway on September 14. He held a 246-point lead when he became embroiled in an ugly on-track incident with local hotshot Ronnie Pressley. Because of the seriousness of the fracus — it required police intervention and the brief hospitalization of Pressley — NASCAR fined Ingram $5,000 and suspended him for two weeks.

While Ingram sat out races at Martinsville (Virginia) and Rougemont (North Carolina), Pearson and Series runner-up Brett Bodine overtook him. When he returned at Charlotte in October he was third, out of the points race. "No question about it," he said later, "the Championship was mine and everybody knew it. If I hadn't missed those races I woulda' won it with no sweat."

He's probably right. After all, Ingram won more races (five) and more money ($152,229) than any other Series regular. Despite two fewer starts, he was second in top-five and top-ten finishes, had a pole position, was second in laps lead, third in times led, first in races led, and completed 91 percent of the available laps. Still, he finished 250 points behind Champion Pearson and 230 behind runner-up Bodine.

Unfortunately for Pearson, his Championship was overshadowed down the stretch by Ingram's misbehavior, fine, and two-race suspension. That's a shame, for he is like his father — a smooth, heady, talented driver who knows exactly how to finish in the money. He deserves better than a hand-me-down title. "I did everything I had to do, raced whoever was on the track, and ran as hard as I could," he said. "I don't apologize for anything. We worked hard for the Championship. We earned it."

Pearson's stats were of Championship calibre. After early-season DNF's at Daytona Beach and Rockingham he completed the next 29 races running, 24 of them in the top 10. For the year he averaged finishing eighth and completed 94 percent of the available laps, most among Series regulars. Down the stretch he was seventh, fourth, fifth, second, first (at South Boston, Virginia), third, fourth, then second to Bodine in his title-clinching run at Martinsville.

The 1986 NASCAR Busch Grand National Champion Larry Pearson. Photo by Mike Slade

The key to his season was consistency. Pearson led just seven times for 200 total laps, compared to Ingram's 19 times for 705 laps. He led just seven races but was among the front-wave finishers in almost every one. The trend paid off in points and — ultimately — the Championship. "We were disappointed that we didn't win but one race," he said, "but we were always right up front. That's what paid off."

As usual, Winston Cup stars stole much of the Series thunder. Dale Earnhardt won five races, Darrell Waltrip and Morgan Shepherd four each, and Tim Richmond one. Among Busch Series regulars, Tommy Houston's four wins ranked behind Ingram's five. Bodine won two, leaving Pearson, Dale Jarrett, L.D. Ottinger, Ronnie Silver, Butch Miller, and Chuck Bown to divide the remaining five. All told, 13 Winston Cup regulars entered at least one Busch Series race.

The '86 Series saw some comings and goings. At 26, Charlie Luck "retired" at

The Championship-winning Chattanooga Chew Pontiac of Larry Pearson is attended to during a brief caution period in the Budweiser 200. Photo by Patty Sands/Motorgraphics

NASCAR/Busch Grand National Series

Series runner-up Brett Bodine. Photo by Mike Slade

Jack Ingram, a five-time winner in 1986 ended the season perhaps the series' biggest loser. Photo by Mike Slade

Runner-up Bodine (#00) battles Jack Ingram (#11), third in points. Photo by Howard Hodge

season's end to go into business with his father. Haskell Willingham, 40, returned after a long absence from NASCAR. Among the bright young newcomers who made an impact (34 combined top 10's) were Larry Pollard, Kenny Burks, Elton Sawyer, Robert Ingram, and Ed Berrier.

They may be the Championship contenders of the future, since it's only a matter of time before Pearson and Bodine move up and the 49-year-old Ingram moves out. But until he does, Ingram must rate as the pre-season pick to win it all in '87. After all, he ruled the '86 season until mid-September.

But they pay off in late-October, and that's when Pearson was the best.

NASCAR's Busch Grand National cars going through a turn at Bristol International Raceway. Photo by Patty Sands/ Motorgraphics

Tommy Houston (#6) scored four '86 wins in his Southern Biscuit Flour Buick. The All Pro Pontiac of L.D. Ottinger (#2) posted one victory. Photo by Howard Hodge

AutoRacing/USA 125

NASCAR/Busch Grand National Series

Promising newcomer Larry Pollard (#98) dices with senior veteran Jack Ingram (#11) during the running of Daytona's Goody's 300. Photo by Patty Sands/Motorgraphics

Davey Allison tackles the road course at Road Atlanta. Photo by Mike Slade

Busch GN Champion Larry Pearson (#21) passes Brad Teague (#75). Photo by Howard Hodge

Charlie Luck (left to right), Jimmy Hensley and L.D. Ottinger. Photo by Mike Slade

Brett Bodine (#00) had his moments when the adrenalin flowed freely — both his and that of those following him. Photo by Mike Slade

AutoRacing/USA 127

NASCAR/Winston Cup

by Randy Hallman, "The Richmond News Leader"

WHEN DALE EARNHARDT WON HIS FIRST NASCAR CHAMPIONSHIP IN 1980, FEW, IF ANY, OF US UNDERSTOOD THAT A REVOLUTION WAS AT HAND. HE WAS 28 YEARS OLD AND ONLY A YEAR BEYOND HIS DAZZLING ROOKIE SEASON. BY STOCK CAR RACING STANDARDS he was a mere cub.

His ascension ended a string of six straight Championships for two of the tour's warhorses — Cale Yarborough and Richard Petty. At the time, most of us thought young Earnhardt's title was an aberration, a harbinger of a future that was some years in abeyance. We felt certain stock car racing's legend-encrusted veterans would regain the throne and hold it well into the '80's.

Au contraire: aprés Earnhardt, le déluge.

In the six seasons since Earnhardt's first title, neither Yarborough nor Petty has been Champion again. A new wave of drivers, none of them 40 when the New Year arrived, has taken over. Darrell Waltrip has worn the NASCAR crown three times, Terry Labonte once. These are superstars not of the old guard, but of the new. The aberration, as it turns out, was the 1983 Championship won by a graying Bobby Allison. He made what may have been a last grand gesture of defiance for the fading luminaries of the '60's and '70's.

Now Dale Earnhardt has won his second NASCAR Winston Cup Championship. His season was a fascinating one, and we shall examine it anon. Before we get to the nuts and bolts of 1986, however, let us consider the flesh and blood of the man who made this his year. Dale Earnhardt did not spring, full grown, from Humpy Wheeler's brow. Raised in Kannapolis, North Carolina, the heart of NASCAR's fertile crescent, Earnhardt was heir to a racing tradition.

"The first time I ever sat in a race car," he says, "I felt like I knew how to race it. I was made to go between the steering wheel and the gas pedal."

True enough. From wheel to pedal there are few who can match Earnhardt. But what about everything else that makes a driver great? In 1980 Earnhardt merely proved he could win the Championship. Now we shall see if he has learned how to *be* a Champion.

Ah, yes, there is a difference. Winning the Championship can happen in a flashpoint. Put a talented driver in a good car, give him a mechanic with a gimmick or two, back them up with a car owner hot to show off how stinking rich he is. With luck you're talking Championship.

Sustaining Championship caliber is another matter. Remaining in contention season after grinding season demands a marshaling of all the myriad skills that make motor sports such an infinitely complex game. Drivers who can go fast are lurking around every stack of slicks. Drivers with the power to make a team great are a rare breed. Those are the ones with driving talent, managerial skills, mechanical savvy, financial acumen, public relations flair, personal magnetism, physical and psychological durability. It takes all that and more now for a driver to get a good NASCAR ride and hold it. He must draw in mechanics who complement his skills. He must attract and keep a sponsor. He must maintain an owner's interest. He must nurture his own stamina and enthusiasm for a tour that holds roughly twice as many races as either Formula One or Indy car racing.

Dale Earnhardt of Kannapolis, North Carolina. Photo by Dan Bianchi

Richard Petty understood the breadth of what goes into a great modern-day team better and sooner than anybody else in stock cars. He was also in the perfect position to make that knowledge work — hence his seven Championships. Yarborough understood, and he was able to seize his opportunity, as was Waltrip. Each has three titles. Allison understood, and his perseverance paid off. After five second-place finishes in 17 seasons, he won his only Championship at 45.

Now comes Earnhardt, Champion a second time at 34. Does he understand?

Six years ago, Earnhardt would never have stopped to ask himself such a question. He had taken an uncomplicated line to the top, and the sport was simple enough to him. You drive hard. You win races. You have a good time. You don't put up with any horse manure. What's to understand?

Earnhardt has mellowed since then, though there are those who would say not

The Wrangler Chevrolet of 1986 NASCAR Winston Cup Champion Dale Earnhardt. Photo by Dan Bianchi

NASCAR/Winston Cup

Terry Labonte's Piedmont Oldsmobile is subjected to the scrutiny of NASCAR inspectors and their merciless templates. Photo by Michael J. Marrer

Following his TranSouth 500 win, Earnhardt takes a moment from the victory circle festivities to cool off. Photo by Patty Sands/Motorgraphics

enough. He is still blunt with words, even blunter with his front bumper. His impatience on and off the track gets him in dutch on occasion. He's still got that same bristly mustache (he shaved it off briefly a couple of years ago, then grew it back almost before the amended publicity photos were delivered) and those same mischievous eyes. The face has weathered well, and so has he. In six years he has gained a new perspective on what it means to win the title.

"The first time I won the Championship, it was like being in a big whirlwind," says Earnhardt. "In '79 I was the Rookie of the Year. In '80 I was Champion. It was like a big wind, and when the wind stopped and the dust settled there was nothing left.

"I didn't realize what the Championship meant. I was young and dumb. I was racing for the cars and the fun. I didn't realize the recognition and the fame and responsibility that went with it. I didn't capitalize on it. I laid back and took it. I appreciated it. I enjoyed it. And when it was over, it was all over.

"I realize the magnitude and potential of the Championship now. I know I need to capitalize on it as a businessman and as a race driver. You don't just use it up like a paper cup. You make the most of it for yourself and your team and your family."

Family has come to mean a great deal to Earnhardt. In 1980 he was a bachelor after a second divorce, majoring in hell-raising. In 1982 he married his current wife, the slender, stunning Theresa. Soon thereafter he was able to gain custody of daughter Kelly King, now 14, and Ralph Dale Jr., 12, his two children by his second wife. Only in the last year has he been able to reacquaint himself with Kerry, his 16-year-old son by his first wife.

"Theresa and the kids have meant everything to me," says Earnhardt. "That's what kept me going this season, that and the memories of my dad."

Earnhardt's dad was Ralph Earnhardt, one of the south's premier short-track drivers of the 1950's and '60's. He was NASCAR's Sportsman Division Champion in 1956. Dale dropped out of school in the ninth grade, as soon as North Carolina law allowed, so he could help his dad full time. They called Ralph Earnhardt "Ironheart," a corruption of his last

Geoff Bodine and his wife, Cathy, exult over his Daytona 500 win. Photo by Patty Sands/Motorgraphics

AutoRacing/USA 131

NASCAR/Winston Cup

The man currently wearing the Winston Cup Crown, Dale Earnhardt, races "The King" of NASCAR, Richard Petty (#43). Photo by Ken Brown

NASCAR/Winston Cup

And the numbers just keep on growing. . .a record crowd packed the stands and infield at Dover's September event. Photo by Ken Brown/Competition Photographers

From Corpus Christi, Texas, Terry Labonte. Photo by Patty Sands/Motorgraphics

name and an approximation of his tough, relentless driving style. Young Dale didn't miss a thing.

"I've been at race tracks all my life, as long as I can remember," Earnhardt says. "I stood on a tire on the back of Daddy's truck to get the best view I could, and went round and round with him every lap he ran. I grew up with a tough kind of racing. I guess my style speaks for itself."

Ralph Earnhardt was only 44 when he died of a heart attack at home in his shop on a September morning in 1973. Dale was 21 and had been racing dirt tracks two seasons. Ralph had been talking about retiring to become his son's crew chief.

"He had been in the hospital with heart trouble," says Earnhardt. "He was on blood thinner, pills, a special diet. But he was home and doing better. And he had just got the house paid for, and all his racing equipment. He was gonna lay back and take it easy. Then he had that heart attack and he was gone. And I miss him more today than I did then. I remember it took me a year just to get over being mad. That was the last funeral I ever went to."

"Ironheart's" spirit lives on in his son. They call Dale Earnhardt "Ironhead," a variation on the old nickname and a none-too-subtle description of his bruising on-track demeanor. Which brings us to the season upon which we now reflect.

Earnhardt opened the season with a near-miss in the Daytona

Following a confrontation with Neil Bonnett, Ricky Rudd's racer gets some in-pit body work. Photo by R. L. Montgomery

In recognition of his 1000th career start, Richard Petty received a proclamation from the state of Michigan. Photo by R. L. Montgomery

AutoRacing/USA 135

NASCAR/Winston Cup

500, running out of fuel three laps from the end. He had been drafting with eventual winner Geoff Bodine, who, like some of Crew Chief Gary Nelson's past drivers, occasionally got Voyager-like mileage.

The tour moved next to the Fairgrounds Raceway in Richmond. Track promoters have vowed for a decade to expand or abandon that funky half-mile oval. But superspeedway plans have a way of running aground, so NASCAR just keeps coming back to the Fairgrounds. And in 1986, Richmond was a hot spot on the tour.

In the February race, on lap 399 of 400, Waltrip made a clean pass on Earnhardt for the lead in Turn Two. As the two

Bill Elliott's Coors Ford up on jacks at Michigan International Speedway. Photo by R. L. Montgomery

Evaluating 1986's war of words, "Earnhardt (right), gruffer than Waltrip (left) and likely to respond to Waltrip's rapier wit with a verbal meat cleaver, gave as good as he got." Photo by Dick Conway

136 AutoRacing/USA

Chevrolets shot down the backstretch, Earnhardt cozied up to the outside rail, then came hard left into Waltrip's right rear fender.

Waltrip never had a chance. He shot nose-first into the rail, gathering Earnhardt with him. A moment later the wreck collected third-place Joe Ruttman and fourth-place Geoff Bodine as well. Kyle Petty had been running fifth in his Thunderbird, so far back he couldn't see the accident, and when all hell broke loose he drove like an angel, creeping past the wreck at rubberneck speed to take his first (and still only) victory. Not exactly a gala coming-out party for Generation III of the Petty Dynasty, but it will have to do for now.

Waltrip was livid, as was his car owner, Junior Johnson.

**The blistering of tires was a season-long problem at Michigan International Speedway.
Photo by R. L. Montgomery**

AutoRacing/USA 137

NASCAR/Winston Cup

In Richmond's victory circle, Kyle Petty may well be thanking the powers above for his first Winston Cup victory. Photo by Ken Brown/Competition Photographers

In 1986, Bobby Allison alone represented the "old guard" in the win column. He collected his trophy and a hug from Miss Talladega 500, Elizabeth Langner, after his victory at Alabama International Speedway's Winston 500. Photo by Patty Sands/Motorgraphics

At Richmond in February, Earnhardt's (#3) old-time racing style became the subject of high-tech monitoring when he put Waltrip (#11) out of the race. Photo by Ken Brown/Competition Photographers

Earnhardt chuckled and called it good, hard racing. Poor Dale. He had learned everything from his pappy, but "Ironheart" didn't have to deal with instant replay. In his day, what you did on the backstretch was your own business, and a man could pay you back if he had the nerve. Now they can roll and re-roll that slo-mo tape while a nationwide audience watches and fancy-pants commentators, most of whom couldn't drive a nail, make noises of disapproval.

Earnhardt had two choices — either admit he had deliberately wrecked Waltrip or concede that he was a clumsy enough driver to have caused the accident. Earnhardt pleaded innocent by reason of clumsiness. NASCAR slapped his wrist with a $3000 fine. Despite the inauspicious start, Earnhardt and car owner Richard Childress didn't turn conservative. Earnhardt continued to charge, and he won for the first time in the sixth race at Darlington, South Carolina, then won the next time out at North Wilkesboro, North Carolina. By the ninth race of the season he was atop the points standings, and once there he never gave up the lead. He was to sweep the races at Charlotte, his home asphalt, and win the November race in Atlanta.

The circuit's balance was evident as 13 different drivers made it to victory lane. Allison became the oldest NASCAR superspeedway winner at 48 with a victory at Talladega in May. His teammate, Bobby Hillin, became the youngest at 22 at the same track (and using the same engine) in July. Save for Allison, the old guard was shut out. Richard Petty's record for most starts plodded past 1000 while his record for most victories was gathering cobwebs at 200. Cale Yarborough was shut out for the first time in 14 years and announced he will field his own team in 1987. David Pearson all but sat out the season, starting just two races.

Bill Elliott, unable to repeat his successful '85 run at the Winston Million, did capture $240,000 for winning The Winston in May. Photo by Mike Slade

Driving his #11 Budweiser Chevrolet, series runner-up Darrell Waltrip won three races in 1986. Photo by Mike Slade

Ricky Rudd earned two victories and fifth spot in the points behind the wheel of Bud Moore's Motorcraft Ford. Photo by R. L. Montgomery

NASCAR/Winston Cup

Rusty Wallace joined Kyle Petty in the first-time winners category, only Wallace did it twice, and without benefit of miracles. Waltrip won three races, Ricky Rudd and Geoff Bodine a pair apiece. Neil Bonnett, who never seemed quite comfortable in his three-year stint as Junior Johnson's second driver, won once, as did Terry Labonte and the resilient Morgan Shepherd.

Bill Elliott's aerodynamically efficient Thunderbird had dominated the 1985 season but General Motors closed the gap with its "stock" rear glass makeovers (Did anybody ever see a street version of one of those Chevy Monte Carlos or Pontiac 2+2's anywhere other than race track VIP parking lots?) and Elliott

Bobby Allison powers his Miller American Buick through the front stretch at Talladega during the running the Winston 500. It was Allison's first victory in several seasons. Photo by Patty Sands/Motorgraphics

On his way to the win, Ricky Rudd (#15) passes Morgan Shepherd on the low side during Dover's Delaware 500. Photo by Ken Brown/Competition Photographers

The Miller Buick of Bobby Hillin, Jr. (#8) and Dave Marcis' Helen Rae Chevy. Photo by Ken Brown/Competition Photographers

Bill Elliott (#9), Bobby Hillin (#8), Darrell Waltrip (#11), Dale Earnhardt (#3), and Rusty Wallace (#27) show the Miller American 400 fans at Michigan some good ole' NASCAR-type racing. Photo by R. L. Montgomery

140 AutoRacing/USA

Motorcraft spark plugs.
THE LIGHTNING BEHIND ITS THUNDER.

It stormed onto the American performance scene. The Thunderbird Turbo Coupe, moved by a sophisticated four-cylinder turbocharged engine that's as powerful as a V-8. And the lightning behind its high-revving thunder: Motorcraft extended-tip spark plugs. Their nickel-chromium-alloy electrodes are designed to cope with the intense heat of today's high-performance engines. There's a Motorcraft spark plug, as well as a full line of quality-made Motorcraft parts, available for all makes of cars and trucks.

Motorcraft from Ford
EXCEEDS THE NEED

NASCAR/Winston Cup

The question is, does Richmond Fairgrounds Raceway go left to right or right to left? At this point, the answer seems up for grabs. Photo by Ken Brown/ Competition Photographers

Earnhardt (#3) and Richmond (#25) indicate hoods and one fender were optional equipment in '86. Photo by Ken Brown/ Competition Photographers

slipped from 11 victories in 1985 to two in 1986. The new phenom was Tim Richmond, who piled up seven victories and four second-place finishes in the season's last 19 races. He and Bodine — both driving Chevies owned by Charlotte, North Carolina, millionaire car salesman Rick Hendrick — won eight poles apiece.

Richmond showed a new maturity to go with his car-control skill. Under the tutelage of veteran Crew Chief Harry Hyde, Richmond found it was no longer necessary to drive 500 miles in a constant, barely controlled spinout. It was Earnhardt, however, who demonstrated his team's strength over the long haul of the season. Earnhardt won five races, second to only Richmond's seven. He completed far more laps (11,162 of a possible 11,447) and led far more miles than anybody else.

In the latter stages of the season, it became increasingly clear that despite Richmond's brilliance, the only driver with the consistency to catch Earnhardt was Waltrip. By the time the tour returned to the Fairgrounds Raceway in September, Waltrip was making a torrid run at Earnhardt. In eight straight races, Waltrip had finished ahead of Earnhardt, and he had escalated the psychological battle, too. Such an onslaught had wilted Elliott the season before. A laconic Georgia mountaineer, Elliott had no taste for the barb-tongued banter that is Waltrip's forte.

Earnhardt, gruffer than Waltrip and likely to respond to Waltrip's rapier wit with a verbal meat cleaver, gave as good as he got. When Waltrip chided Earnhardt for "stroking" to preserve his points lead, Earnhardt parried with a reminder that Waltrip has a reputation for being too timid on the circuit's

The 1986 NASCAR Champion Spark Plug Rookie of the Year Alan Kulwicki (#33) leads Rookie runner-up Mike Waltrip (#23) into Turn One at Martinsville. Photo by Mike Slade

Running three abreast during Atlanta's Motorcraft 500 are Buddy Baker (#88), Rick Wilson (#4) and Eddie Bierschwale (#6). Photo by Patty Sands/Motorgraphics

After having been pulled from the car with heat exhaustion, Richard Petty watches the remainder of Bristol's Valleydale Meats 500. Photo by Patty Sands/Motorgraphics

AutoRacing/USA 143

NASCAR/Winston Cup

Winners of the Ingersoll-Rand Pit Crew Championship, the Gary Nelson-led Levi Garrett team in action. Photo by Kay Presto

NASCAR/Winston Cup

With the help of RJR's Roger Baer (left), his wife Theresa and Miss Winston Denise Lowrey, Dale Earnhardt displays THE WINSTON CUP. Photo by Patty Sands/Motorgraphics

As there is a new generation of drivers, so is there a new generation of crew chiefs. The renowned Bud Moore (left) shares a contemplative moment with Ernie Elliott. Photo by Mike Slade

fastest tracks, Daytona and Talladega. If that thrust hit home, Waltrip didn't let it show. He simply recalled that Earnhardt allowed "the oldest man in racing," Allison, to outduel him at Talladega.

At the Fairgrounds, Waltrip qualified second to Earnhardt's fifth, and immediately began to predict that in the race he would continue to whittle — if not chop — away at Earnhardt's points lead. Instead, Waltrip's bid to overtake Earnhardt suffered a mortal blow. He lasted just 61 laps before his engine expired. He finished last in the 29-car field. Earnhardt finished second and virtually wrapped up the title.

He finished the job of clinching the Championship in the next-to-the-last race of the season at Atlanta International Raceway. That was a rare feat under the NASCAR points system, which is

Richard Childress went from nice guy but unsuccessful driver to nice guy and Winston Cup Champion car owner. Photo by Al Steinberg

contrived to make the Championship too close to call until the final lap of the season is in the books. Earnhardt clinched the title in style, dominating the Atlanta race and winning it by more than a lap. Afterward, a reporter asked why he bothered to keep stretching the lead after he had the race safely in hand.

"When you go to kick ass, kick ass," said Earnhardt.

Hey, the Champ doesn't mince words.

With Earnhardt's name inked in as the new Champion, the season's denouement was left to Waltrip, who had announced in July that 1986 would be his last season driving for Junior Johnson. In their six seasons together, they had been everything a great team should be, leading the circuit with 43 victories, winning the Championship three years and contending the other three.

Waltrip had been lured away from Johnson by Rick

Dan Elliott, crew member and brother of Bill Elliott, keeps cool during the exceedingly hot running of the Talladega 500. Photo by Patty Sands/Motorgraphics

Junior Johnson may well know more about how to chase a championship than anyone else in racing. Photo by Mike Slade

AutoRacing/USA 147

NASCAR/Winston Cup

Tommy Ellis goes high. Terry Labonte goes low. Neil Bonnett goes sideways. Photo by Bill Zmirski

NASCAR/Winston Cup

Leonard Wood, Crew Chief for Kyle Petty, has produced 77 superspeedway victories, an all-time NASCAR record. Photo by Kay Presto

Neil Bonnett scored one win in '86. Photo by Ken Brown/ Competition Photographers

Former racer Dick Brooks (right) interviews Tim Richmond during a rain delay of the Southern 500. Photo by Mike Slade

At 22, Bobby Hillin, Jr. became the youngest driver to win a big-league NASCAR race when he won the Talladega 500. Photo by Ken Brown/ Competition Photographers

150 AutoRacing/USA

Hendrick, stock car racing's newest plutocrat. Already owner of the two fastest cars on the circuit — the Chevies driven by Bodine and Richmond — Hendrick wanted a third team. He has paired Waltrip, whose strength has been on short tracks, with Waddell Wilson, the builder of demon superspeedway engines. Their future looks intriguing, to say the least.

Waltrip's departure from Johnson's team set off ripples of driver changes. Terry Labonte got the Johnson ride. Sterling Marlin replaced Labonte on the Billy Hagen/Wayne King team. Ron Bouchard got Marlin's job on Hoss Ellington's team, and so on. It was a driver's market. Marlin, who has yet to win a major-league race, was the object of a contract dispute that the owners had to settle with a buyout.

By the time the tour got to Riverside for the final event, the ride-hopping was virtually finished. The usually glib Walltrip,

About the only language common to both Tim Richmond (left) and his Crew Chief Harry Hyde (right) is the language of cars, speed and winning. Photo by Mike Slade

Cockeyed with happiness after winning Daytona's Pepsi Firecracker 400, Richmond is joined in victory circle by team owners Mr. and Mrs. Rick Hendrick (left) and Folgers Team spokesperson T. G. Sheppard (right). Photo by Patty Sands/ Motorgraphics

AutoRacing/USA 151

NASCAR/Winston Cup

Junior Johnson's Budweiser Racing Chevys lead the pack around Daytona's banking. Photo by Sidell Tilghman

AutoRacing/USA 153

NASCAR/Winston Cup

Racing at Dover Downs, Terry Labonte (#44), Dale Earnhardt (#3), J. D. McDuffie (#70), Harry Gant (#33), and Joe Ruttman (#26). Photo by Howard Hodge

Benny Parsons wasn't quite so relaxed when he won the 1986 Winston Invitational at Atlanta. Photo by Al Steinberg

154 AutoRacing/USA

saying goodbye to six years of mutual respect and shared success with Johnson, was moved to silence. In the minutes before the start, Waltrip walked from his pits to a nearby gas pump and cradled his head in his arms for a moment.

"I was really all choked up," he said. "My eyes were filling up and my stomach was all knotted up...that's the first time I've ever driven a car feeling like that."

Comes now 1987, and Earnhardt and car owner Richard Childress may only now be hitting their stride. Last season was their third together since reuniting, and they are showing signs of becoming the kind of team that can defend the Championship. The two were together briefly in 1981 when Earnhardt was between teams. Childress, owner and driver of his own "independent" team, stepped aside as driver and hired out his services as car owner and team manager.

When Earnhardt moved to another team in 1982, Childress could have gone back to driving, but he had gone 0-for-285 in 11 seasons behind the wheel, and Mrs. Childress hadn't raised any mental midgets. Having Earnhardt behind the wheel had been a revelation. Childress knew his shot at success was not as driver but as car owner and team manager.

"I don't think I'd ever have been the caliber of driver Dale is," says Childress. "He's got a talent, a gift. I had fun driving, but I don't think I was a natural-born race driver."

Few are, and fewer still are natural-born Champions.

Harry Gant leads Neil Bonnet (#12), Geoff Bodine (#5) and Joe Ruttman (#26). Photo by Howard Hodge

NASCAR/Winston Cup

In Bristol's victory circle, Rusty Wallace celebrates his first Winston Cup victory after the Valleydale Meats 500. Photo by Patty Sands/Motorgraphics

After qualifying on the pole for Pocono's Miller High Life 500, Geoff Bodine was leading the race when subjected to a rain delay. When the race resumed, his leading manner ended. Bodine finished ninth — the last man on the lead lap. Photo by Howard Hodge

Bill Elliott put his Coors Ford into two 1986 victory circles. Photo by Al Steinberg

Neil Bonnett (#12) passes on the outside of Bill Elliott (#9) during the Daytona 500. Photo by Howard Hodge

156 AutoRacing/USA

On his way to a win at Watkins Glen, Tim Richmond put the Folgers Chevrolet into seven victory circles in 1986. Photo by Howard Hodge

NASCAR/Winston Cup

Not even damage from a crash could stop Tim Richmond from winning the fog-shortened Summer 500 at Pocono. Photo by Howard Hodge

The Rick Hendrick-owned cars of Tim Richmond (#25) and Geoff Bodine (#5) dominated qualifying, earning eight poles each. Photo by Howard Hodge

158 AutoRacing/USA

As Buddy Baker (#88) slips by, Harry Gant (#33) and Joe Ruttman (#26) have a bone-jangling confrontation on Daytona's high banks. Photo by Howard Hodge

Stock cars do not race in any kind of wet conditions, including fog. The field awaits the lifting of a low-hanging cloud at Pocono to embark upon the Summer 500. Photo by Howard Hodge

AutoRacing/USA 159

The Wershow-Ash-Lewis Auctioneers/Thompson Building Materials Pontiac Grand Prix 2+2 of the 1986 NASCAR Winston West Champion Hershel McGriff. Photo by James C. Taylor/Courtesy of RJR

NASCAR/Winston West

by Owen Kearns, Jr.

HERSHEL MCGRIFF WAS CONCISE BUT CLAIRVOYANT IN OUTLINING HIS EXPECTATIONS FOR THE 1986 NASCAR WINSTON WEST STOCK CAR SEASON. "THIS YEAR," SAID THE 58-YEAR-OLD RACING LEGEND, "SHOULD TOP EVERYTHING ELSE."

And it did: McGriff finally captured the Winston West Championship.

The casual observer might wonder how *any* year could better the Portland, Oregon, native's past accomplishments, which include:

— Winning the 1985 Mexican road race at the expense of the top European factory sports car teams and their Formula One drivers;

— Logging a top-10 finish (in the same car) in the first Southern 500 at Darlington, South Carolina;

— Winning four NASCAR (then-called) Grand National stock car races at the tail end of an abbreviated season but on a pace that would have given McGriff, not Lee Petty, the title had McGriff raced all year long;

— Teaming with son, Doug, in the 24 Hours of Le Mans, behind the wheel of a 4,000-pound stock car, to the delight of thousands of French spectators.

Casual spectators, however, cannot perceive McGriff's depth of attachment for Winston West. He's been an on-and-off fixture in the series since its beginning, in 1954, winning his first of 31 races that first season. Although Jack McCoy and Ray Elder have won more races — and Elder, from Caruthers, California, claimed six Championships — McGriff is the acknowledged heart and soul of a series which had more than its share of ups and downs through several eras of stock car racing.

McGriff had come close to filling the void in his trophy shelf. In 1972, in a 30-race season, he won 12 races, finishing 22 times in the top five. But because points were awarded for laps completed, and McGriff fell out of a late-season race shortly after its start, Elder won by 40 1/4 points. Last year, McGriff entered the next-to-final race of the schedule trailing Jim Robinson by just five points. Engine failure in that event doomed the title bid.

No one was saying 1986 *had* to be the year but... Despite running four miles a day and having the stamina of a 30-year-old, McGriff wasn't getting any younger. And the morale of his team, led by veteran Ivan Baldwin, was at issue, as well, following two, snake-bitten campaigns.

As it turned out, the mettle of driver, car builder and team was tested as severely — or more so — than in 1984 or 1985. At the mid-point of the year, his Wershow-Ash-Lewis Auctioneers/Thompson Building Materials Pontiac Grand Prix 2+2 virtually demolished following a bout with the Calgary first turn wall, McGriff was virtually counted out.

McGriff and company, however, came off the canvass with three straight victories to record the most amazing come-back in Winston West history. Trailing eventual Rookie of the Year Chad Little of Spokane, Washington, by 25 points following the Canadian 500 catastrophe, McGriff staged a 41-point turnaround over the final four of eight events to beat the 24-year-old law student by 16 strokes.

A disappointed Little, the third rookie in five years to narrowly miss a Championship never won by a novice, expressed the sentiments of virtually all fellow competitors. "I have to admit," he observed, "that there's nobody I'd like to have seen win it as much as Hershel McGriff, except myself."

McGriff, when he'd finally won the most-pursued prize, was a bit numb. "A lot of my friends," he said, "are probably more excited than I am."

The season the shortest in 33 years but the richest with more that $1 million in posted awards, began on the 2.52-mile road course at Sears Point International Raceway near Sonoma, California. Robinson, from North Hollywood, California, was gunning to join Elder as the only driver to win four consecutive titles. The 187-mile event nearly

One of the most popular drivers to ever wear a Champion's crown, Hershel McGriff. Photo by James C. Taylor/Courtesy of RJR

NASCAR/Winston West

Bill Schmitt scored two wins in his California Cooler Chevrolet finishing third in the points. Photo by David Allio/ Courtesy of RJR

produced a stunning upset as first-year driver Terry Petris put his Petris Homes/Marchman Roofing/3-Way Chevrolet in the lead with six laps remaining. He held off Robinson's Oldsmobile for a couple of circuits but settled for second when his car slid wide in one of the track's tight turns. McGriff, who'd led early, was a lap behind in sixth place, without brakes.

The racing shifted to Riverside, California, for the Budweiser 400, a joint Winston Cup/Winston West affair with separate points awarded for west coast drivers. McGriff, with 14 victories on the 2.62-mile road course was the Winston West favorite, bolstered by his 13th place qualifying effort in a new car. Suspension failure at the end of Riverside's back straightaway, on the second lap, put McGriff off the course at 160 MPH. Glen Steurer's Stick Only Chevrolet was the top finishing Winston West entry for the third consecutive time while Little's Northland Peterbilt/Western Truck Brokers Ford was second. McGriff limped in ninth, 23 laps behind overall winner Darrell Waltrip.

The second Peterbilt Winston Washington 500 at Monroe, Washington's Evergreen Speedway made Little's year. In 1985, Derrike Cope drove George Jefferson's Ford to victory in the 500-lap event on the 0.646-mile oval but switched to another team at season's end. That opened up the seat for Little, a green but promising newcomer.

Jefferson, whose cars have won 10 times in Winston West, is a superb tactician. In a three-way Washington 500 battle with Cope, in the Western Peterbilt Ford, and Winston Cup superstar Bill Elliott, in the Coors/Melling Ford, Little set an exact pace and won the $90,000 race when Elliott — holding a one-second lead — broke an axle with 50 laps to go. McGriff, runner-up in '85, was third with handling problems.

Cut tires were the big story at Race City Speedway, a new, 0.42-mile high-banked oval in Calgary. They sent McGriff, Petris and Steurer into the crashwall and were a factor in a late-race crash which blunted Little's challenge to 1977 and 1979 Winston

The series runner-up and 1986 NASCAR Winston West Rookie of the Year Chad Little. Photo by David Allio/Courtesy of RJR

West Champion Bill Schmitt. The 50-year-old Schmitt, who hadn't won in his California Cooler Chevrolet since 1984, had a seven-lap advantage over Little at the finish. His $14,300 victory helped Schmitt become the first Winston West driver to win move that $300,000 in a career.

When the going got tough, McGriff got going. The scene shifted to Tacoma, Washington, the site of NASCAR's first through-the-streets event. Baldwin and Hershel McGriff, Jr., worked round-the-clock to rebuild the Pontiac. McGriff

Rather than capturing his fourth consecutive Winston West title, Jim Robinson took only one win in 1986, finishing fourth in the points battle. Photo by David Allio/ Courtesy of RJR

NASCAR/Winston West

In the Tacoma Grand Prix victory circle with Linda Vaughn, Hershel McGriff was unaware that he is the only driver to compete in both the first NASCAR superspeedway race (Darlington) and the first NASCAR street race (Tacoma). Photo by David Allio

practiced a backup car and ultimately qualified fifth, the car rolling to the line with the nose in primer. Cope, who'd competed in several early Winston Cup races, sat on the pole and battled Ruben Garcia's Suncrest Motorhomes Chevrolet in the early going. Garcia DNF'd with a broken driveline on the 32nd lap and Cope seemed a sure winner until having to pit for gas just short of the finish. McGriff, running a steady pace, won while Little — victim of tire problems while running second — wound up 10th.

An early contender for NASCAR's Winston Cup rookie honors, Derrike Cope was forced by the reality of inadequate financing to return to the Winston West wars. Photo by Patty Sands/Motorgraphics

Cope again was on the pole at 1.95-mile Portland International Raceway but never led a lap, spinning wildly in the first turn at the start. The 300-kilometer race settled down to a Garcia-McGriff duel with McGriff — again — destined for second place until fate intervened. Garcia spun out 19 laps short of the checkered flag. Little was fifth, a lap behind.

At Willow Springs Raceway, near southern California's Edwards Air Force Base, Cope won his third consecutive pole but again had difficulty staying on the track. So did McGriff, who got into a shoving match with several cars entering the first turn of the 125-mile Suncrest Motorhomes 200. Result: spin and cut tire and last place in the 24-car field. Miraculously, McGriff slashed his way back into the lead by the 17th lap and out-dueled Cope to become the first Winston West driver to win three straight races since 1976. Little, who'd led briefly, slipped back with an oil leak but salvaged fifth.

Riverside's Winston Western 500 finale was anticlimactic. McGriff entered the race with a 10-point lead and when Little's Ford exited with engine failure on the 54th lap, the title was delivered. McGriff's Pontiac also failed to finish but, this time, it had lasted long enough. Schmitt, one of only two Winston West drivers running at the finish, was three laps behind winner Tim Richmond.

McGriff won nearly $70,000, a one-season record, giving him nearly $300,000 for his career. More than one-third of that was won in 1985-86, underlining the monetary growth of the series.

Some felt McGriff might retire, having finally scaled the last mountain. They were wrong. "That's never crossed my mind," McGriff said. "When the time comes, it'll be just as big a surprise to me as it is to you."

McGriff still thinks there's plenty of winning to be done.

"Hey," he told reporters interviewing him after the Winston Western 500, "I can go right out now and run another 500 (kilometers) if I can borrow Tim's car!"

The Tacoma Dome arena was turned into a stock car garage when the Winston West show came to town. Photo by David Allio/Courtesy of RJR

IROC

Photo by Michael J. Marrer

The Budweiser International Race of Champions (IROC), with one decade under its wheels, consisted of four races in 1986. Two superspeedway events combined with two road course races to test the talents of twelve drivers representing the best of the abilities the diverse sport of auto racing can generate. The series' first race, held in February at Daytona International Speedway, was won by Al Unser. Al Unser, Jr. kept the family's winning ways in focus by capturing the second (Mid-Ohio) and fourth (Watkins Glen) events. Cale Yarborough managed to out-Unser the Unsers in the third event and drove into Victory Circle at Talladega's Alabama International Motor Speedway.

The series Championship, worth $164,100, was won by Al Unser, Jr. Following him in the point standings were: Bill Elliott, Cale Yarborough, Al Unser, Sr., Darrell Waltrip, Harry Gant, Bobby Rahal, Klaus Ludwig, Hans Stuck, Hurley Haywood, Jochen Mass, and Rick Mears.

Photo by Howard Hodge

Photo by Mike Slade

Formula I
Detriot Grand Prix

The Renault-powered John Player Special Team Lotus 98T of Brazilian Ayrton Senna first sat on the pole and then in victory circle at the Detroit Grand Prix. Photo by Bob Brodbeck

The pit set-up for Team Lotus. Photo by Steve Swope

In the Detroit pits, Team Haas-Ford USA crew members work on the Neil Oatley-designed Lola of Alan Jones. Photo by Bob Brodbeck

The Marlboro McLaren-TAG MP4/2C of 1986 World Champion Alain Prost Photo by Bob Brodbeck

Series runner-up Englishman Nigel Mansell put his Patrick Head-designed Canon Williams-Honda FW11 on the outside front row at Detroit. Photo by Bob Brodbeck

AutoRacing/USA 169

Formula Atlantic

by Steve Nickless, "SportsCar" Magazine

THE "REGIONAL PRO SERIES" CONCEPT NEATLY RESUSCITATED NORTH AMERICAN FORMULA ATLANTIC RACING IN 1983. THREE SEASONS LATER THERE IS MUCH OF THE OLD MAGIC IN EVIDENCE AS WELL. A NINE-ROUND 1986 WEST COAST ATLANTIC RACING (WCAR) series on the Pacific coast and a nine-round E-Z Wider-sponsored ECAR equivalent in the east and midwest brought even more of the luster back to what was once this continent's pre-eminent stepping-stone series.

WCAR, a loosely formal organization founded by SCCA Director Jon Norman and fellow Atlantic entrants Gudrun and Rick Shea, and Tim Fortner, bloomed in 1986: Quality fields yielded nine superb events on some of the west coast's finest tracks and the title went to the wire with no fewer than four drivers having a real mathematical shot in the final race. (One — electrifying returnee Tom Phillips — skipped in favor of prepping for an Indy Car debut but the other three — Dan Marvin, Ted Prappas and Roberto Quintanilla — qualified one-two-three! Team Tui Ralt driver Prappas clinched the Championship by shadowing race winner Quintanilla to the flag as former champ Marvin lost a wheel nut and a lap-and-a-half in the pits.)

ECAR, founded and managed by Vicki O'Connor's Pro-Motion Agency (which put Pro Sports 2000 racing on the map in this country), capitalized on an outstanding 1985 premier with bigger purses and greater prestige in 1986. This Championship, too, went to the wire (Young Canadian Scott Goodyear, a five-race winner, won the Florida finale and the Championship, having traded victories all summer long with the Englishman, Calvin Fish).

With at least one established manufacturer set to take on dominant chassis builder Ralt in 1987 and the administration of the west coast series being assumed by the eager and apparently well funded Stefan Petroff Industries organization, Formula Atlantic racing is riding a fresh wave of enthusiasm.

It's carbureted 1.6-liter Cosworth music to the ears....

The 1986 WCAR Champion Ted Prappas earned three pole positions and won an equal number of races in his Team Tui Ralt. Photo by Jay Smith/Courtesy of SPI

The 1986 ECAR E-Z Wider Champion Scott Goodyear won five of the series' nine events in his Tom Mitchell Racing Tricon Ralt RT-4. Photo by Peter Gloede

Goodyear leads the field at Mid-Ohio. Photo by Ken Brown/Competition Photographers

Formula Atlantic

Dan Marvin's talents are evident not only on the race track but also in his choice of reading material. Photo by John Zimmermann

Prappas flanked by series runner-up Roberto Quintanilla (right) and third-place man Dan Marvin (left). Photo by Jay Smith/Courtesy of SPI

ECAR runner-up Calvin Fish after victory at Summit Point. Photo by Ken Brown/Competition Photographers

172 AutoRacing/USA

COMMENTARY

by Brock Yates

FOR MORE YEARS THAN I CAN REMEMBER I HAVE BEEN BEHAVING AS THE "CHICKEN LITTLE" OF INTERNATIONAL MOTOR RACING, PREDICTING TIME AND AGAIN THAT THE ECONOMIC HOUSE OF CARDS THAT SUPPORTS THIS SPORT WILL ULTIMATELY COLLAPSE OF its own weight. For the same amount of time I have been dead wrong, each season witnessing what I expect to be a major financial crisis and then viewing — with some relief — the continued prosperity of the sport. But now it looks as if the day of reckoning is approaching. Repent, you sinners, or we will be facing the equivalent of the stockbrokers of 1929 standing precariously on their window ledges contemplating the last big leap.

The harsh fact is that the economic situation worldwide which has brought immeasurable prosperity to the sport is about to fade into the middle distance. We have seen billions, literally billions, of dollars injected into automobile racing since the boom-days began in the early 1960's. It started in the United States with the great tire war between Goodyear and Firestone and the struggle between Ford Motor Company and Chrysler Corporation (with the shadow-like participation of General Motors). It has been estimated that during the decade of the 1960's these economic powerhouses infused international motorsports with more than $100 million dollars in support in both overt and convert ways. But even then in those halcyon days there was little in the way of series sponsorship. Most races were run as free-standing events with little or no overall sponsor support.

But that all changed in the 1970's. Major automobile manufacturers dropped out, in part because of governmental pressures, and in part in response to changing public concern about fuel economy and the environment. The sport then dove into the new world of event sponsorship. It began in a big way when S.C. Johnson, the manufacturer of car waxes, gave major support to the SCCA Can-Am series. USAC responded with support from Marlboro and in the south R.J. Reynolds became a major player in NASCAR stock car racing with its Winston Cup. A few years later IMSA received a giant boost, thanks to RJR's Camel brand. This opened the flood gates for massive sponsorship participation at all levels. Virtually everybody in the sport was on the street hustling any number of cock-a-mamie schemes guaranteed to sell every imaginable product from toilet seats to roach wrappers.

Much of the marketing justification for such sponsorships was based on what was expected to be the boom in motorsports television. Those of us who were around in the wild days of the 1960's recall motor racing being touted as "the sport of the 70's." In retrospect it is more than likely that motorsports was the sport of the 1960's. That is when the modern era was created and with it the blind optimism that the economics of the business would continue to increase on an exponential basis. For awhile television was a big player. Certainly ABC's prime-time telecast of the Indianapolis 500, coupled with CBS's live telecasts of the Daytona 500 inspired whoozy dreams on the part of motorsports aficionados. It was fantacized that a day would come when automobile racing would displace or at least rival the National Football League and professional baseball as the number-one television spectator sport. After all, was it not endlessly and tediously quoted that motor racing was the number one spectator sport in the United States (if horse racing and its betting mentality was discounted)? However, the stark reality is that that enthusiasm — which has fragmented throughout dozens of types of motorsports — has never been transplanted into big numbers on national television. While the Indianapolis 500 and the Daytona 500 have attracted impressive rating numbers, they look miniscule when compared to those generated by the World Series or the Super Bowl or by any number of major, mainstream sporting events. In the last five years we have experienced a steady decline in the number of televised races on the networks and more importantly, a radical drop in the amount of dollars being paid in rights fees. Two examples: NBC has steadily reduced its once widespread coverage of the CART Indianapolis racing series, and in 1987 will televise only a handful of events. They will hand off the rest to the worthies at ESPN, whose reputation for low-ball production values has, in the minds of many, *diminished*, not increased, the appeal of motorsports to the masses. Moreover, CBS has radically reduced its motorsports commitment, as has ABC — which in the 1970's was extremely active in televising the sport.

Worse yet, the dollars being infused via television's rights fees have almost ended. There was a day in the not so recent past when even the most podunk, bush-league NASCAR stock car race could demand television rights fees of $50-to-$100 thousand. Today any number of automobile races on the CART, NASCAR, and IMSA schedules are available for no rights fees at all, and

COMMENTARY

in fact, many promoters are quietly prepared to ante up their own money to get an event on television.

Unfortunately, while a massive modification in the economic foundation of racing has been taking place, i.e. diminishing returns from television and the subsequent awareness by big dollar sponsors that the sport has been oversold in terms of its nationwide exposure and attendent commercial value, nothing has been done by most of the major sanctioning bodies to control cost. We have reached a point today where a serious effort to compete with an Indianapolis-type car costs at least $2 million and perhaps as much as $6 million per year. The Formula One series is based on a ludicrous financial structure with probably $20 million necessary to win or at least seriously compete for the World Championship. IMSA Camel GT competition with its miniscule purses requires budgets of over $1 million to be an active player. Only NASCAR and its Winston Cup cars have maintained any semblance of price reality. A major effort with a Winston Cup car can be mounted for something in the neighborhood of a million dollars, but considering the high level of interest of some types of sponsors and the very healthy purses being generated on the NASCAR schedule, it remains the most viable of the major world series. And the fact that this series grows in participation each season — while the number of cars in IMSA and CART remain in stasis — only amplifies the relatively solid economic foundation that part of the sport enjoys.

Sadly the worst appears yet to come. The hostile takeover attempt by Sir James Goldsmith of the Goodyear Tire and Rubber Company can only bode ill for that august firm's participation in motorsport. It has long been a contention of those within the company that their motorsport budget would at some time have to be brought into line. But the management realizes that they are participants in a kind of welfare state necessary to keep a number of motorsport series operating. Until now that has prevented Goodyear from dropping by the wayside. But the mandated strictures caused by the Goldsmith effort have perhaps given Goodyear a valid excuse to pull back. Much of the generous support from Akron will become a thing of the past. This can only adversely affect many major racing teams that have taken for granted the supply of free or low cost race tires in years past when estimating their bloated annual budget. Not only does Goodyear appear to be a lessened force in the years to come but its partner in town, BFGoodrich (now known as Uniroyal Goodrich), is also reducing its racing activities for a number of reasons. Part of this has to do with economies of scale, others have to do with new emphasis on marketing.

It is also possible that Detroit will begin to refocus its motorsports efforts in the future. The new reality that over 50 percent of all new automobiles are purchased either by women or with direct influence from them has already caused Chevrolet to alter its advertising campaign. There is every likelihood that other manufacturers, both imported and domestic, will follow suit. That could mean reduced participation in motorsports. The Champion Sparkplug Company, one of the oldest and most devoted supporters of automobile racing, is rapidly diminishing as a force. To be sure other big time accessory manufacturers like Bosch, PPG etc. in company with cigarette and beer companies, may continue to absorb the losses but that cannot be expected to last forever.

So what is to be done? The answer is simple. Over the years motor racing has operated on two levels: One, as pure entertainment, a sporting attraction for which people pay good money to watch interesting and exciting competition. On the second level it was a technical enterprise. Major manufacturers developed new products and competed with them in a test environment. As we know, the second reason has slowly disappeared. Car-makers use computers and test tracks to develop their products. Mercedes-Benz is an example, perhaps the most technologically advanced automobile manufacturer in the world (or certainly one of the two or three) maintains that motorsport is essentially valueless as a testing ground. Technology has long since outrun motorsports as a viable ground for developing most new products. In fact costs and absurd performance levels have forced the banning of such advanced devices as turbines, moveable air foils, skirts, Wankel rotary engines, four-wheel-drive, and any number of other sophisticated components that could be used in creating the ultimate, technologically perfect racing machines.

Therefore it would appear the primary mission of

motorsports is that of providing entertainment. That goal is best accomplished at present by the Winston Cup series. Massive crowds are attracted to closely contested races. The vehicles are basic, even crude, by comparison to contemporary Formula One cars. But their entertainment factor is without comparison. The same can be said for ASA and All Pro short track stock car racing or the World of Outlaw Sprint Car series. Here men compete with cars that are strong, simple and easily maintained, yet are essentially equal in performance. These series run under strictly measured rules that prevent costs from escalating to the ridiculous levels that will ultimately cause the CART series to become an exotic enclave, much like Formula One, where a tiny, elite cadre of excellent drivers and superb automobiles race against each other but in a closed-loop system.

There may be room for one or two such series. As long as the Indianapolis 500 exists as the greatest race in the world, CART can probably maintain itself (although a day may soon come when 33 Indy-type cars will not be able to fill the grid.) Formula One will remain as an absurd exercise in extravagance. But the grass roots of motorsports, especially in the United States, must get off the dole. Organizers must recognize that the television dollars of the past are gone forever. They must recognize that the sport is not capable of displacing football and baseball in the United States or even to contest secondary sports for supremacy. Automobile racing is unfortunately fragmented by literally dozens of different permutations that do not overlap.

The doors of potential sponsors have been pounded into submission. Many of those doors are locked now that marketing evaluations have determined that the sport is not the magic formula to sales that it has long been heralded to be. We must drive ahead in motorsports but it cannot be done with the Pollyanna-ish notions that the money wells of the television networks, the cable networks and the major sponsors are bottomless. Unless costs are brought into line in the immediate future, racing could be remembered as the sport of the 1960's that died in the 1990's.

SCCA/Bendix Trans-Am

by Bill Mitchell

THE 1986 SCCA BENDIX TRANS-AM WAS A RENEWAL OF THE GREAT FORD-CHEVY BATTLES OF THE LATE SIXTIES, BUT WITH A NASTY DIFFERENCE. ON THE SURFACE IT WAS JUST LIKE MARK DONOHUE VS PARNELLI JONES; CAMARO VS MUSTANG; US VS THEM. BUT BENEATH the surface lay the vicious undertow of emotions stemming from the division of 1985's all-conquering Roush/Protofab team into Roush Racing (Ford) and Protofab Racing (Chevrolet). At the close of '86, Wally Dallenbach, Jr., and the Lincoln-Mercury Mercur Division of Ford each retained custody of their '85 titles... in spite of each other. (Indeed, it was Dallenbach who initiated the contact with Chevrolet which led to the establishment of Protofab Engineering — the design and development arm — and Protofab Racing — the race team.) After the separation the Roush and Protofab teams revealed very different personalities: Protofab and Dallenbach went racing by the book. Jack Roush threw away the book and did whatever it took to win.

Dallenbach became the first driver to win consecutive Trans-Am Driver's Championships since Bob Tullius in 1977-78. And he was the first ever to successfully defend his title after having switched manufacturers.

Dallenbach's achievement becomes all the more remarkable when one realizes the formidable obstacles faced by Protofab last spring. The newly formed team did not have cars, sponsors, transporters, or even a place to work. What they did have was a talented crew — the heart if not the soul of Roush/Protofab — and a contract with Chevrolet. And they had an ace in the hole — Bob Riley, who was anxiously awaiting his April 1 retirement date from Ford so he could re-emerge as President of Protofab Engineering.

The season began at Riverside. There, Dallenbach qualified the brand-new Protofab Camaro on the pole by nearly a second. A broken distributor rotor sidelined him on the season's first race-lap but he came back to win the next three events: Sears Point, Portland and Detroit.

The Detroit race also saw the introduction of a new Protofab Camaro, this one powered by a V6 engine and driven by '78 Trans-Am Champion Greg Pickett, another ex-Roush/Protofab driver. The 4.5-liter V6, which is really 3/4's of a 360 V8, was allowed to run 250 pounds lighter than the 5.1-liter V8. That made for a more nimble car, easier on tires and brakes. At Mid-Ohio, the next race, Pickett won following a first-turn accident which eliminated his Protofab teammates. Then at Brainerd, Pickett passed Roush's lead drivers, Pete Halsmer and Scott Pruett, in the final five laps for victory, the fifth in a row for Protofab and Chevrolet. This win established the V6 as the car to beat. The introduction of the V6's gave Protofab another weapon, one which Dallenbach chose to utilize after Road America.

Protofab had seemingly accomplished their objectives. They had built the best normally aspirated Trans-Am car the series had ever seen. On tight tracks it was heads and shoulders above the opposition. But for all their early glory, Protofab was destined to win just one of the final seven races.

Ford had decreed that Roush would campaign the Merkur XR4Ti in '86 rather than the V8 Capri, which was soon to go out of production. This meant developing both a new chassis and a new motor. Ford tried to get permission to run the Probe GTP motor but the SCCA turned them down. That left Lee White, Roush's new Team Manager, less than six months to design, build and test the Merkur four-cylinder turbo motor. And White, who came to Roush from Paul Miller's Porsche team, knew the Camaros weren't the only competition for his turbo-motor. Meanwhile, Roush hedged all bets by keeping V8 Capris.

Roush also had to find two new drivers to replace Dallenbach and Ribbs, who had gone to NASCAR. He chose veteran Pete Halsmer and young Scott Pruett. Halsmer had an engineering degree from Purdue and a great deal of experience in turbo-charged cars, ranging from CART to IMSA GTP. Pruett was a Kart legend who drove for Roush/Protofab in a couple of '85 IMSA

From Basalt, Colorado, Wally Dallenbach, Jr. Photo by Randy McKee

The Protofab Racing Chevrolet Camaro of 1986 SCCA Bendix Brakes Champion Wally Dallenbach. Photo by Bill Stahl

SCCA/Bendix Trans-Am

The Paul Newman Fan Club as conceived and organized by Dallenbach (center) and Kneifel (right). Photo by Werner Fritz

GTO races. The '86 plans called for Pruett to concentrate on GTO while Halsmer led the Merkur developmental effort. However, for the Riverside opener Pruett would compete in an IMSA GTO event in Charlotte on Saturday, then fly cross-country to Riverside for Sunday's Trans-Am race. Since he couldn't qualify, he had to start at the back of the grid in his Capri. In a very dramatic race, Pruett charged through the field to win his first Trans-Am. Halsmer, also competing in the Trans-Am for the first time, took second in the Merkur's initial outing. Chris Kneifel, at the wheel of another Roush Capri, completed the top-three picture by finishing third.

The Motorcraft/Mac Tools Merkur began demonstrating its potential in qualifying with poles at Portland (Halsmer) and Detroit (Klaus Ludwig). The first Merkur victory came at Road America, the season's seventh event, in a 60-mile heat-race which determined starting positions for the 100-mile main event.

Halsmer and Dallenbach dueled throughout the race with Halsmer claiming victory at the end.

It was Halsmer's teammates, Scott Pruett and Chris Kneifel, who earned points in the next four races, bringing the Lincoln-Mercury Merkur Division back into the battle for the Manufacturer's Championship. Roush knew that a winning melody needed both woofers and tweeters, and he had both in the big, booming V8 Capris and the turbo Merkur which emitted a whistle whenever the driver shifted gears.

The race at Road Atlanta, the 11th in the series, was decisive, controversial and wet. Dallenbach captured the pole with a remarkable on-and-over-the-edge lap on what should have been a Merkur track. But it was all for naught as a rain shower washed over the field as they sat on the grid. This race would not go to the fastest, but rather to the best survivor. That proved to be Chris Kneifel who drove his Merkur to his first Trans-Am victory after

Chris Kneifel fends off a congress of Camaros. Photo by Bruce Schulman

SCCA/Bendix Trans-Am

Jack Roush. Photo by Randy McKee

leader Jim Miller collided with Pete Halsmer.

This might have been dismissed as just an unfortunate racing incident between an over-anxious driver trying to win his first race and a veteran driver trying to deal with a stuttering, stumbling car. But then Protofab provided the SCCA with an audio tape of the radio transmission between Halsmer and his car chief Rick Dilcher. Therein Dilcher (following orders) told Halsmer to block Miller. The sanctioning body fined Halsmer $2,000 for, "rough and dangerous driving."

That was when the series got nasty. Suddenly Roush was showing everyone the "Wally bars" he had installed on the rear of all his cars: additional material designed to protect vital components from contact from the rear. And suddenly the season was being reviewed in a different light. What about the collision between Kneifel and Jim Miller at Riverside which knocked Miller out of the lead? Or the four car, first turn crash at Mid-Ohio which eliminated Dallenbach, Miller and Halsmer? Or the heavy collision between Halsmer and Miller at Lime Rock (Halsmer was running without front brakes; Miller braked early to let him by and the courtesy put both cars into the bank)? And what about the contact between Dallenbach (the chaser) and

One half of the Roush Racing moveable garage. Photo by Mike Slade

180 AutoRacing/USA

LINCOLN-MERCURY-MERKUR THUNDERS TO 5-CAR SWEEP, WINS THIRD STRAIGHT CHAMPIONSHIP CUP.

MERKUR XR4TiS FINISH 1-2 IN ST. PETERSBURG ROUT.

Lincoln-Mercury-Merkur captured its third consecutive Trans-Am Manufacturer's Championship with an impressive five-car sweep of the final race at St. Petersburg, Fla.

Pete Halsmer, driving a Motorcraft/Mac Tools Merkur XR4Ti, claimed the victory, edging past teammate Klaus Ludwig in a Budget-sponsored Merkur XR4Ti with just one mile left in the contest.

It was the third win in a row for the Merkur XR4Ti, a race-prepared version of the sports coupe sold by Lincoln-Mercury-Merkur dealers. With the victory, Lincoln-Mercury-Merkur won its third Trans-Am Manufacturer's Championship Cup.

All told, the turbocharged four-cylinder Merkur XR4Ti won four checkered flags in this, its very first year of Trans-Am racing. A satisfying record. And a good indication of the satisfying performance that awaits with one test drive of a Merkur XR4Ti. For more information, visit a Lincoln-Mercury-Merkur dealer, or call **1-800-822-9292**.

MERKUR MOTORSPORT
LINCOLN-MERCURY-MERKUR

SCCA/Bendix Trans-Am

Halsmer or Pruett (the leaders); was that banging by Dallenbach who had the V6 which was faster in the corners or blocking by Halsmer and Pruett in their faster cars.

The Manufacturer's Championship was on the line in the two Florida races and both teams brought in late-season pinch hitters. Chevrolet added Willy T. Ribbs in the Brooks Racing Camaro and Ford added Klaus Ludwig in the Budget-Rent-a-Car Merkur normally driven by Mike Miller. There might have been more pinch hitters, but an "arms limitation" agreement between top-level executives of Chevrolet and Ford kept the others out.

The races at Tamiami and St. Petersburg were a Merkur show. At Tamiami Pete Halsmer led from the pole until an exhaust manifold failure slowed him. Klaus Ludwig won after dropping to 22nd as a result of a first lap spin caused, not by a Chevrolet driver, but by Ludwig Heimrath, Jr., in his Porsche 944 Turbo. At St. Petersburg Roush was simply overwhelming as Halsmer and Ludwig dueled flatout for the entire race before

Mike Miller drove his Budget Rent-a-Car Capri to fifth place in the series. Photo by Mike Slade

182   AutoRacing/USA

Although Jim Miller's year in the Protofab Camaro wasn't without its rough spots, he supported his team admirably with some fine driving. Photo by Peter Gloede

From Anaheim, California, Les Lindley finished seventh in points. Photo by Randy McKee

SCCA/Bendix Trans-Am

Jim Sanborn (#35) leads Jerry Kuhn (#51) and Kerry Hitt (#19) around a very wet Tamiami Park. Photo by Bill Stahl

Tommy Riggins leads Jim Fitzgerald (#38) and Jim Derhaag (#40) down the straight at Road America. Photo by Bruce Schulman

Ludwig Heimrath, Jr. fills the mirrors of race winner Chris Kneifel at Road Atlanta. Photo by Sidell Tilghman

Slithering through the rain at Road Atlanta, Ludwig Heimrath, Jr. had the field covered with his Porsche 944T until clutch and transmission problems forced him to retire. Photo by Ken Brown/Competition Photographers

The Motorcraft/Mac Tools Merkur XR4Ti of series runner-up Pete Halsmer. Photo by Ken Brown/Competition Photographers

Elliott Forbes-Robinson scored six top-five finishes in his Performance Motorsports Buick Somerset. Photo by Ken Brown/Competition Photographers

SCCA/Bendix Trans-Am

Leading Jerry Clinton (#63), Peter Dus (#46) and Pete Halsmer (#3) over the crest at Lime Rock is Paul Newman (#33) who went on to win. Photo by Randy McKee

pole-sitter Halsmer, who had lost the lead to Ludwig at the start, passed Ludwig on the last lap. Roush Racing finished 1-2-3-4-5 with their combination of woofers and tweeters. Protofab and Chevrolet had been soundly beaten.

In the past, Chevrolet has historically down-played their connection with race teams. The official position was that Chevy built good parts which winning teams chose to use. Their relationship with Protofab was a bold step forward into the limelight. The trouble was that when Chevrolet chose to come out of the closet they stepped into Ford's living room. Ford began with a small but acknowledged factory effort in 1981 and the program grew until it dominated in '84 and '85. Chevrolet now has to decide whether to come all the way out or go back into the closet.

Dallenbach had quietly clinched the Driver's Championship at Tamiami but the drama of the Manufacturer's Championship often seemed to overshadow his accomplishment. He was a frustrated Champion, feeling the Chevrolet team had been "out-knobbed" and "out-spent" by Roush Racing. But throughout the final races when he had to chase a superior car, he displayed moments of great talent which should lead him on to the levels to which he aspires.

There was fantastic racing in the '86 Bendix Trans-Am. In the

The F.S.I. Sprinkler/Lindley Chevrolet Camaro. Photo by Peter Gloede

SCCA/Bendix Trans-Am

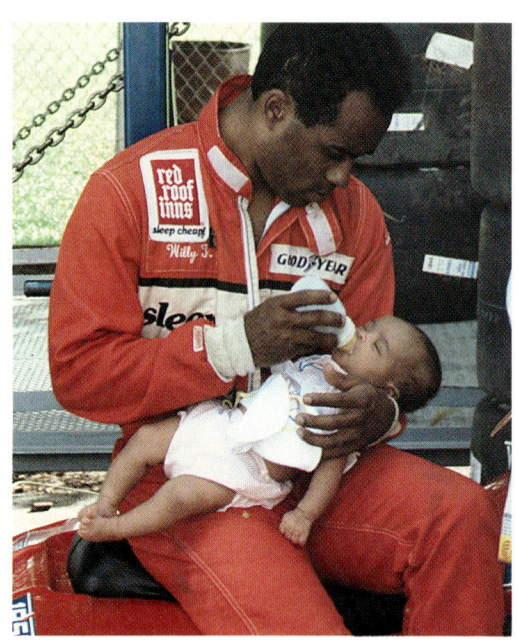

Willy T. Ribbs feeds newborn daughter Sasha during a break in the racing action. Photo by Paul Tyler

Designer Bob Riley, recently of Ford, now President of Protofab Engineering. Photo by Rich Chenet

Pete Halsmer from Anaheim, California. Photo by Dan Bianchi

Chris Kneifel, from Lake Forest, Illinois, finished third in points. Photo by Drew Gloede

Performance Motorsports Team drivers John Schneider (left) and Elliott Forbes-Robinson. Photo by Peter Gloede

Scott Pruett made selected appearances in the Motorcraft/Mac Tools Merkur XR4Ti and finished eighth in points. Photo by Bruce Schulman

SCCA/Bendix Trans-Am

middle of the season came 460 miles of racing at four tracks with the leader never more than five seconds ahead of second place, which was a different manufacturer with a different engine combination (V8 VS V6 VS 4-cylinder turbo or V6 turbo). But the raw human emotion which fueled the season was eventually distilled into cold metalic parts and pieces which made the Merkur a superior car. The Merkur didn't arrive in time to contest the Driver's Championship, though Halsmer did finish second. Arrive in time it did, however, to capture the Manufacturer's Championship. And it may so continue for several years.

It would be simplistic to say a Ford-Chevy battle is as simple as, "us VS them" — not with all the personal ties among the participants, to say nothing about "the others." Was Chevrolet driver Jim Miller not going to talk to Merkur driver Mike Miller, his younger brother? And how could Dallenbach and Kneifel plan their great practical jokes on Paul Newman without crossing factory lines occasionally?

After an exhange of press releases, Newman escalated the practical jokes war at Detroit when he hired an airplane to tow a message over the pre-grid: "Chris and Wally, call Mommy." Dallenbach and Kneifel retaliated at Road America by arranging for a bus-load of senior citizens, wearing "Paul Newman Fan Club" sweatshirts, to invade Newman's pit and

Regardless of who did what to whom and with what motivation, this was the result of the confrontation between Halsmer and Jim Miller at Road Atlanta. Photo by Ken Brown/Competition Photographers

Former Trans-Am Champion Greg Pickett contested eight of the '86 Trans-Ams, scoring two wins. Photo by Mike Slade

Paul Newman of Westport, Connecticut. Photo by Peter Gloede

The Protofab Camaros of Dallenbach (#8) and teammate Jim Miller negotiate Lime Rock. Photo by Randy McKee

192 AutoRacing/USA

SCCA/Bendix Trans-Am

loudly demand autographs and photos. But Newman got the ultimate revenge at Lime Rock. He began avenging himself by acting the part of a Pied Piper (with actress Marsha Mason and actor Tom Cruise assisting), leading the crowd surrounding his pits on a tour through the Roush and Protofab pits. The multitude converged on the teams busily involved in pre-race preparations and were led by Newman around the cars, through the semis, and were even helped to sit in the race cars. But the ultimate joke was when the 61-year-old actor won the race by passing his former Can-Am driver, Elliott Forbes-Robinson, right after the Halsmer-Miller accident and then held on for his second Trans-Am victory.

And there were others in the '86 Trans-Am, though they didn't win any races. Forbes-Robinson and John Schneider returned in the Performance Motorsports Buick Somersets. They had proven the worth of the V6 last year with two wins and the addition of Buick's fuel injection this year made them early season favorites in some books. But they got off to a late start building their new cars and never really caught up. They also faced the tough task of

Swelling the ranks of the Ford forces as Ford lunged for the Manufacturers' Championship at season's end, Klaus Ludwig won Tamiami and finished second at St. Petersburg. Photo by Bruce Schulman

SCCA/Bendix Trans-Am

fighting the factories with a largely independent effort. EFR made fine showings in finishing second five times. At Tamiami he nearly beat Klaus Ludwig but the power of the Merkur negated EFR's advantage in the corners.

Tommy Riggins also ran a limited Trans-Am schedule in a Buick Somerset. He benefited from better aerodynamics than the bricks. . .er, Buicks of EFR and Schneider, but suffered from mechanical problems, largely a result of his limited budget. A third at Brainerd was his best placing. He certainly accomplished the most with the least.

The final factory team was Ludwig Heimrath, Jr., in the Porsche 944 Turbo. This small team appeared at the Riverside opener but did not qualify following a series of engine and car problems. The motor then went back to Andial for development. It reappeared at Mosport and displayed some of the highest MPH readings before breaking. Heimrath's best showing was at Road Atlanta in the wet. The powerful turbo Porsche might be expected to be an unruly handful in wet conditions but Heimrath

At the wheel of the Brooks Racing Camaro at the season's last two events, Willy T. Ribbs' task was to pile up points for Chevy. He finished fifth at Tamiami but was sidelined with a broken drive shaft at St. Petersburg. Photo by Bruce Schulman

SCCA/Bendix Trans-Am

tamed it and led the race until gearbox woes sidelined him.

"The Independents" were what the drivers without factory connections called themselves (although some did have small factory assistance). Eppie Wietzes was the best of these as he accomplished wonders with his under-financed Camaro. Like fellow Canadian Heimrath, he was at his best in the wet at Road Atlanta.

Les Lindley and Jerry Miller were the first drivers to try the Chevy V6. Lindley was second in the points early in the season with a fourth at the Riverside opener his best finish. Jerry Miller was down on power with his Armour Camaro but the rain at Road Atlanta gave the ex-sprint car driver a fifth, his best result in two years of Trans-Am racing.

Jim Derhaag ran a Pontiac Trans-Am with a 9:1 low-compression motor, an economy formula designed by the SCCA to help independents. Derhaag was named the series' "Most Improved Driver" for 1986.

The Newman-Sharp Racing Nissan 300ZX Turbo on the streets of Detroit. Photo by Steve Swope

SCCA/Volkswagen Cup

by Bill Mitchell

ALISTAIR OAG WON THE VOLKSWAGEN CUP CHAMPIONSHIP IN HIS SIXTH YEAR IN THE SERIES. OAG'S TWO WINS AT LAGUNA SECA AND ON THE MILWAUKEE MILE, COMBINED WITH THREE SECONDS AND FIVE OTHER TOP-SIX FINISHES, EARNED HIM THE title ahead of Al Salerno, who won four races. Oag is just the third Champion in the nine year history of the VW Cup, as Paul Hacker and Gary Benson won four titles each.

But Oag was more of a force in the series than two wins would indicate. He led more laps (89) and miles (133) than Salerno and earned two poles, equal to Salerno and more than anyone else. He totally dominated the Milwaukee race by leading from pole to checkered flag.

Drivers tend to stay in the VW Cup for quite a while because the racing among the near-stock Golfs is very intense and the financial rewards are commensurate with the costs. Paul and Karl Hacker finally moved on (to the IMSA Firehawk series) after a decade in VW's, including the Scirocco/Bilstein series in '76-'77.

Perhaps the best race of the year was at Pocono, where the wide-open spaces of the tri-oval allowed the Golfs to run in trains of a dozen cars or more. Chuck Hemmingson won his first VW Cup race at Pocono and was the only driver, other than Oag and Salerno, to win more than one race. He finished fifth in the Championship.

The Behms, father Les and son Mark, finished third and fourth in the points. They finished 1-2 at Road America, their home track, but both were disqualified for illegal modifications to their cars, giving the win to Salerno. The other drivers to win were veteran showroom stock driver Ray Kong and VW Cup veteran Kurt Mathewson.

Alistair Oag. Photo by Ken Brown/ Competition Photographers

The #3 Volkswagen Golf of 1986 Volkswagen Cup Champion Alistair Oag shows his style at Mid-Ohio. Photo by Ken Brown/ Competition Photographers

AutoRacing/USA 197

SCCA/Volkswagen Cup

Series runner-up Al Salerno won four races in '86. Photo by Peter Gloede

Mark Behm leads the pack at Road America with Oag and Les Behm filling his mirrors. Photo by Peter Gloede

SCCA/Escort Endurance Championship

by Bill Mitchell

CORVETTE 12, PORSCHE 0. SO READ THE SCOREBOARD AFTER TWO YEARS OF THE SCCA ESCORT ENDURANCE CHAMPIONSHIP. THE PLASTIC FANTASTICS FROM CHEVROLET HAVE DOMINATED THE TUTONIC TURBOS FROM PORSCHE. AND IT WASN'T AS IF PORSCHE hasn't been trying: SCCA gave them a special options package and they took a couple Corvettes to their test grounds at Weissach for study. At Mosport, the Canadian course with the longest straight in the series, where the 944 Turbo was reckoned to have its best chance, they imported Al Holbert, Derek Bell, Price Cobb, Drake Olson and a host of other pros to drive. But at the end of the year, the tee-shirts read Corvette 12, Porsche 0.

Bakeracing dominated the Super Sports class with four wins in their Corvettes. Kim Baker's drivers, Bobby and Tommy Archer, won the SportsCar Drivers Cup as well, while Baker, Mitch Wright and John Dinkel also assisted behind the wheel. The team used Goodyear Eagles, thus Goodyear's Chairman of the Board presented Baker with a new Corvette for '87 and $5000 per race — hardly good news for either Porsche or the other Corvette teams.

SSGT was the name of the premier class in '85. Then the Corvette and Porsche 944 Turbo were raised into Super Sports (along with Ferrari, Lotus and a host of exotics which did not choose to race). The normally aspirated Porsche 944 dominated the '86 version of SSGT. The Delta G team of Geoff Provo, Barney Gardner and Gregg Doran won the first two SSGT races but didn't leave the west coast when the series did. The Carlsen Porsche team did travel east and won at Nelson Ledges and Atlanta with Paul McIntosh (the SportsCar Drivers Cup winner), Kees Nierop, Larry Bleil, Bruce MacInnes and Scott Maxwell.

Team Shelby again won SSA with their Dodge Shelby but had stiff competition from the Mitsubishi Starions of Dave Wolin. Drivers of the Chrysler Team were Garth Ullom and Tim Evans (winners of the Drivers Cup), and Chrysler engineers Neil Hannemann and Jack Broomall.

Honda's CRX-Si again dominated the SSB class. Last year the Quantum Engineering Hondas won SSC in such convincing fashion that the entire SSC was consolidated with SSB. The result: the Quantum Hondas again won the Championship, but they only won three of six events. Wiley Timbrook's Starion won at Portland and the 16-valve VW Scirocco GTX won the final two races.

Goodyear dominated the intense tire battle with 12 wins and captured three class Championships. Yokohama had five wins and was on the Hondas which won SSC. Toyo (four), BFGoodrich, General, and Firestone also won races.

And if you think the '86 series was a hot-bed of manufacturer involvement, wait for '87 and the new Showroom Stock Truck class!

The 1986 SCCA Escort Endurance Super Sports Champion Bakeracing Corvette driven by Tommy and Bobby Archer. Photo by Gene Rosintoski

The 1986 SCCA Escort Endurance SSGT Champion Carlsen Racing Porsche 944T. Photo by Ken Brown/Competition Photographers

The 1986 SCCA Escort Endurance SSA Champion Team Shelby Dodge. Photo by Ken Brown/Competition Photographers

The Bakeracing Corvette (#4) goes inside the 1986 SCCA Escort Endurance Champion Quantum Engineering Honda CRX-Si (#33). Photo by Ken Brown/Competition Photographers

The key word in Escort racing is, "Endurance." Missing body work? Not to worry. A cattywhompus corner? Big deal! We came to race! Photo by Ken Brown/Competition Photographers

AutoRacing/USA 201

Until now, you had to move pretty fast to use our newest synthetic lubricants.

What was once reserved only for world class drivers is now available to the world.

Now, three additional Mobil synthetic lubricants join Mobil 1® in protecting cars that drive 200 MPH. And under.

They're the very same lubricants that have helped Formula 1, CART, USAC, SCCA and IMSA drivers succeed time after time in the world's most grueling races.

Take the blistering Indy 500. Three of the top 5 finishers in 1986 used Mobil synthetic lubricants—including Mobil Synthetic Universal Grease. Nothing can protect bearings, joints and linkages better.

Mobil Synthetic Gear Lubricant is race-proven, too—not only at Indy but at endurance competitions all over the world. The fact is, no conventional gear lube can perform as well as Mobil's synthetic.

The same goes for Mobil's race-proven Synthetic Universal ATF: simply put, it outperforms all conventional automatic transmission fluids.

So now, together with Mobil 1, your whole car can benefit from the high performance and protection of Mobil synthetic lubricant technology. Just call 1-800-662-4525 for availability and more information. And hurry.

Because lubricants like these go very, very fast.

Mobil®
The synthetic lubricants with the proven track record.

IMSA/Firestone Firehawk Endurance

by Dave Arnold

ONWARD, UPWARD, BIGGER, BETTER AND MORE... THAT'S ABOUT THE ONLY WAY TO DESCRIBE THE 1986 SEASON OF IMSA'S FIRESTONE FIREHAWK ENDURANCE CHAMPIONSHIP SERIES.

The Firehawk series' "numbers" increased dramatically in 1986, with the series' ten races averaging 64 cars per event. And with 20 American, Japanese and European manufacturers competing with 39 different models of cars, it was the largest participation series in the entire solar system.

With a typical laid-back Southern California attitude and some meticulous preparation, Max Jones and 19-year-old Tom Kendall took the overall title. The winners of four races, they knocked off $55,000 for their effort in the Datsun Alley Nissan 300ZX Turbo, including $17,000 out of the $70,000 year-end points fund.

In the Sports class, Ron Christensen took the Championship right down to the final 84 minutes of racing. Needing only a ninth place by Ray Korman and Christensen at Firebird to ice the title, the Korman Autoworks BMW 325e was tapped by another car early in the race, was rolled and there went the title, at least for Ray. Christensen, not yet having been in the car and thus still eligible to score points, bought 84 minutes of cockpit time in Carl McGinn's BMW and was able to nose out Dorsey Schroder in one of Paul Rossi's three Dodge Shelby Turbos.

In the Touring class, Toyota MR2 driver Craig Horning also took his title down to the last race. Although he won only twice during the season with mentor Bob Henderson as his co-driver, he was able to stay consistently high in the standings.

Despite considerable manufacturer pressure, IMSA steadfastly refuses to allow any "killer" cars in the series. Thus, preliminary car lists for 1987 not only do not permit Porsche 944's, but also exclude the 5.7-liter Camaros and Firebird. The TPI 5.0-liter powerplant seems to be the hot tip for 1987, but then the Mustang GT's have more power, the Nissan Turbos are trimmed up better, Korman and Christensen may run a BMW M3, and heaven help us, here we go again!

The Datsun Alley/Kendall Nissan 300ZX T which Tom Kendall and Max Jones drove to the 1986 IMSA Firestone Firehawk Endurance Overall Championship. Photo by Ken Brown/Competition Photographers

IMSA/Firestone Firehawk Endurance

The Korman Autoworks BMW 325e which, except for the last 84 minutes of '86 competition, Ron Christensen drove to the 1986 IMSA Firestone Firehawk Endurance Sports Class Championship. Photo by Ken Brown/ Competition Photographers

Craig Horning wheeled his Toyota MR2 to the 1986 Firestone Firehawk Endurance Touring Class Championship. Photo by Ken Brown/ Competition Photographers

IMSA/Barber Saab Pro Series

The Forest City Saab Mondiale-Saab of 1986 IMSA Barber Saab Pro Series Champion Willy Lewis, of Portland, Maine. Photo by Gene Rosintoski

IMSA/Barber Saab Pro Series

Contestants in the 12-race series raced specially designed, identically prepared Mondiale racers powered by stock turbocharged 16-valve Saab engines. All preparation is done by the staff of Skip Barber Racing. Photo Courtesy of Saab

The mirrors of Willy Lewis (#80) are filled with Richard Myhrie (#17) as he charges for the checkered flag. Lewis beat Myhrie by .3 second. The average margin of victory for the season was 1.5 seconds. Photo Courtesy of Saab

Robby Unser, son of Bobby Unser, finished the series points battle in the fourth position. Photo by Ken Brown/Competition Photographers

Eric Kielts, from Oak Park, Michigan, finished third in points. Photo by Gene Rosintoski

AutoRacing/USA 207

IMSA/Camel GTP

by Bill Oursler, "National Speed Sport News"

IN THIS COMPUTER-ORIENTED SOCIETY STATISTICS MAY BE CONSIDERED A REFLECTION OF REALITY. HOWEVER, THERE IS A PROBLEM OF INTERPRETATION FOR THOSE USING THE FIGURES FOUND IN THAT REFLECTION. A PRIME EXAMPLE IN THE DIFFICULTY IN DETERmining what is true can be found in the 1986 Camel GT Prototype year. There, although IMSA president John Bishop found a novel and long sought variety of marques in the winner's circle, Porsche walked off with yet one more successful Camel season to celebrate.

It is axiomatic in motorsport that he who spends the most, given equal portions of luck and foresightedness, will have the joy of savoring the largest rewards. The problem for Bishop is that only Porsche appears ready to put large amounts of money and time into winning.

Over the years Bishop has tried a number of ways to overcome the financial deficiencies found in the budgets of those racing against Porsche. Unfortunately, he has so far been unable to influence the course of history on any permanent basis.

In short, Bishop doesn't appear to be able to live with Porsche, or operate without them. Moreover, every time he tries to tame the tiger, both Porsche's customers and Porsche's rivals wind up spending additional funds because of the company's research programs and the need to keep abreast of them.

And that, in turn, has not only reduced the number of players on the prototype scene, but introduced an element of player whose legal problems have done little to enhance the reputation of either the series or the sport. In 1986, parading through the courts either on their way to trial or jail for drug related offenses were both John Paul, Senior and Junior, the 1982 Camel titlists; the Whittington Brothers, Don and Bill; and the '84 Camel crown winner, Randy Lanier.

Yet, despite the negative publicity, there were many who felt that 1986 was a season that may well be remembered as the highwater mark of American prototype racing.

As the teams prepared for the Daytona SunBank-sponsored 24-Hour enduro which inaugurated the '86 Camel campaign, there was much to anticipate. This was due to the goings on two months earlier in the Eastern Airlines-backed '85 finale at the France family's Florida facility. There both Chevrolet and BMW displayed a competitiveness which left the promise that perhaps the stranglehold of Porsche's Group C-based 962 might be broken.

Certainly Bishop and his rulemakers had that in mind when they tinkered with the Camel scriptures by adding 150 pounds to the 962's weight and banning the in-cockpit turbo boost knobs that had allowed the thirsty Porsche's to circulate on econo-cruise until those few occasions when they needed the maximum fuel guzzling performance from their turbos.

Unfortunately, the '86 version of the Camel title chase didn't start out on the path IMSA had hoped it would. First BMW withdrew from the race when one of it's March chassis cars caught fire and burned to the ground during testing at Road Atlanta. Then Rick Hendrick's pole sitting Lola-based Corvette expired early, turning Daytona once more into a fratricidal 962 contest. With all the front runners suffering from a variety of continuing ills, the least troubled Lowenbrau team of Al Holbert, Derek Bell, and Al Unser, Jr., crossed the finish line first.

From Warrington, Pennsylvania, Al Holbert. Photo by Dan Bianchi

In the end Holbert would collect his second consecutive and fifth total Camel Drivers' Crown on the basis of that Daytona performance, plus a string of top-five finishes, including victories at Lime Rock, Mid-Ohio, the July Watkins Glen event, Portland and Road America. (Sharing the duties with Holbert in the longer events was Bell, the younger Unser substituting when the Britisher was off running in the World Sports Car Championship tour.)

If Holbert took personal pleasure from his efforts, they were only part of a Porsche mosaic that also handed Holbert, as the head of Porsche's North American competition program, both the prototype chassis and engine titles as well.

The Holbert Racing Lowenbrau Porsche 962 of 1986 IMSA Camel GTP Champion Al Holbert. Photo by Peter Gloede

IMSA/Camel GTP

The team victorious at the conclusion of the 24 Hours of Daytona: (from the right) Al Unser, Jr., Derek Bell, Al Holbert and a sponsoring representative. Photo by Peter Gloede

In Miami, the prototype set spent practice and qualifying rebuilding their cars after continually tagging the concrete barriers lining the temporary course. There, Bob Wollek, with the help of the '85 Le Mans winner Paola Barilla put Bruce Leven's Bridgestone-Bayside 962 into victory lane.

Then at the annual Sebring 12-hour airport grind, it was the Bob Akin led Coca Cola team with Hans Stuck (who would go on to win the '86 Le Mans classic partnered by Holbert and Bell) and the late Jo Gartner who posted the third straight 962 triumph of the year.

Road Atlanta, which followed Sebring, provided the perfect setting for Bishop's hoped-for breakthrough as Sarel Van der

A quiet moment for the Champion, Al Holbert. Photo by Drew Gloede

Chevrolet Corvette GTP co-driver Doc Bundy, co-tenth in points. Photo by Drew Gloede

AutoRacing/USA 211

IMSA/Camel GTP

Englishman Derek Bell teamed with Holbert, finishing third in points. Photo by Dan Bianchi

Driving the Bob Akin Motor Racing Coca-Cola Porsche 962, Bob Akin (left), Hans Stuck (right) and Jo Gartner (who, in May, was killed in a European racing incident) teamed for victory at the 12 Hours of Sebring. Photo by Peter Gloede

The Bob Akin Motor Racing Coca-Cola Porsche 962. Photo by Ken Brown/Competition Photographers

212 AutoRacing/USA

BIRDS OF PREY.

Flexing their wings at America's toughest road racing courses in our Firestone Firehawk Endurance Championship series. And taking off across the country as more and more drivers see how these street legal tires fly at the track.* Our Firestone V-speed rated Firehawk SV™ and H-speed rated Firehawk GT™ performance radials.** Catch them at your Firestone retailer. And attack the streets for yourself.

Firestone FIREHAWK

Firestone

*Tires in our Firehawk series are modified from street use only by shaving the treads to racing depth. **See your Firestone retailer for written speed rating and tire safety information.

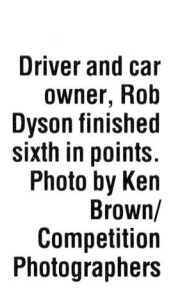

IMSA/Camel GTP

Driver and car owner, Rob Dyson finished sixth in points. Photo by Ken Brown/ Competition Photographers

From Bonn, West Germany, Klaus Ludwig. Photo by Anne Peyton

John Morton co-drove the #68 BFGoodrich Porsche, finishing the season ninth in the points battle. Photo by Ken Brown/ Competition Photographers

Merwe and Doc Bundy scored Chevrolet's first GTP win with a strong showing in their Hendrick Racing Corvette V6 turbo.

Ironically, at Riverside Bundy totaled the Hendrick entry in a spectacular accident which also destroyed the Ford Probe of Lynn St. James as well as the Jaguar XJR-7 of Chip Robinson (fortunately without serious injury to any of the participants). Although Van der Merwe and Bundy would come back, with the exception of winning the inaugural West Palm Beach street affair, the rest of the season was one of unfulfilled promise for the Chevy pair.

While Riverside was a disastrous weekend for some, for the troubled Dyson team it offered concrete hope. After destroying

The Valvoline Porsche 962 of A. J. Foyt, Danny Sullivan and Arie Luyendyk finished second at the 24 Hours, 1 minute, 49.15 seconds behind Holbert's team. Photo by Peter Gloede

IMSA/Camel GTP

Series runner-up Price Cobb, of Dallas, Texas, co-drove the Dyson Racing Porsche 962 to the Porsche Cup North America Championship. Photo by Dan Bianchi

The Dyson Racing Porsche made three '86 trips to victory circle. Photo by Bill Stahl

At Watkins Glen on its way to its sole victory, the #18 BMW GTP fielded by McLaren North America. Photo by Bill Stahl

France's Bob Wollek finished eighth in points, competing in Bruce Leven's Bridgestone Bayside Porsche 962. Photo by Dan Bianchi

"The Kids" BMW GTP contingent of Davy Jones (left) and John Andretti scored BMW's lone GTP victory. Photo by Dan Bianchi

AutoRacing/USA 217

IMSA/Camel GTP

Sharing an eyeful with Jochen Mass (right), 1986 CART Champion Bobby Rahal (left) made occasional forays into IMSA GTP competition at the wheel of a Ford Probe. Photo by Al Steinberg

During the '86 IMSA season, David Hobbs, partnered with John Watson in the #19 BMW, had more opportunity to display his verbal talents than his driving skills. Photo by Drew Gloede

The Electramotive Engineering Nissan GTP ZX-T. Photo by Peter Gloede

one car, and severely wounding a second during early in the season, Dyson's team quickly constructed a replacement Porsche for Riverside which brought Dyson and Price Cobb the win in the Southern California desert.

Although the coming months would bring further troubles and crashes — incidents that eventually would cause Dyson to fire last year's North American Porsche Cup winner, Drake Olson — there would be two other impressive victories. The first of these came in Charlotte in May when Olson and Cobb combined to put the Porsche ahead of the field. The second occured at Sears Point where Cobb put the car into the lead and then left Dyson to successfully defend the position against the best drivers in IMSA.

Jaguar XJR-7: V12-Powered Research Lab.

Jaguar XJ-S: V12-Powered Luxury Coupe.

For more than thirty years motorsports have played a critical role in the development and refinement of Jaguar automobiles. From Silverstone to Le Mans to Daytona, Jaguar race cars have provided an invaluable test bed for passenger car design while writing a grand and glorious racing legend.

Today a new 220 mph XJR-7 prototype bears the Jaguar marque. Featuring significant advances in aerodynamics, engine management technology and chassis design, the XJR-7 race car is designed to win races and to generate engineering advances for tomorrow's Jaguars.

The XJ-S grand touring coupe is the product of more than a quarter century of Jaguar racing and high performance research. Equipped with a smooth production version of the V-12 engine that powers the XJR-7, it accelerates briskly and can reach a speed of 140 mph. Four-wheel independent suspension and power rack and pinion steering make it a most agile road machine.

Yet the XJ-S offers far more than performance. Inside, it is rich with rare wood and fragrant leather. Uncommonly silent, even at speed, the XJ-S is a significant departure from the typically loud high performance automobile. To complement its hushed and luxurious environment, the Jaguar XJ-S offers the dulcet tones of a powerful 4-speaker stereo sound system. Automatic climate control, a trip computer and a wide range of other power and convenience accessories help make driving a distinct pleasure.

Progeny of race cars, flagship of the marque, the Jaguar XJ-S is a legend for tomorrow. Drive it today at your Jaguar dealer.

For the name of the Jaguar dealer nearest you, call this toll-free number today: 1-800-447-4700.
Jaguar Cars Inc., Leonia, NJ 07605.

ENJOY TOMORROW. BUCKLE UP TODAY.

JAGUAR
A BLENDING OF ART AND MACHINE

IMSA/Camel GTP

The Group 44 Jaguar XJR-7 of Bob Tullius and Chip Robinson closed the '86 season with a victory. Photo by Trackside Photo

Leven's Bridgestone Bayside Porsche had an affinity to city streets, winning the Miami Grand Prix and the Columbus Grand Prix. Photo by Bill Stahl

The Hendrick Motorsports Chevrolet Corvette GTP, driven by Sarel Van der Merwe and Doc Bundy, posted two '86 wins. Photo by Bill Stahl

AutoRacing/USA 221

IMSA/Camel GTP

The Group 44 Jaguar XJR-7 entries exhibit the wear-and-tear of endurance racing. Photo by Peter Gloede

With the exception of Columbus' street show which saw Wollek, with the help of GTO champion Scott Pruett, give Bridgestone its second 962 season win, the rest of the Camel slate was strictly a manufacturers' affair.

Klaus Ludwig made the Ford brass happy with the first-ever Probe GTP triumph at the Laguna Seca sprint in May. BMW celebrated its only winners' circle appearance at Watkins Glen in September where the youthful duo of John Andretti and Davy Jones held their rivals at bay. Lastly, Bob Tullius and Chip Robinson gave Jaguar it's solo victory of '86 with a steady drive in the Eastern Daytona finale.

South African Sarel Van der Merwe co-drove the Chevrolet Corvette GTP to a shared tenth in points. Photo by Drew Gloede

IMSA veteran Hurley Haywood partnered Brian Redman in the #04 Jaguar XJR-7, finishing in a three-way tie for tenth in points. Photo by Gene Rosintoski

IMSA/Camel GTP

Al Holbert, no stranger to Victory Circle with 46 IMSA career wins. Photo by Bill Stahl

At Laguna Seca Klaus Ludwig drove the Team Zakspeed USA Mustang Probe to its sole '86 victory. Photo by Bruce Schulman

In the blackness of night, lights become life-like entities, tracing the paths carved by contestants of the 24 Hours of Daytona. Photo by Sidell Tilghman

IMSA/Camel GTP

Jim Busby (#67) holds off the Porsche-powered March (#00) of Jim Adams and Oscar Larrauri's Porsche at Miami. Photo by Peter Gloede

With several new twists designed to further reduce the competitive advantages of the 962, 1987 could well be another tremendous year for the Camel prototypes. How well that equation will stand up once the season gets underway is another question, since BMW has pulled out, Jaguar has cut back to a limited schedule, and Ford has handed over its Probe operation to the privateers.

In this case the real truth behind the figures seems to be that the more things change, the more money needs to be spent, and there are limits to that exercise. The hope is the Camel GTP hasn't reached them yet.

BFGoodrich team owner Jim Busby, co-driver of the #67 Porsche. Photo by Peter Gloede

Chip Robinson, co-driver of the #44 Jaguar XJR-7, finished the points race in fifth. Photo by Drew Gloede

IMSA/Camel Lights

by Bill Oursler, "National Speed Sport News"

PAINT THE 1986 CAMEL LIGHTS SEASON IN THE HUES COLORING THE OUTSIDE OF THE ROTOR CASINGS FOR THE MAZDA WANKEL BRIGADE. HOWEVER, LIKE PORSCHE IN THE GT PROTOTYPE CATEGORY, THE JAPANESE MANUFACTURER FACED DETERMINED CHALlenges from its rivals among this smaller engined sports racing set.

Indeed, the early money went to the new Pontiac Fiero team. The effort featured a chassis designed by Spice Engineering in England, the winners of the '85 Group C-2 crown, the equivalent of the Camel Light division on the FIA's World Sports Car tour. However, despite an impressive debut that saw Bob Earl win at Laguna Seca and Charlotte in the car's first two appearances, '86 turned out to be a time for sorting as opposed to dominating for the Pontiac camp.

Other car makers successfully displaying their engine technology included Buick which collected the honors at Miami; Ferrari which showed the way at West Palm Beach and Road America, and Chevrolet which earned the first place Camel Lights trophy at the Daytona finale.

Again the dominant chassis was the British built Argo. Tiga, another English export, and the Italian-constructed Alba, also shared the limelight of victory circle. The only non-brand name in the Camel Lights equation was the home-commissioned Mazda prototype of New Jersey car dealer Pierre Honegger, driven to first place by David Loring at Lime Rock.

As for the drivers, Jim Downing, the long time IMSA star and a man who knows more about Argos than even Argo itself, once again emerged with the category crown. Downing was, as usual, a model of consistency, putting a host of top five finishes together with wins at Riverside, Portland and Sears Point to fashion his latest title season.

From Atlanta, Georgia, Jim Downing. Photo by Craig Fischer

At the wheel of the Spice Engineering Pontiac Fiero GTP Bob Earl finished the year fifth in points. Photo by Peter Gloede

The STS-Mike Meyer Racing Mazda Royale of series runner-up Jim Rothbarth and Mike Meyer, third man in the points chase. Photo by Ken Brown/Competition Photographers

The Certified Brakes Racing Mazda Argo of 1986 IMSA Camel GTL Champion Jim Downing and John Maffucci, fourth in points. Photo by Craig Fischer

IMSA/Camel GTO

by John Phillips, III
Senior Editor, "Automobile" Magazine

IF ONE WERE TO SIMPLY EXAMINE THE YEAR-END CAMEL IMSA GTO STATS, ONE WOULD GET THE NOTION THAT 1986 WAS AN OUT-AND-OUT CAKEWALK — A VERITABLE MUSTANG ROMP — FOR 27-YEAR-OLD SCOTT PRUETT. AFTER ALL, THE HANDSOME NATIVE OF Roseville, California, won seven races, collected nine pole positions set seven outright qualifying records and earned 11 top-five finishes. What could be simpler?

In point of fact, there was nothing simple about it. "Look at the manufacturers' battle," explains Pruett. "Ford beat Chevrolet by four points (256 versus 252); believe me, I was feeling the pressure."

Pruett, a go-karting whiz with 13 titles to his credit, contested his first full season of automobile racing in '86. But he had two distinct advantages. "First," said team owner Jack Roush, "he's driving a car that has had the benefit of three years of sorting. And second, Scott's simply got that fire in his eye, that instinct in his gut.". The prodigious horsepower of Roush's legendary five- and six-liter Ford engines certainly helped, too. And Pruett, when asked his recipe for success, answers: "I think maybe I have an edge in concentration and a real, well, sort of *killer* determination."

Pruett also had killer competition, most of it menacingly emanating from the Chevrolet camp. A thinly disguised, full-fledged GM factory project, Jack Baldwin's Peerless Racing Camaro, was the epitome of high-tech construction: carbon-fiber tub (the first such application in a road-racing sedan), experimental gearboxes using automatic transmission fluid, front uprights from an Indy car, even on-board computer-controlled shock absorbers. In Baldwin's experienced hands, the car flew, winning five times. Jim Miller, who co-drove to victory with Baldwin at the six-hour Riverside race, said: "The car's so sophisticated, it holds the road like a ground-effects car. It takes time to learn to drive."

Chevy's hopes were further buttressed by Brooks Frybarger's Camaro, with fast-and-flashy Willy T. Ribbs at the wheel. Ribbs actually started the season in an aging Thunderbird, but after a controversial bumping incident with Scott Pruett at Miami,

Scott Pruett, from Roseville, California. Photo by Drew Gloede

both Willy and Brooks abandoned the FoMoCo minions. The team's new Camaro, unfortunately, did not appear until the season was 10 races old, nor was it the technological equal of the Peerless car. Ribbs nonetheless piloted the blue-and-white racer to victories at Sears Point and Columbus. But the latter was the most controversial meeting of the year.

With Ford and Chevrolet separated by only one point in Columbus, the gloves really came off. Ribbs tapped Pruett out of the lead in the early stages. Baldwin bounced off Mustang driver Pete Halsmer. Then Pruett, as if in retaliation, slammed Baldwin's Camaro, forcing it, in a shower of shattering body panels, into the wall. Thus invoking the wrath of IMSA, all three drivers earned fines and were put on probation. But the Ford-Chevrolet feud would not be settled until the season finale, at Daytona.

Unfortunately, the unceasing combat between Pruett and Baldwin largely obscured standout performances by Bruce Jenner (Ford Mustang) and Dennis Aase (Toyota Celica).

Jenner actually scored more top-five finishes — an even dozen — than teammate Pruett, and was crucial to Ford's title. "Bruce takes a lot of criticism because he's a celebrity," says Roush Racing crewman Alan Ladyman, "but he rarely hurts the car and knows how to race for points — which is the way a lot of people have won IMSA titles." Jenner was eventually second in the Championship, 21 points behind Pruett and 16 points in front of Chevrolet's Jack Baldwin.

Finishing a strong fourth in points was Aase, in Dan Gurney's radical, turbocharged, 450-horsepower Toyota. Although the Toyota made a dubious debut, burning at Riverside, the car later came into its stride, taking powerhouse victories at Road America and Watkins Glen. "The Elkhart win was sweet," said Aase, "because it was a 500-miler. Until then, our car had a reputation for being unreliable."

230 AutoRacing/USA

The Roush Racing Motorcraft Ford Mustang of 1986 IMSA Camel GTO Champion Scott Pruett. Photo by Ron McQueeney

IMSA/Camel GTO

In 7-Eleven livery, the Roush Racing Ford Mustang of Bruce Jenner. Photo by Peter Gloede

Series runner-up Bruce Jenner. Photo by Drew Gloede

At Sears Point defending GTO Champion Jack Baldwin's Peerless/Hendricks Levi Garrett Chevrolet Camaro leads GTU contestant Felix Mancinez. Photo by Craig Fischer

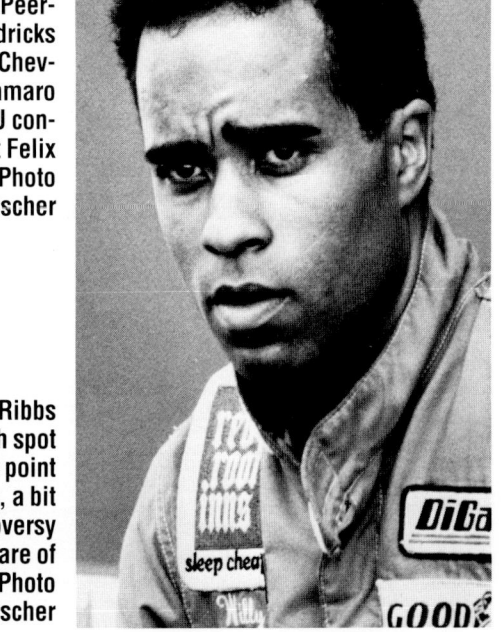

Willy T. Ribbs earned fifth spot in the point standings, a bit of controversy and his share of respect. Photo by Craig Fischer

IMSA/Camel GTO

Willy T. Ribbs' Brooks Racing Chevrolet Camaro on its way to victory at Columbus. Photo by Steve Swope

Craig Carter drove the Dingman Brothers Racing Valvoline Pontiac to the sixth slot in the standings. Photo by Al Steinberg

Later at Watkins Glen, the AAR Toyota claimed the pole, shattered the GTO record by over two seconds ("That was a pretty berserk lap," joked Aase) and won going away from Ribbs and Baldwin.

So impressive was the Toyota's design — with twin-plug engine and Hewland transaxle — that it and the Peerless Camaro are pre-season favorites for the '87 title.

Meanwhile, Pruett's Championship-winning performance drew more than curious interest from men who can do much to advance the Californian's career. "You'd see the Roush team unload the trailer," enthused Porsche GTP owner Bruce Leven, "and 10 minutes later, Scott would put the car on the pole at a track he'd never seen before. Behind the wheel, he's got such grace, it's amazing."

Amazing grace, you might call it.

At the wheels of their All American Racers Toyota Celica T's, Dennis Aase (#98) and Chris Cord (#99) finished the series fourth and seventh in points, respectively. Photo by Anne Peyton

During a midnight pit stop during the 24 Hours of Daytona, Bill Elliott exits from the Roush Racing Folgers Mustang as teammate Ricky Rudd buckles into the driver's seat. Photo by David Allio

IMSA/Camel GTU

by John Phillips III
Senior Editor, "Automobile" Magazine

"I ALWAYS HOLD BACK AT THE START," SAYS TALL, BLOND, BASHFUL TOM KENDALL, IMSA's 1986 CAMEL GTU CHAMPION. "THEN WHEN THINGS QUIET DOWN, I START TO MOVE. BUT I GUESS I PICK THINGS UP REAL QUICK. I THINK A LOT. ALL OF THE TIME I'M THINKING, 'race, race, race.' You see a lot of people out here profilin' around. I just concentrate on what I'm doing."

Kendall, who clinched the title at the tender age of 19, comes by his see-what-can-be-learned attitude honestly. When he wasn't racing his '81 Mazda RX-7 (the same car that previously earned GTU titles for Jim Downing and Jack Baldwin), he was in school at UCLA, near his home in California. "My goal was just to get the checkered flag — to learn something from everyone, from every race. I guess, in 1986, I was a full time student," he explains.

Not only did Kendall learn from every race, but he was also a winner four times (at Laguna Seca, Charlotte, Sears Point and Lime Rock), and was a top-five finisher in 15 of the year's 17 events. The one time he didn't finish was at Mid-Ohio, where, in torrid pursuit of Bob Earl, Tom crashed into a sandbank. "It was stupid of me," remembers Kendall. "It wasn't mature driving."

Young Kendall's desire to drive maturely is understandable. His year-long competition came from four die-hard veterans: Roger Mandeville, Amos Johnson, Bob Earl and Terry Visger. Of the group, Mandeville (Mazda RX-7) and Earl (Pontiac Fiero) seemed the most likely to sweep Championship honors.

Roger Mandeville won twice as many races as Kendall, including the last three contests of the season. Although Roger was almost always the fastest Mazda competitor on any given weekend, he insists his strategy was to run the slowest pace possible. "We are determined to run a tortoise pace," he says. "We race against the track, not our competitors. We set a strategy, a pace, and follow it no matter what." Curiously, Mandeville meant to contest only half a season of GTU. He was building a Mazda GTO racer (which he eventually unveiled at the Daytona finale), and the new car's construction demanded almost as much of Roger's attention as his GTU bid.

The youngest Champion in IMSA history, Tom Kendall from La Canada, California. Photo by Ken Brown/Competition Photographers

Only on five occasions did Mandeville fail to finish in the top five. But at each of those races, Kendall scored heavily, and at the year's end, Kendall's consistency paid a handsome dividend: a slim seven-point edge over Mandeville.

Employing the same sort of consistency was fellow RX-7 driver Amos Johnson, with 11 top-five finishes and a stunning win in the Daytona 24 Hours. Johnson finished the season third in the point standings.

Kendall, Mandeville and Johnson easily clinched the Manufacturers' Championship for Mazda, but as the season began, all three had predicted 1986 would be the year of the Pontiac. Bob Earl, with six victories in his Fiero in 1985, seemed set to stomp the RX-7s, which he called, "antiquated." Sure enough, Earl's Fiero was consistently a guided missile in qualifying. But all year long, the Mr. Goodwrench Fiero was felled by gremlins after it dashed to the fore. The list of infuriating failures included clutches, motors, transmissions, input shaft, flywheels, and electrical maladies. And two of the car's victories were earned when the Fiero simply got better gas mileage than the Mazdas. "If nothing else, we get the high-mileage award," said Earl of his wins at Mid-Ohio and Portland. But while Earl was joking, he and the Huffaker team were intensely disappointed with the car's performance. "We had expected to mash Mazdas," said a crew member. Earl and teammate Terry Visger finished fourth and fifth in the year-end standings.

And so it was that a teenager who, before '86, had contested only four GTU events, won the 1986 IMSA Camel GTU Championship. Tom Kendall is tied with Johnny Jones as the youngest pilot to secure an IMSA title. And, having simultaneously clinched the Firestone Firehawk series, Kendall is the only driver in history to have won two IMSA titles in a single season. Through it all, Kendall somehow managed to squeeze in a semester

The CCR Mazda RX-7 of 1986 IMSA Camel GTU Champion Tom Kendall. Photo by Peter Gloede

IMSA/Camel GTU

The winningest active GTU driver and series runner-up Roger Mandeville. Photo by Craig Fischer

Bob Earl ended the season fourth in the GTU points battle. Photo by Craig Fischer

The on-track discrepancy of IMSA GT racing: The GTU Mazda of Roger Mandeville stares down the tunnels of a GTP vehicle. Photo by Craig Fischer

Out of Spartanburg, South Carolina, the Mandeville Auto Tech Mazda RX-7. Photo by Gerald Schallié

IMSA/Camel GTU

of school — both at UCLA and on the track.

Says last year's GTU champ Jack Baldwin: "Tom really deserves the title. He won because he's consistent. And I'll tell you something else. Tom's probably the only driver in all IMSA who doesn't have an enemy — everybody loves the guy."

Sometimes, nice guys finish first.

The Team Highball Mazda RX-7, GTU winner of the 24 Hours of Daytona, took Amos Johnson to third in points. Photo by Craig Fischer

Bob Earl (#55) and Huffaker Engineering teammate Terry Visger (who finished fifth in points) wend their way around Sears Point. Photo by Craig Fischer

240 AutoRacing/USA

IMSA/Kelly American Challenge

by J.J. O'Malley

IRV HOERR HAD REASONS TO BE SKEPTICAL GOING INTO THE 1986 KELLY AMERICAN CHALLENGE SEASON. AFTER ALL, THE HANDSOME 38-YEAR-OLD DRIVER FROM PEORIA, ILLINOIS HELD THE SERIES POINTS LEAD THE PAST TWO YEARS, ONLY TO LOSE THE TITLE TO Tommy Riggins. Hoerr virtually had the '84 title sewed up, when mechanical failure hit only four laps from the finish while leading the Daytona finale. Hoerr held the series lead early in the '85 season, before Riggins won six straight races to wrap up the title.

But following the nightmares of the past two years, 1986 was a dream come true. When Hoerr suffered his only DNF of the year — after leading 18 laps at Columbus — the title had long been decided in his favor. Hoerr's white ATS Olds Toronado won nine of the 11 races, won nine poles, had the fastest lap nine times, and set 17 track records. He won the first five races of the year before finishing second to Patty Moise at Portland, with veteran Clay Young going on to win at Columbus.

Even though it was Hoerr's year, he had to share the limelight with two top women.

Moise set series history with her victory at Portland, and it came as no surprise — she posted three consecutive runner-up finishes early in the year. With sponsorship for her Buick Somerset from Red Roof Inns and the support of veteran NASCAR Winston Cup Crew Chief David Ifft in the pits, Moise was a factor at nearly every track, and finished a strong, albeit distant, second in the point standings.

Robin Dallenbach came on strong late in the year in her Olds Calais, taking second at Columbus. The same Robin McCall who made brief NASCAR Winston Cup appearances for J.D. Stacy, she ended the year with a double dose of good news. She was named the series' Most Improved Driver and landed a ride as co-driver with Hoerr on the championship ATS Oldsmobile team for 1987.

A Kelly veteran since 1979, Young finished up the year strong after a string of bad luck early in the season in his Dole Fresh Fruit Pontiac Trans-Am, preceeding his victory at Columbus with a second at Watkins Glen. Young's victory was not without its drama. Misunderstanding a radio report from his pit — and glancing at a checkered flag near trackside — Young pulled into the pits with five minutes remaining in the race, thinking it was over. Fortunately, he quickly realized his mistake, returned to the track, and beat Dallenbach to the real checkered flag.

Once the series' answer to Rodney Dangerfield, Dick Danielson earned plenty of respect. The Milwaukee driver won the pole at Road America and set the fastest lap at the Meadowlands in an unsponsored Buick Somerset prepared by himself and a few friends. He posted six top-three finishes, and will enter the '87 campaign as a contender for the title.

Another bright young driver was Steve Clark. Finishing an impressive third at the Glen, Clark wound up the year tied for sixth with another Colorado charger, Dallenbach.

After two straight titles, in 1986 Riggins was only an

The ATS Oldsmobile Toronado of 1986 IMSA Kelly American Challenge Champion Irv Hoerr of Peoria, Illinois. Photo by Peter Gloede

IMSA/Kelly American Challenge

The Red Roof Inns Buick Somerset of series runner-up Patty Moise. Photo by Craig Fischer

infrequent visitor to the Kelly American Challenge, yet was quickly involved with what proved to be a changing of the guard. The season opened at Road Atlanta with a series of bizarre incidents involving most of the top contenders. As the field came around the penultimate turn of the first lap, Danielson tagged Moise, both spun and were collected by Clark, eliminating all three. On the next lap, Riggins saw a yellow flag at the start/finish line, and realizing a full-course caution was in effect, he let off the power and triggered a three-car collision with Hoerr sandwiched between Riggins and Young. Young was forced to retire, while Hoerr managed to out-duel Riggins in a battle of battered cars.

From there on, everything went Hoerr's way. He didn't have to worry about losing the Championship again with late-season misfortunes — his victory at Road America in the series' eighth race clinched the elusive title.

On the down side, Kelly Services announced the end of its 77-race sponsorship

Third man in the points battle, Clay Young in his Pontiac Firebird. Photo by Ken Brown/Competition Photographers

The Buick Somerset of Dick Danielson. Photo by Craig Fischer

IMSA/Kelly American Challenge

of the series over the past eight years. While the American Challenge picture otherwise looks bright for 1987, chances are fans and competitors will still be calling it the Kelly series for a long time to come.

Robin Dallenbach earned the series' Most Improved Driver Award in her Lucas Truck Service Oldsmobile Calais. Photo by Peter Gloede

Driving his Buick Somerset, Steve Clark tied with Dallenbach for the sixth place in the points. Photo by Ken Brown/Competition Photographers

IMSA/Champion Spark Plug Challenge

by J.J. O'Malley

DOUG PETERSON INTENDED FOR THE 1986 CHAMPION SPARK PLUG SEASON TO BE A LEARNING YEAR WORKING WITH THE NEW HONDA ACURA INTEGRA. WAS HE IN FOR A SURPRISE!

Peterson's development work came through better than expected. He became a contender in IMSA's ProFormance series point race with a third at Lime Rock, a second at Mid-Ohio and back-to-back wins at Portland and Sears Point. He then won the Championship as Tommy Archer stumbled in the final two races of the year. He became the tenth different champion in as many years in this series for front wheel drive compact sedans, climaxing a very competitive season in which seven drivers won races.

"Initially, I felt I would be happy just to be around at the end of each race," said the California driver. "We were looking at the season as a development year, and any results were secondary. Compared to the Archers, Kal Showket and Team Highball, we had little experience in this kind of racing."

Peterson's experience in the Champion Spark Plug Challenge was limited to nine "forgettable" races in 1983 and 1984. The winner of three GT-4 SCCA National Championships, Peterson moved to Honda in 1985 and drove a CRX to the GT-5 national title. With the introduction of the Acura set for April — right about the time of the Road Atlanta opener — both Peterson and Honda decided that the Champion Spark Plug Challenge would be the series to showcase the Acura's performance image. Also involved was Mugen Competition of Japan — which does Honda's Formula 1 and Formula 2 engines — supplying Peterson's initial engine and transmission.

Peterson and Comptech co-owner Don Erb then went to work. Their maroon car finished fourth at Road Atlanta. Not only were they around for the finish of every race, they ran every lap, with their worst finish a seventh at Charlotte. Erb was named the series' TRW Mechanic of the Year for his efforts.

Peterson's Championship highlighted an intense year of excellent on-track competition. Nine different manufacturers participated, with Mazda edging out Chevrolet for the TRW Manufacturer's Cup on the basis of having one more victory after the two finished the year tied with 147 points.

The front-runner for the title was '84 Champion Tommy Archer, who joined his brother Bobby in a pair of Cars and Concepts Chevy Cavaliers, reminiscent of their two-car Renault punch of 1984. Tommy won at Lime Rock while Bobby won at Watkins Glen, and Tommy held the points lead with two rounds remaining. But Tommy crashed while racing Peterson for second place at Road America, giving the Honda driver the points lead going into the series finale at Daytona. Tommy Archer then needed a strong finish to win the title, but his brakes failed while he was racing for the lead to give him his second straight DNF.

One thing which remained the same was the steady performance of Kal Showket. The Alabama driver took his Full Time Racing Dodge Daytona to four victories, becoming the

The Comptech Racing Acura Integra of the 1986 IMSA Champion Spark Plug Challenge ProFormance Champion Doug Peterson of Sunnyvale, California. Photo by Ken Brown/Competition Photographers

IMSA/Champion Spark Plug Challenge

The interior of Peterson's Championship Acura Integra. Photo by Ken Brown/Competition Photographers

series' all-time leading winner with 19 career triumphs. But once again, Showket remained the bridesmaid, finishing second in the point standings for the third time in the last four years.

Mazda won the manufacturers' race by virtue of victories by three different drivers. Amos Johnson won at Riverside in a 626, while defending Champion Dennis Shaw triumphed at Mid-Ohio in a GLC and Dave Jolly won at Laguna Seca in a GLC.

A new feature of the 1986 Champion Spark Plug Challenge was the ProStock class. Designed as a means for the defunct Renault Cup and Firestone Firehawk Compact competitors to continue racing, the new group provided plenty of action. Nearly doubling the sizes of the fields, the ProStocks brought plenty of racing to the middle and back of the pack, while giving the front runners traffic to work around.

It was a familiar name at the front of the new class as Paul Hacker won three of the 11 rounds which combined with six second place

Tommy Archer, third man in ProFormance points, takes the inside line from Peterson with his Cars & Concepts Chevrolet Cavalier. Photo by Anne Peyton

The #08 Synthoil International Volkswagen Golf of 1986 IMSA Champion Spark Plug ProStock Champion Paul Hacker fills the mirrors of his teammate, brother and third man in ProStock points, Karl Hacker (#00). Photo by Trackside Photo.

IMSA/Champion Spark Plug Challenge

finishes (five scored consecutively) to edge out Randy Pobst for the title. Pobst was the series' leading winner with five victories, while Karl Hacker won two races to finish a distant third in the points. Volkswagen GTI's dominated the class, winning all the races and taking the first seven positions in the driver point standings.

The series will take on a new look in 1987. With the Champion Spark Plug organization ending its sponsorship after nine seasons, the series will be called the International Sedan Series and for the first time, different tire manufacturers will be able to participate, instead of one specified make of tire. The goal — "Tire War."

The Sprectro Oils Volkswagen Golf of ProStock series runner-up Randy Pobst (#91) fights Karl Hacker for the line going into Turn One at Sears Point. Photo by Craig Fischer

The Full Time Racing Dodge Daytona of ProFormance series runner-up Kal Showket. Photo by Ken Brown/Competition Photographers

248 AutoRacing/USA

Off-Road

by Tom Blattler

ADVANCED TECHNOLOGY, HIGHLY EXOTIC ENGINES AND OUTSTANDING HANDLING SOUNDS MORE LIKE THE CART INDY CAR SCENE OR THE IMSA PROTOTYPE WARS.

But how about off-road racing?

The three off-road campaigns — SCORE International, High Desert Racing Association (HDRA) and the Mickey Thompson short course series — took giant leaps forward in 1986 with the advancement of suspension packages, shock absorber rates and high-RPM foreign powerplants. Everything from the single-seat buggies to the big trucks and from the mini-pickups to the limited two-seaters has seen a tremendous jump in technology. Very seldom does a team enter today's off-road world with a home-built vehicle and come out victorious.

In fact, several well-known sports and formula car designers, such as Trevor Harris, have now joined the off-road efforts. Their background and knowledge assist the constructors in preparing the tough machinery to handle the even tougher terrain.

"The cars and trucks have really become sophisticated," said Walt Lott, president of HDRA who has been involved in the sport for more than 20 years. "The sport has become much more professional and that's good. But, we still have classes for the little guy to compete. And the factories, who spend a lot of money to win, have their respective classes."

Just two years ago, the off-road sport was in turmoil with constant bickering between HDRA and SCORE, both on rules and organizational ideas. But with the assistance of various vehicle and tire manufacturers, the two associations dropped the hatchets and shook hands. Since that moment, off-road racing has flourished. Contingency sponsors, media coverage and entries have grown rapidly and, in 1987, the southwest-based sport is expanding to the Rocky Mountains.

"Everything is on an upward swing," explained Sal Fish, president of SCORE International. "Our entries have been up 27 percent and sponsors continue to become involved. The factories are also utilizing off-road racing in a lot of their advertising."

In addition to the desert action, the growth of Mickey Thompson's short course continued with events in Detroit, Indianapolis, Houston, and San Diego, as well as the Los Angeles area. The slam-bang action is extremely crowd-pleasing, but one question still remains: Why isn't this excitement on television? With six desert races being televised on ESPN, the Thompson events would be a natural for the type of entertainment the viewing audience is looking for. Mickey, why no TV?

On the competition side, the action was hot and heavy. The hotly contested Grand National truck division saw road racing and rally veteran Steve Millen take his Toyota to the title on the eight-race Thompson series. With wins at Indianapolis, Detroit, Houston, and San Bernardino, Millen, who also saw action in the '86 ARS and IMSA GT series, was the class of the field.

In the desert, Las Vegas veteran Jack Ramsay piloted his 1600cc buggy to the overall points title while legendary Dodge

Overall titlist Jack Ramsay takes command of the Great Mojave 250. Photo by Trackside Photo

Off-Road

Heavy-Metal Champion Walker Evans. Photo by Trackside Photo

Defending and current Mini-Metal Champion Spencer Low. Photo by Trackside Photo

man Walker Evans took the Heavy-Metal truck crown. Spencer Low drove his Nissan to the Mini-Metal pickup Championship, the only repeat winner of the three major titles.

Individual performances again highlighted the desert tour with both veterans and newcomers making news:

* For the fourth time, Mark McMillin took the overall Baja 1000 win in his sleek Porsche-powered single-seat buggy.

* In that same race, former Indy car racer Roger Mears, teaming with Sherman Balch, nipped former buggy star Larry Ragland by just 13 seconds after a thousand-mile, classic Nissan-Chevy Class 7 battle.

* Toyota's Ivan Stewart lead the Class 1 (unlimited class single-seater) points for most of the season with his full-bodied truck only to place second to McMillin at season's end.

* Veteran Manny Esquerra won six straight Class 7 races with his Ford before getting caught in the Mears-Ragland duel at Baja.

Grand National Truck Champion Steve Millen (#3) appears to be of two minds: The nose of his Toyota seems bent on bashing his teammate Ivan Stewart while his front wheels seem to seek a path past. Photo by Trackside Photo

Off-Road

Roger Mears on his way to his 20th World Championship at Riverside. Photo by Trackside Photo

* 17-year-old Rob Gordon, co-driving with Frank Arciero, Jr., won the prestigious Frontier 500 and defeated his father, Bob, who placed second overall.
* Rick Hagle and Steve Tetrick battled all season for the Class 10 title before Hagle pulled it out with wins at the Frontier 500 and Baja 1000.
* Rod Hall continues his usual dominance in Class 4 with his Dodge four-wheel-drive scoring another points title.

Overall, off-road racing experienced another banner season with a growth in entries, sponsors and media awareness. But most importantly, technology was the big news in the sport of dust, rocks and sage brush.

Rob Gordon and co-driver Frank Arciero, Jr. on the way to victory in the Frontier 500. Photo by Trackside Photo

The winner of six consecutive Class 7 races, Manny Esquerra. Photo by Trackside Photo

252 AutoRacing/USA

The Porsche-powered Chenowth buggy of Mark McMillin, four-time overall winner of the Baja 1000. Photo by Trackside Photo

Pikes Peak

The Audi Sport Quattro S1, driven by Bobby Unser, was first in the Rally Division, setting a new Pikes Peak Hill Climb record of just over 11 minutes. Photo by Su Kemper

Audi's Jo Hoppen (right) and an Audi engineer (left) enjoy the congratulations received by Unser on his 13th Pikes Peak Hill Climb Championship. Photo by Trackside Photo

Bobby Regester took the Open Wheel Class win. Photo by Trackside Photo

The Ford Thunderbird of Leonard Vahsholtz took Stock Car Class honors. Photo by Trackside Photo

John Crawford drove his Dodge Shelby Turbo to victory in the Production Rally Class. Photo by Trackside Photo

Look what happens when a rally driver relies on Audi technology:

1982 Pro-Rally Winner
1983 Pro-Rally Winner
1984 Pro-Rally Winner
1985 Pro-Rally Winner
1986 Pro-Rally Winner

John Buffum clinched the 1986 North American Rally Cup Championship recently with a win at the Defi-Ste.-Agathe, in Ste.-Agathe des Monts, Quebec.

His turbocharged Audi Quattro covered the 200-mile course of the two-day race with ease, besting the 56-car field in near-record time.

This victory earned Buffum an unprecedented fifth straight National Drivers Championship.

In the five years John has been driving for Audi, he has won 40 of 52 SCCA Pro-Rallies.

The combination of John Buffum's skills and Audi technology is not only winning rallies, it's the field work by which Audi engineers refine and design what goes into the Audi you drive today.

Which is why today's Audi Quattros are perhaps among the most advanced automobiles you can buy. Both the 4000CS Quattro and 5000CS Turbo Quattro utilize the same basic rally-winning, all-wheel drive system, as found on John's Audi, to help you achieve maximum traction and control on any roads you drive.

If you're ready to get behind the wheel of the car which has technologically proven itself in some of the world's toughest road rallies, then you're ready for an Audi.

You're ready for an Audi.

© 1986 Audi

SCCA/Pro Rally Series

By Su Kemper

NOW IN ITS 13TH YEAR, THE SCCA PRO RALLY SERIES CONTINUES TO SUFFER FROM ACUTE GROWING PAINS. DISGRUNTLED BY THEIR TREATMENT THE PREVIOUS SEASON WHEN THEY SPONSORED THE NATIONAL SERIES, BRIDGESTONE TIRE GRACEFULLY DECLINED ITS option for 1986. Sponsorless, the Series moved into the new year with the usual great hopes for the future, but soon found itself leaderless, as well. Bob Radford, a multi-year TSD rally champion himself, was pressed into service as Pro Rally Manager in late 1984. But his form of administration, good as it may have been, drew nothing but grumbling from the grass-roots rallyists and by mid-year he had resigned to pursue other interests. Then former rally organizer Dave Thompson was handed the reins. Short on experience, but long on enthusiasm, he was determined to make a go of the series. For a time he enjoyed the input from John Buffum, newly appointed Pro Rally Advisor to SCCA President Nick Craw. But the rank and file soon began muttering "conflict of interest," so nine-time series Champion Buffum resigned, relegating himself to being just another contestant.

Well, sort of. For at the wheel of a short wheelbase Sport Quattro, Buffum won six of the seven Pro Rally events, claiming the overall series driving Championship and the manufacturers title for Audi. His arch-rival, Rod Millen, was back with yet another hybrid 4WD Mazda RX-7, but this time the car was giving away as much as 150 horsepower to Buffum's new Quattro. Still, in a surprise victory, Millen won the Sunriser Forest Rally in Ohio, largely due to the excellent handling of the car on the freshly pea-graveled stage roads. Unfortunately, another promising Open class protagonist, Jon Woodner, was never able to successfully challenge the Buffum-Millen show. Despite an impressive looking "customer" Peugeot 205 T-16, Woodner finished out the season firmly in third, with six third places to his credit.

It was a good year (again) for Dodge. They were the big winners in the Production GT class with Doug Shepherd, driving a Shelby Turbo, winning all seven events. With no other manufacturer earning any points in this class all season, Dodge easily won the manufacturers crown. In the production class, long-time rallyist John Crawford, in an Omni GLH, only won two events during the year but with his other high placings was able to capture his first-ever rally title. It was an exciting race throughout the year, with no fewer than four drivers winning various events, but Crawford and Dodge came out on top.

With the Olympus Rally in Washington state now a full qualifying round in the World Rally Championship, one would expect that the numbers of competitors in Group A would grow steadily in 1986. Statistically they did, but not in the magnitude one would have expected. Detroit's well-known abhorrence of anything "not invented here" likely swayed SCCA's thinking, and that organization continued to eschew international rules. So there wasn't much incentive to field a homologated car, although a few far-sighted souls did take the plunge, with Group A the obvious choice. The number of entries in the class never topped 12 at any given event, even with the knowledge that a WRC would soon be in their own backyard.

John Buffum. Photo by Trackside Photo

Even so, the competition was keen throughout the year with five different drivers winning the first five events. Only two, former Canadian rally Champion Walter Boyce and New Zealander Clive Smith, went on to take double victories during the season. In what proved to be the closest race of the year, Boyce, in a VW Golf GTI, pulled ahead to capture the class title by a mere three points over Chad DiMarco in a 4WD Subaru RX Turbo. And for the second year, Toyota easily clinched the manufacturers crown in this division with three outright wins during the season. Chrysler racing honcho Dick Maxwell grumbled that it was "impossible for an American manufacturer to build a competitive Group A car," but if the Olympus Rally is successful in improving the general public's awareness of a great sport, maybe that will change.

AutoRacing/USA 257

SCCA/Pro Rally Series

The Audi Sport Quattro of 1986 SCCA Pro Rally Overall Champion John Buffum and his co-driver, Tom Grimshaw. Photo by Trackside Photo

The Dodge Shelby Turbo of 1986 SCCA Pro Rally Production GT Champion Doug Shepherd and his co-driver, Ginny Reese. Photo by Trackside Photo

The Dodge Omni GLH of 1986 SCCA Pro Rally Production Champion John Crawford. Photo by Su Kemper

SCCA/Pro Rally Series

The Volkswagen Golf GTI of 1986 SCCA Pro Rally Group A Champion Walter Boyce and his co-driver, Jim Brandt. Photo by Trackside Photo

Track Profiles/1986

Alabama International Motor Speedway

Talladega, Alabama
2.66-mile, 33°-banked tri-oval

Atlanta International Raceway

Hampton, Georgia
1.522-mile oval with turns
banked 24°

Brainerd International Raceway

Brainerd, Minnesota
3.0-mile, 10 turn road course

Burke Lakefront Airport

Cleveland, Ohio
3.0-mile, 10 turn
road course

Charlotte Motor Speedway

Charlotte, North Carolina
1.5-mile tri-oval with turns
banked 24° to 26°
2.25-mile, 12 turn
road course

Columbus Grand Prix

Columbus, Ohio
2.67-mile, 11 turn road course

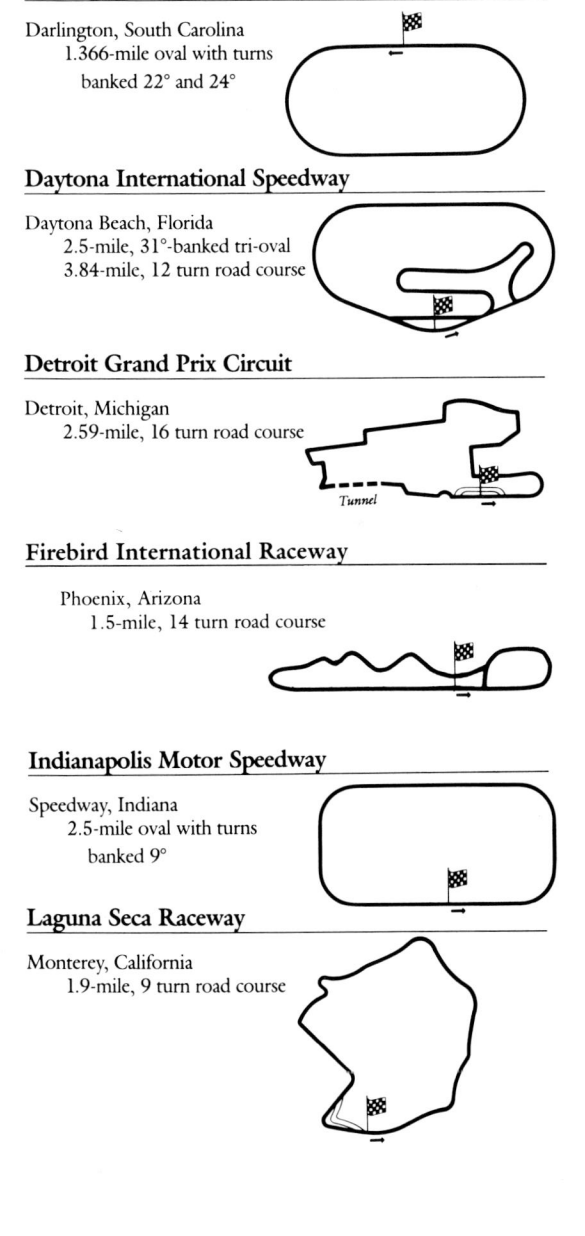

Darlington International Raceway

Darlington, South Carolina
1.366-mile oval with turns
banked 22° and 24°

Daytona International Speedway

Daytona Beach, Florida
2.5-mile, 31°-banked tri-oval
3.84-mile, 12 turn road course

Detroit Grand Prix Circuit

Detroit, Michigan
2.59-mile, 16 turn road course

Tunnel

Firebird International Raceway

Phoenix, Arizona
1.5-mile, 14 turn road course

Indianapolis Motor Speedway

Speedway, Indiana
2.5-mile oval with turns
banked 9°

Laguna Seca Raceway

Monterey, California
1.9-mile, 9 turn road course

AutoRacing/USA 261

Track Profiles/1986

Lime Rock Park
Lime Rock, Connecticut
1.53-mile, 11 turn road course

Long Beach Grand Prix Circuit
Long Beach, California
1.67-mile, 11-turn road course

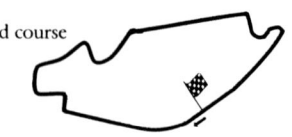

Meadowlands Sports Complex
East Rutherford, New Jersey
1.682-mile, 9-turn road course

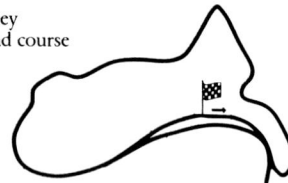

Miami Grand Prix Circuit
Miami, Florida
1.87-mile, 12-turn road course

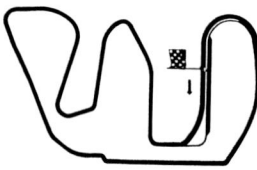

Michigan International Speedway
Brooklyn, Michigan
2.0-mile oval with turns banked
1.9-mile, 9-turn road course

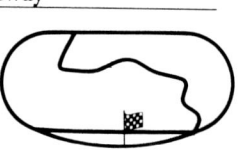

Mid-Ohio Sports Car Course
Lexington, Ohio
2.4-mile, 15 turn road course

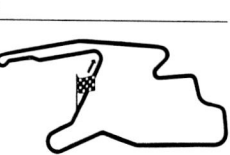

Mosport Park
Durham Region, Ontario, Canada
2.459-mile, 10 turn road course

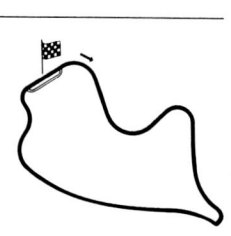

Phoenix International Raceway
Phoenix, Arizona
1.0-mile, semi-banked oval

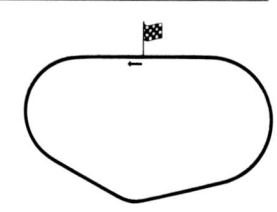

Pocono International Raceway
Long Pond, Pennsylvania
2.5-mile tri-oval with turn 1 banked 16°, turn 2 banked 8°, and turn 3 banked 6°.
2.5-mile, 9 turn road course

Road course runs clock-wise.

Portland International Raceway
Portland, Oregon
1.915-mile, 9 turn road course

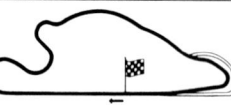

Riverside International Raceway
Riverside, California
2.62/3.3-mile, 9 turn road course

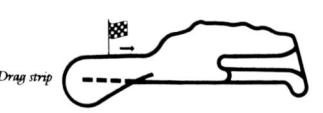

Drag strip

Road America
Elkhart Lake, Wisconsin
4-mile, 11 turn road course

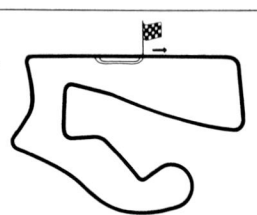

Road Atlanta
Braselton, Georgia
2.52-mile, 12 turn road course

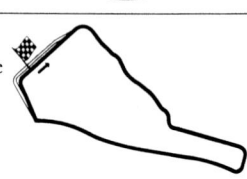

Sanair Super Speedway
Quebec, Canada
1.33-kilometer tri-oval

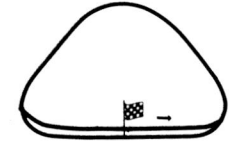

262 AutoRacing/USA

Sears Point International Raceway

Sonoma, California
2.523-mile, 12 turn road course

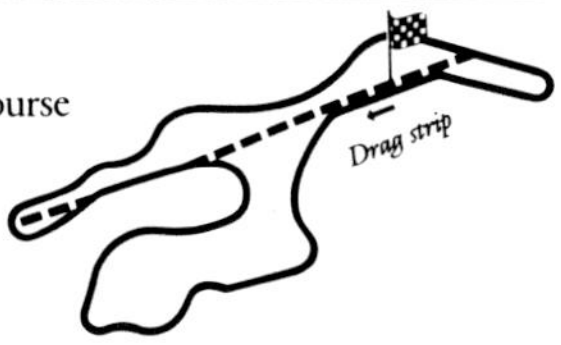

Seattle International Raceway

Kent, Washington
2.25-mile, 10 turn road course

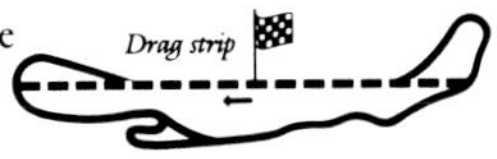

Sebring Airport

Sebring, Florida
4.86-mile, 12-turn road course

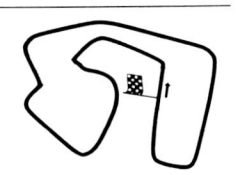

St. Petersburg Grand Prix

St. Petersburg, Florida
2.00-mile, 8 turn road course

Summit Point Raceway

Summit Point, West Virginia
2.0-mile, 10 turn road course

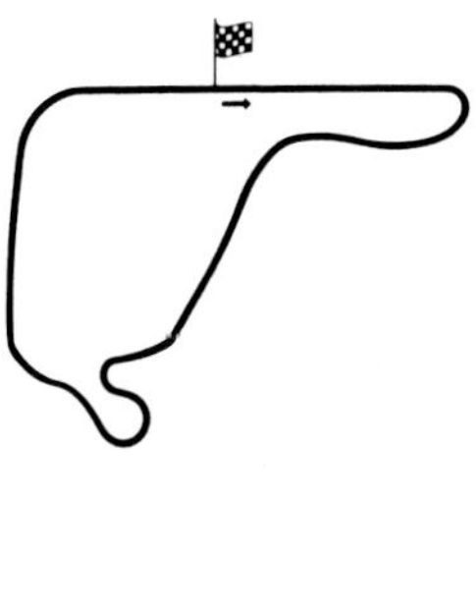

Tamiami Park

Miami, Florida
1.742-mile, 8 turn road course

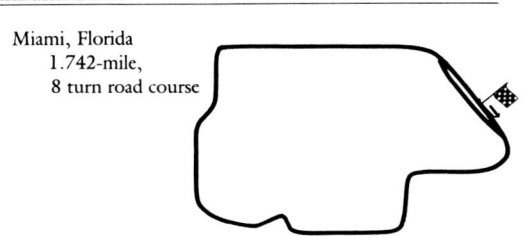

Trois-Rivieres Circuit

Trois-Rivieres, Quebec, Canada
2.1-mile, 15 turn road course

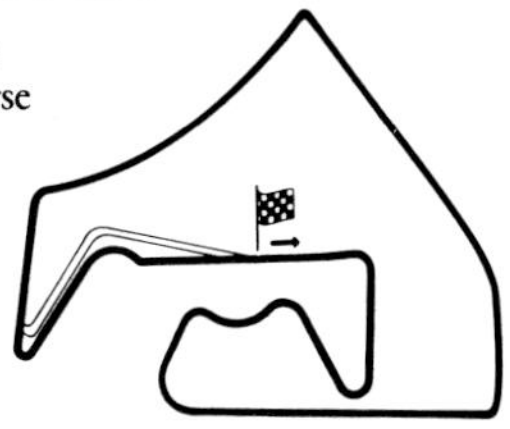

Watkins Glen Grand Prix Circuit

Watkins Glen, New York
3.377-mile, 11-turn road course

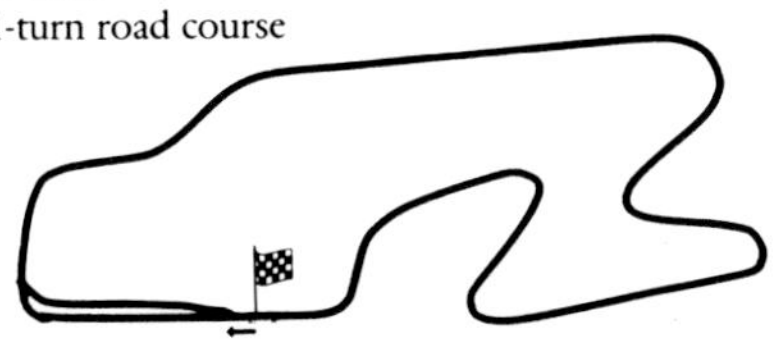

Wisconsin State Fair Park Speedway

Milwaukee, Wisconsin
1.0-mile oval with turns banked 9°

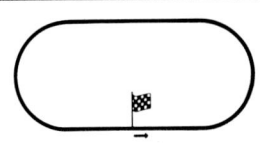

Results Charts

CART/PPG INDY CAR WORLD SERIES

DRIVER	POINTS	PHOENIX INT'L RACEWAY April 6 Q/F	TOYOTA GRAND PRIX OF LONG BEACH April 13 Q/F	WISCONSIN STATE FAIR PARK SPEEDWAY June 8 Q/F	PORTLAND INT'L RACEWAY June 15 Q/F	MEADOWLANDS SPORTS COMPLEX June 29 Q/F	BURKE LAKEFRONT AIRPORT July 6 Q/F	CANADIAN NATIONAL EXHIBITION July 20 Q/F	MICHIGAN INT'L SPEEDWAY August 2 Q/F	POCONO INT'L RACEWAY August 17 Q/F	MID-OHIO SPORTS CAR COURSE August 31 Q/F	SANAIR SUPER SPEEDWAY September 7 Q/F
1. Bobby Rahal	179	9 / 16*	12 / 18*	7 / 6	8 / 20*	7 / 3	10 / 15*	2 / 1	3 / 10*	4 / 14*	4 / 1	3 / 1
2. Michael Andretti	171	2 / 15*	7 / 1	1 / 1	2 / 2	1 / 20*	3 / 2	9 / 19*	6 / 11*	1 / 11*	7 / 10	4 / 6
3. Danny Sullivan	147	6 / 4	1 / 11*	18 / 11	4 / 11*	5 / 1	1 / 1	5 / 2	9 / 25*	9 / 16*	2 / 3	8 / 5
4. Al Unser, Jr.	137	8 / 12	2 / 2	10 / 8	6 / 3	4 / 9	4 / 8	10 / 4	20 / 8	22 / 6	5 / 5	10 / 2
5. Mario Andretti	136	1 / 7	3 / 5	4 / 5	7 / 1	2 / 24*	5 / 3	3 / 3	10 / 21*	3 / 1	1 / 24*	5 / 8
6. Kevin Cogan	115	4 / 1	10 / 17*	8 / 12*	12 / 14*	11 / 21*	8 / 23*	8 / 5	12 / 22*	5 / 2	8 / 4	2 / 4
7. Emerson Fittipaldi	103	5 / 3	4 / 16*	11 / 24*	1 / 12*	9 / 2	2 / 13*	1 / 17*	13 / 20*	11 / 19*	3 / 21*	6 / 3
8. Rick Mears	89	3 / 19*	9 / 20*	5 / 3	9 / 16*	20 / 19*	7 / 4	15 / 8	1 / 12*	6 / 8	11 / 17*	1 / 18*
9. Roberto Guerrero	87	15 / 8	13 / 24*	6 / 18*	3 / 13*	3 / 4	9 / 17*	6 / 20*	4 / 24*	7 / 21*	6 / 2	7 / 17*
10. Tom Sneva	82	14 / 2	15 / 4	3 / 2	16 / 4	12 / 17*	13 / 5	12 / 9*	8 / 18*	29 / 15*	13 / 12*	9 / 13*

Q = Qualifying
F = Finished
* = Not running at the finish

70th INDIANAPOLIS 500

DRIVER	CAR	Q	F
Bobby Rahal	Budweiser TrueSports March 86CC	4	1
Kevin Cogan	7-Eleven March 86CC	6	2
Rick Mears	Pennzoil Z-7 March 86CC	1	3
Roberto Guerrero	True Value/Emerson Elec March 86CC	8	4
Al Unser, Jr.	Domino's Pizza Lola T8600C	9	5
Michael Andretti	Kraco/STP/Lean Machine March 86CC	3	6
Emerson Fittipaldi	Marlboro March 86CC	11	7
Johnny Rutherford	Vermont American March 86CC	12	8
Danny Sullivan	Miller American March 86CC	2	9
Randy Lanier	Arciero March 86CC	13	10
Gary Bettenhausen	Vita Fresh March 86CC	29	11
Geoff Brabham	Valvoline Spirit Lola T8600 C	20	12
Raul Boesel	Coppertop Duracell Lola T8600 C	22	13
Dick Simon	Coppertop Duracell Lola T8600 C	33	14
Arie Luyendyk	MCI — Race for Life Lola T8600 C	19	15*
Pancho Carter	Coors Light Lola T8600 C	14	16*
Ed Pimm	Skola/Pace March 86CC	10	17*
Josele Garza	Schaefer/Machinists March 86CC	17	18
Roberto Moreno	Valvoline Spirit II Lola T8600 C	32	19*
Jacques Villeneuve	Living Well/Ind. Bus March 86CC	15	20*
Chip Ganassi	Bryant/Machinists March 86CC	25	21*
Al Unser	Hertz Penske PC-15 CH	5	22*
Danny Ongais	Goodwrench/Panavision March 86CB	16	23*
A. J. Foyt	Copenhagen/Gilmore March 86CC	21	24*
Rich Vogler	Byrds Kentucky Fried Chicken March 86CC	27	25*
George Snider	Calumet Farms March 86CC	31	26*
Johnny Parsons	Pizza Hut/Machinists March 86CC	28	27*
Tony Bettenhausen	Bettenhausen Racing March 86CC	18	28*
Jim Crawford	Team ASC March 86CB	26	29*
Scott Brayton	Hardee's/Living Well March 86CB	23	30*
Phil Krueger	Squirt/Moran March 85CC	24	31*
Mario Andretti	Newman - Haas Racing Lola T8600 C	30	32*
Tom Sneva	Skoal Bandit March 86CC	7	33*

CART/PPG INDY CAR WORLD SERIES

DRIVER	POINTS	MICHIGAN INT'L SPEEDWAY September 28 Q/F	ROAD AMERICA RACEWAY October 4 Q/F	LAGUNA SECA RACEWAY October 12 Q/F	PHOENIX INT'L RACEWAY October 19 Q/F	TAMIAMI PARK November 9 Q/F
1. Bobby Rahal	179	8 / 1	1 / 5	2 / 1	1 / 3	4 / 8
2. Michael Andretti	171	3 / 2	7 / 2	4 / 3	4 / 1	10 / 18*
3. Danny Sullivan	147	16 / 2	12 / 6	5 / 2	3 / 2	9 / 26*
4. Al Unser, Jr.	137	11 / 21*	9 / 11	11 / 23*	10 / 6	19 / 1
5. Mario Andretti	136	10 / 10*	6 / 9	1 / 4	5 / 4	5 / 11
6. Kevin Cogan	115	14 / 4	4 / 20*	8 / 9	6 / 14*	6 / 4
7. Emerson Fittipaldi	103	7 / 3	5 / 1	9 / 7	7 / 5	8 / 20*
8. Rick Mears	89	1 / 8	8 / 3	3 / 17*	2 / 20*	14 / 3
9. Roberto Guerrero	87	2 / 22*	24 / 4	6 / 5	8 / 16*	1 / 2
10. Tom Sneva	82	9 / 5	12 / 12*	15 / 22*	19 / 18*	13 / 22*

NASCAR BUSCH GRAND NATIONAL

DRIVER	POINTS	DAYTONA INT'L SPEEDWAY February 15 Q/F	NORTH CAROLINA MOTOR SPEEDWAY March 1 Q/F	HICKORY SPEEDWAY March 9 Q/F	MARTINSVILLE SPEEDWAY March 23 Q/F	BRISTOL INT'L RACEWAY April 5 Q/F	DARLINGTON INT'L RACEWAY April 12 Q/F	SOUTH BOSTON SPEEDWAY April 19 Q/F	LANGLEY SPEEDWAY May 3 Q/F	GEORGIA INT'L SPEEDWAY May 10 Q/F	DOVER DOWNS INT'L SPEEDWAY May 17 Q/F	CHARLOTTE MOTOR SPEEDWAY May 24 Q/F
1. Larry Pearson	4551	1 / 41*	3 / 32*	6 / 4	4 / 2	6 / 8	15 / 10	5 / 2	16 / 11	4 / 12	4 / 5	4 / 5
2. Brett Bodine	4531	10 / 23	1 / 24*	3 / 8	1 / 20*	4 / 19*	7 / 3	2 / 8	5 / 10	2 / 6	1 / 3	8 / 2
3. Jack Ingram	4301	31 / 6	2 / 1	2 / 1	18 / 25*	13 / 5	13 / 8	8 / 1	9 / 2	7 / 3	6 / 2	11 / 6
4. Dale Jarrett	4261	11 / 22*	25 / 15	5 / 9	6 / 5	8 / 24*	6 / 20	2 / 1	1 / 5	2 / 7	5 / 4	15 / 37*
5. L. D. Ottinger	4153	8 / 35*	4 / 10	11 / 3	9 / 4	17 / 15	12 / 6	16 / 14	13 / 7	9 / 5	7 / 8	17 / 32*
6. Tommy Houston	4121	15 / 27*	5 / 3	4 / 5	31 / 15	9 / 4	11 / 7	4 / 23*	3 / 1	3 / 25*	8 / 23*	5 / 28*
7. Ronnie Silver	3967	22 / 24*	17 / 18	14 / 1	25 / 23*	24 / 11	29 / 15	17 / 3	17 / 4	12 / 4	16 / 11	33 / 21
8. Jimmy Hensley	3950	39 / 18	14 / 12	10 / 17	13 / 18	31 / 13	14 / 9	7 / 5	6 / 25*	15 / 15	15 / 14	18 / 17
9. Charlie Luck	3847	29 / 10	8 / 8	13 / 7	12 / 14*	32 / 12	28 / 35*	15 / 7	12 / 6	10 / 24	12 / 6	41 / 11
10. Larry Pollard	3726	20 / 13	22 / 17	24 / 18	23 / 16*	28 / 14	32 / 14	20 / 11	10 / 9	11 / 7	11 / 10	34 / 16

NASCAR BUSCH GRAND NATIONAL

DRIVER	POINTS	SOUTH BOSTON SPEEDWAY May 31 Q/F	HICKORY SPEEDWAY June 7 Q/F	ORANGE COUNTY SPEEDWAY June 14 Q/F	INDIANAPOLIS RACEWAY PARK June 21 Q/F	SOUTH BOSTON SPEEDWAY June 28 Q/F	ROAD ATLANTA July 6 Q/F	OXFORD PLAINS SPEEDWAY July 14 Q/F	SOUTH BOSTON SPEEDWAY July 19 Q/F	HICKORY SPEEDWAY July 26 Q/F	LANGLEY SPEEDWAY August 2 Q/F	ORANGE COUNTY SPEEDWAY August 16 Q/F
1. Larry Pearson	4551	2 / 3	6 / 7	4 / 4	16 / 2	7 / 2	6 / 7	36 / 18	6 / 4	9 / 6	7 / 7	17 / 12
2. Brett Bodine	4531	6 / 5	3 / 3	3 / 6	2 / 26*	3 / 22*	1 / 1	7 / 1	2 / 1	5 / 1	2 / 2	12 / 3
3. Jack Ingram	4301	3 / 1	4 / 4	5 / 3	21 / 3	3 / 3	1 / 1	18 / 19	3 / 4	1 / 8	1 / 3	10 / 19*
4. Dale Jarrett	4261	1 / 6	2 / 2	1 / 2	7 / 3	1 / 1	17 / 21*	1 / 40*	1 / 3	5 / 12*	3 / 4	1 / 1
5. L. D. Ottinger	4153	4 / 4	20 / 6	13 / 7	13 / 4	12 / 5	4 / 12	12 / 5	27 / 28*	9 / 24*	2 / 25*	15 / 18*
6. Tommy Houston	4121	7 / 2	1 / 1	2 / 1	1 / 5	4 / 24*	16 / 2	21 / 23*	21 / 8	7 / 18	11 / 26*	1 / 5
7. Ronnie Silver	3967	25 / 14	17 / 5	15 / 22	14 / 5	14 / 8	9 / 20	14 / 18	37 / 16	17 / 6	24 / 8	8 / 20*
8. Jimmy Hensley	3950	13 / 11	12 / 18	11 / 11	25 / 1	6 / 3	15 / 12	26 / 13	13 / 7	7 / 9	10 / 3	11 / 1
9. Charlie Luck	3847	19 / 9	18 / 10	18 / 20	22 / 15	15 / 11	14 / 9	— / —	25 / 17	6 / 17	21 / 19	21 / 5
10. Larry Pollard	3726	9 / 13	8 / 8	19 / 14	11 / 9	21 / 14	13 / 8	— / —	5 / 9	4 / 3	9 / 8	9 / 21*

NASCAR BUSCH GRAND NATIONAL

DRIVER	POINTS	BRISTOL INT'L RACEWAY AUGUST 22 Q F	DARLINGTON INT'L RACEWAY AUGUST 30 Q F	RICHMOND FAIRGROUND RACEWAY SEPTEMBER 6 Q F	DOVER DOWNS INT'L SPEEDWAY SEPTEMBER 13 Q F	MARTINSVILLE SPEEDWAY SEPTEMBER 21 Q F	ORANGE COUNTY SPEEDWAY SEPTEMBER 28 Q F	CHARLOTTE MOTOR SPEEDWAY OCTOBER 4 Q F	NORTH CAROLINA MOTOR SPEEDWAY OCTOBER 18 Q F	MARTINSVILLE SPEEDWAY NOVEMBER 2 Q F
1. Larry Pearson	4551	9 18	6 7	5 4	4 5	5 2	13 1	4 3	2 4	5 2
2. Brett Bodine	4531	1 1	12 3	1 19	7 3	2 4	1 3	3 7	7 5	1 1
3. Jack Ingram	4301	4 25*	7 6	12 9	5 15	— —	— —	9 15	4 31*	7 8
4. Dale Jarrett	4261	18 4	4 17	6 2	2 22*	6 5	4 6	11 12	5 3	4 6
5. L. D. Ottinger	4153	7 27*	5 5	10 8	9 4	11 3	17 17*	5 4	3 24*	6 3
6. Tommy Houston	4121	13 24*	11 9	3 3	3 2	1 1	3 5	7 10	6 10	3 22
7. Ronnie Silver	3967	13 8	19 18	18 5	11 14*	18 13	24 4	29 39*	37 36*	8 14
8. Jimmy Hensley	3950	14 21*	21 12	2 7	17 8	4 6	2 18*	30 19	16 6	2 4
9. Charlie Luck	3847	17 9	18 19	23 13	10 9	14 20*	8 2	41 38*	14 7	11 9
10. Larry Pollard	3726	6 10	26 34*	9 15	8 23*	17 12	22 15	42 21	24 17	24 7

Q = Qualifying
F = Finished
* = Not running at the finish

NASCAR WINSTON CUP

DRIVER	POINTS	DAYTONA INT'L SPEEDWAY FEBRUARY 16 Q F	RICHMOND FAIRGROUND RACEWAY FEBRUARY 23 Q F	NORTH CAROLINA MOTOR SPEEDWAY MARCH 2 Q F	ATLANTA INT'L RACEWAY MARCH 16 Q F	BRISTOL INT'L RACEWAY APRIL 6 Q F	DARLINGTON INT'L RACEWAY APRIL 13 Q F	NORTH WILKESBORO SPEEDWAY APRIL 20 Q F	MARTINSVILLE SPEEDWAY APRIL 27 Q F	ALABAMA INT'L SPEEDWAY MAY 4 Q F	DOVER DOWNS INT'L SPEEDWAY MAY 18 Q F	CHARLOTTE MOTOR SPEEDWAY MAY 25 Q F
1. Dale Earnhardt	4468	4 14*	10 3	5 8	1 2	6 10	4 1	5 1	3 21*	14 2	2 3	3 1
2. Darrell Waltrip	4180	6 3	3 5*	4 5	15 4	7 3	10 2	10 4	2 27*	24 34*	6 5	15 5
3. Tim Richmond	4174	37 20	15 22	2 16	2 7	3 8	2 5	3 12	1 20	12 12	7 32*	2 2
4. Bill Elliott	3844	1 13	9 21	9 7	5 3	12 5	21 8	13 9	9 31*	1 24*	21 7	5 6
5. Ricky Rudd	3823	22 11	8 30*	14 28*	23 26	8 2	8 26*	14 2	4 1	20 36*	1 4	13 8
6. Rusty Wallace	3762	9 8	6 10	20 12	7 8	14 1	13 6	15 10	5 30*	16 13	19 26*	9 10
7. Bobby Allison	3698	3 42*	23 4	6 34*	17 9	10 6	12 3	6 6	11 8	2 1	10 2	18 12
8. Geoff Bodine	3678	2 1	1 8*	3 20*	8 10	1 24*	1 40*	1 3	6 17	3 27	3 1	1 31*
9. Bobby Hilton, Jr.	3546	25 4	4 6	24 39*	41 16	16 28*	18 38*	19 13	23 6	10 4	20 8	22 15
10. Kyle Petty	3537	7 16	12 1	12 11	38 28	17 9	27 9	9 8	12 5	9 31*	12 19	17 20

Q = Qualifying
F = Finished
* = Not running at the finish

NASCAR WINSTON CUP

DRIVER	POINTS	RIVERSIDE INT'L RACEWAY JUNE 1 Q F	POCONO INT'L RACEWAY JUNE 8 Q F	MICHIGAN INT'L SPEEDWAY JUNE 15 Q F	DAYTONA INT'L SPEEDWAY JULY 4 Q F	POCONO INT'L RACEWAY JULY 20 Q F	ALABAMA INT'L MOTOR SPEEDWAY JULY 27 Q F	WATKINS GLEN AUGUST 10 Q F	MICHIGAN INT'L SPEEDWAY AUGUST 17 Q F	BRISTOL INT'L RACEWAY AUGUST 23 Q F	DARLINGTON INT'L RACEWAY AUGUST 31 Q F	RICHMOND FAIRGROUNDS RACEWAY SEPTEMBER 7 Q F
1. Dale Earnhardt	4468	10 5	8 2	11 6	5 27*	10 7	2 26*	10 3	12 5	5 4	21 9	5 2
2. Darrell Waltrip	4180	1 1	9 40*	16 5	23 4	6 4	15 25*	2 2	4 3	10 1	10 5	2 29*
3. Tim Richmond	4174	3 2	3 1	1 15	9 1	5 1	3 2	1 1	2 2	2 6	1 1	4 1
4. Bill Elliott	3844	12 11	11 5	8 8	2 16	4 35*	1 27*	27 4	1 1	9 19	14 3	17 9
5. Ricky Rudd	3823	8 3	14 4	18 10	33 6	13 2	20 3	7 7	18 21	4 23*	15 6	8 24*
6. Rusty Wallace	3762	6 4	7 6	7 19	12 8	11 27*	22 35*	4 6	7 6	12 14	16 23	6 19
7. Bobby Allison	3698	11 7	12 13	5 11	6 15	12 5	21 10*	11 12	8 24	3 8	11 2	10 8
8. Geoff Bodine	3678	2 39*	1 9	4 3	18 29*	2 3	10 23*	8 19	6 4	1 3	2 8	21 13
9. Bobby Hilton, Jr.	3546	23 32*	37 10	12 7	8 3	17 33*	13 1	18 28*	11 13	19 9	6 7	22 10
10. Kyle Petty	3537	16 41*	25 8	31 32*	13 5	23 8	6 9	16 9	22 28*	15 30*	24 14	20 20*

Q = Qualifying
F = Finished
* = Not running at the finish

NASCAR WINSTON CUP

DRIVER	POINTS	DOVER DOWNS INT'L SPEEDWAY SEPTEMBER 14 Q F	MARTINSVILLE SPEEDWAY SEPTEMBER 21 Q F	NORTH WILKESBORO SPEEDWAY SEPTEMBER 28 Q F	CHARLOTTE MOTOR SPEEDWAY OCTOBER 5 Q F	NORTH CAROLINA MOTOR SPEEDWAY OCTOBER 19 Q F	ATLANTA INT'L RACEWAY NOVEMBER 2 Q F	RIVERSIDE INT'L RACEWAY NOVEMBER 16 Q F
1. Dale Earnhardt	4468	3 21	2 12	14 9	3 1	10 6	4 1	8 2
2. Darrell Waltrip	4180	21 14	4 4	4 1	5 9	5 3	9 39*	2 4
3. Tim Richmond	4174	2 26	3 10	1 11	9 1	1 27*	1 20	8 4	1 1
4. Bill Elliott	3844	7 27*	15 11	2 16	6 7	15 7	1 3	5 23*
5. Ricky Rudd	3823	11 1	10 28*	7 7	16 4	4 2	25 25	3 19
6. Rusty Wallace	3762	8 13	8 1	5 4	15 8	7 19	14 13	11 8
7. Bobby Allison	3698	10 20	9 21	16 22*	29 41*	18 25*	21 16	9 7
8. Geoff Bodine	3678	1 28*	1 2	3 2	2 6	2 32*	3 38*	4 3
9. Bobby Hilton, Jr.	3546	12 9	30 17	8 15	27 26	12 11	10 15	18 6
10. Kyle Petty	3537	20 3	7 6	24 14	41 13	17 10	32 7	16 15

Q = Qualifying
F = Finished
* = Not running at the finish

Results Charts

NATIONAL HOT ROD ASSOCIATION 1986 SUMMARY

TOP FUEL	Winternationals Pomona, Calif.	Gatornationals Gainesville, Fla.	Southern Nationals Atlanta, Ga.	Cajun Nationals Baton Rouge, La.	Springnationals Columbus, Ohio	Grandnationals Montreal, Canada	Summernationals Englishtown, N.J.	Mile-High Nationals Denver, Colo.	NorthStar Nationals Brainerd, Minn.	U.S. Nationals Indianapolis, Ind.	Keystone Nationals Reading, Pa.	Chief Nationals Dallas, Tex.	Fallnationals Phoenix, Ariz.	Winston Finals Pomona, Calif.	BONUS RACES	Winston World Championship Points
GARLITS	4	W	3	W	10	3	9	15	W	W	W	2	5	5	W	11,936
GWYNN	W	6	9	15	6	W	W	9	9	2	9	2	2	W	4	11,412
LAHAIE	9	2	7	7	9	2	2	7	2	3	W	8	W	4	3	10,618
AMATO	3	7	5	5	2	5	5	3	12	4	3	9	3	2	2	9,484
KALITTA	2	5	10	9	W	6	7	14	11	16	13	3	12	6	5	7,346
ORMSBY	*	15	8	2	5	15	3	12	14	12	4	6	7	7	8	6,952
PASTORINI	11	4	W	14	3	9	6	11	5	6	7	10	16	12	6	6,950
SNOW	5	9	2	3	8	7	15	16	4	5	12	13	10	16	7	6,906
BECK	7	3	6	4	16	11	4	5	10	7	5	12	—	—	—	6,318
MULDOWNEY	10	13	12	6	*	4		6	3	14	10	11	—	3	—	5,526
MINOR	16	—	—	10	—	—	W	—	15	—	14	2	9			—
EDDIE HILL	*	*	*	16	12	—	10	2	6	11	11	5	8	11	—	—

FUNNY CAR																
BERNSTEIN	3	3	9	9	2	W	W	2	9	3	2	W	W	W	5	12,786
OSWALD	*	5	10	3	W	9	3	W	4	4	W	3	6	3	W	10,510
MEYER	10	6	5	2	5	4	5	6	7	2	15	4	5	2	4	8,712
FORCE	2	7	6	5	3	2	2	7	10	6	9	12	12	14	2	8,200
WEST	7	10	3	4	6	3	7	3	5	5	10	6	3	9	3	8,100
McCULLOCH	9	W	W	14	13	9	14	9	2	8	7	11	4	11	7	7,720
McEWEN	*	2	15	W	4	5	6	10	W	*	13	2	8	*	6	7,496
HEAD	*	14	2	8	9	12	13	—	8	15	11	16	2	7	—	5,932
GROSE	W	15	7	7	11	10	8	12	6	*	4	5	—	*	8	5,865
TUTTLE	14	9	—	—	7	6	9	11	12	11	3	*	*	*	—	4,250
MIKE DUNN	8	—	—	—	—	—	—	—	W	—	13	9	5	—		—

PRO STOCK																
GLIDDEN	16	5	2	8	10	5	3	W	W	W	5	W	W	W	6	12,834
JOHNSON	2	11	W	W	2	9	W	2	9	5	9	2	6	5	5	10,992
ALLEN	5	4	3	5	6	4	4	3	2	2	2	3	3	3	W	10,166
LEAL	4	2	4	2	W	W	9	5	14	6	6	9	7	7	2	9,886
LEPONE	9	12	6	3	3	3	7	7	15	11	11	4	13	13	3	7,034
HARDY	8	7	13	13	8	10	15	9	3	8	10	8	2	*	—	6,474
COONCE	10	9	5	7	12	11	2	10	10	4	11	9	6	8	8	6,336
ECKMAN	6	6	8	10	4	6	11	11	8	13	16	7	14	11	7	6,316
BEVERLEY	—	14	9	16	*	7	10	*	12	3	W	6	5	4	—	6,300
RIVERA	12	3	15	6	11	8	5	8	5	12	15	12	11	*	4	5,914
CAMPANELLO	—	W	*	*	16	*	16	—	7	7	*	—	12	*	—	—
IACONIO	W	10	10	12	7	16	*	14	16	*	*	*	15	15	—	—
HUTCHENS	15	13	*	9	5	2	6	6	13	9	3	—	—	—	—	—
MANCHESTER	—	—	7	—	—	—	—	11	*	—	—	—	—	2	—	—

Legend:
W race winner
* did not qualify
— did not participate

(Positions based on Winston points earned in each event)

INTERNATIONAL HOT ROD ASSOCIATION 1986 SEASON SUMMARY

PRO FUNNY CAR	Winter Nationals Darlington, S.C.	Bayou Nationals Eunice, La.	Pro-Am Nationals Rockingham, N.C.	Winston Spring Nationals Bristol, Tenn.	Gateway Nationals Fairmont City, Ill.	Northern Nationals Milan, Mich.	Summer Nationals Cincinnati, Ohio	Popular Hot Rod Nationals Martin, Mich.	World Nationals Norwalk, Ohio	U.S. Open Rockingham, N.C.	Fall Nationals Bristol, Tenn.	Winston Points
MARK OSWALD	—	W	6	3	W	2	W	2	3	2	W	W	7,366
PAUL SMITH	2	3	W	7	4	6	8	8	4	6	3		5,351
TOM McEWEN	—	6	3	4	2	7	3	4	7	—	7		4,651
ED McCULLOCH	—	2	5	8	3	3	6	—	3	7	5		4,416
KENNY BERNSTEIN	—	—	2	2	—	W	—	W	W	—	—		3,750
STEVE HODKINSON	8	7	4	—	—	—	—	5	3	—			2,866
SCOTT KALITTA	—	4	8	6	—	5	—	5	—	4	—		2,510
DOC HALLADAY	—	—	—	—	—	8	2	—	—	5	6		1,780
TIM GROSE	—	—	—	W	—	4	—	3	—	—	—		1,755
RIC DESCHNER	—	—	—	8	—	—	14	—	—	—			1,691
DALE PAULDE	W	—	—	—	—	—	—	—	—	—	—		—
RAYMOND BEADLE	—	—	—	—	—	—	—	—	—	2	—		—
D. A. SANTUCCI	—	—	—	—	—	—	—	—	—	—	2		—

PRO STOCK												
RICKIE SMITH	4	4	2	3	4	3	2	W	2	W	4	7,706
DARRELL ALDERMAN	W	9	8	2	3	2	4	4	4	4	9	6,981
ROY HILL	3	2	3	8	2	8	5	6	W	2	6	6,821
BOB GLIDDEN	—	W	—	6	W	W	W	8	15	15	W	6,711
BILLY EWING	2	6	6	—	5	6	3	2	16	5	7	5,911
TERRY ADAMS	16	5	5	5	—	10	6	5	9	3	3	4,756
JIM RUTH	12	10	16	7	13	5	8	10	5	9	5	4,711
TIM NABORS	9	12	4	—	14	13	9	7	3	6	16	4,576
BOB OLSON	14	7	—	4	11	12	7	14	6	—	11	3,941
BRUCE ALLEN	—	3	W	W	8	7	—	—	—	8	—	3,705
BUDDY INGERSOLL	—	—	—	—	—	—	—	—	15	12	2	—

Legend:
W race winner
— did not participate

(Positions determined by comparitive elapsed times in round eliminated with the quicker car given the higher finishing position.)

IMSA/CAMEL GTP

DRIVER	POINTS	DAYTONA INT'L SPEEDWAY FEBRUARY 2 Q F	MIAMI GRAND PRIX FEBRUARY 23 Q F	SEBRING INT'L RACEWAY MARCH 22 Q F	ROAD ATLANTA APRIL 6 Q F	RIVERSIDE INT'L RACEWAY APRIL 27 Q F	LAGUNA SECA RACEWAY MAY 4 Q F	CHARLOTTE MOTOR SPEEDWAY MAY 18 Q F	LIME ROCK PARK MAY 26 Q F	MID-OHIO SPORTS CAR COURSE JUNE 8 Q F	WEST PALM BEACH JUNE 22 Q F	WATKINS GLEN JULY 6 Q F
1. Al Holbert	210	8 1	4 6	2 3	2 3	4 28*	2 4	3 18*	5 1	2 1	8 4	4 1
2. Price Cobb	155	2 32*	— —	— —	— —	10 1	5 3	4 1	1 2	4 6	— —	11 4
3. Derek Bell	154	8 1	4 6	2 3	2 3	4 28*	— —	3 18*	13 4	2 1	8 4	4 1
4. Darin Brassfield	121	5 3	17 20*	6 2	9 6	9 2	9 18*	8 5	8 8	9 9	4 2	14 7
5. Chip Robinson	101	9 6	12 22*	9 53*	7 4	11 43*	6 2	— —	3 5	3 2	2 10	2 9
6. Rob Dyson	92	2 32*	— —	— —	— —	10 1	— —	— —	— —	— —	— —	— —
7. Bob Wollek	91	1 52*	3 1	3 69*	— —	6 3	— —	7 21*	6 3	10 4	6 17*	5 50*
8. Bob Akin	89	— —	— —	— —	4 1	6 19*	13 4	— —	2 2	12 6	— —	11 4
9. John Morton	82	— —	— —	— —	6 2	11 5	12 10	— —	8 5	9 18*	11 10	10 5	12 38*
10. Doc Bundy	81	— —	— —	— —	1 1	7 44*	— —	6 4	10 7	8 3	1 1	1 15
Sarel Van der Merwe	81	— —	1 28*	— —	1 1	— —	— —	6 4	10 7	8 3	1 1	1 15
Hurley Haywood	81	12 24*	8 4	8 44*	12 18*	14 47*	6 2	— —	7 26*	12 5	7 3	9 43*

Q = Qualifying
F = Finished
* = Not running at the finish

IMSA/CAMEL GTP

DRIVER	POINTS	PORTLAND INT'L RACEWAY JULY 27 Q F	SEARS POINT INT'L RACEWAY AUGUST 3 Q F	ROAD AMERICA AUGUST 24 Q F	WATKINS GLEN SEPTEMBER 21 Q F	COLUMBUS GRAND PRIX OCTOBER 5 Q F	DAYTONA INT'L SPEEDWAY OCTOBER 26 Q F
1. Al Holbert	210	5 1	8 2	6 1	4 2	— —	4 6
2. Price Cobb	155	17 11	2 1	10 2	13 3	7 4	16 2
3. Derek Bell	154	6 7	8 2	— —	4 2	— —	4 6
4. Darin Brassfield	121	15 12	14 7	12 11	11 25*	4 2	18 3
5. Chip Robinson	101	3 2	9 15*	9 41*	9 14	8 36*	6 1
6. Rob Dyson	92	17 11	2 1	10 2	13 3	7 4	16 2
7. Bob Wollek	91	9 10	1 6	— —	12 1	— —	10 5
8. Bob Akin	89	— —	— —	16 6	5 9	13 9	15 4
9. John Morton	82	14 14	15 17*	12 11	11 25*	14 6	18 3
10. Doc Bundy	81	2 8	12 14*	— —	15 4	2 35*	1 14
Sarel Van der Merwe	81	2 8	12 14*	1 58*	15 4	2 35*	1 14
Hurley Haywood	81	13 9	10 3	11 33*	14 5	9 3	13 25*

Q = Qualifying
F = Finished
* = Not running at the finish

IMSA/CAMEL GTO

DRIVER	POINTS	DAYTONA INT'L SPEEDWAY FEBRUARY 2 Q F	MIAMI GRAND PRIX MARCH 2 Q F	SEBRING INT'L RACEWAY MARCH 22 Q F	ROAD ATLANTA APRIL 5 Q F	RIVERSIDE INT'L RACEWAY APRIL 27 Q F	LAGUNA SECA RACEWAY MAY 4 Q F	CHARLOTTE MOTOR SPEEDWAY MAY 17 Q F	MID-OHIO SPORTS CAR COURSE JUNE 7 Q F	WEST PALM BEACH JUNE 22 Q F	WATKINS GLEN JULY 6 Q F	PORTLAND INT'L RACEWAY JULY 27 Q F
1. Scott Pruett	196	16 2	1 15*	20 1	2 1	19 2	2 1	2 3	1 1	1 1	23 2	6 1
2. Bruce Jenner	175	16 2	4 5	20 1	8 38*	19 2	9 6	2 3	7 2	5 5	23 2	6 1
3. Jack Baldwin	159	46 10*	3 1	12 25*	1 3	16 1	1 29*	1 1	2 3	2 22*	17 1	5 4
4. Dennis Aase	98	21 5	12 22	17 22*	— —	— —	3 2	— —	4 10	3 12*	18 7	3 29*
5. Willy T. Ribbs	92	— —	2 4	— —	— —	— —	— —	— —	— —	— —	16 14*	2 2
6. Craig Carter	70	— —	— —	— —	— —	23 9	6 5*	— —	5 4	4 2	28 11*	— —
7. Chris Cord	60	21 5	— —	17 22*	36 41*	— —	— —	— —	4 10	— —	18 7	4 22*
8. Chet Vincentz	59	— —	21 33*	— —	9 2	— —	— —	6 26*	8 20*	17 4	27 3	— —
9. Tommy Riggins	57	17 7	6 2	15 16*	7 40*	23 9	7 3	3 2	5 4	6 15*	28 11*	— —
10. Kikos Fonseca	46	63 3	— —	47 8*	15 6	33 10*	15 7	— —	— —	7 3	35 6	— —

Q = Qualifying
F = Finished
* = Not running at the finish

IMSA/CAMEL GTO

DRIVER	POINTS	SEARS POINT INT'L RACEWAY AUGUST 3 Q F	ROAD AMERICA AUGUST 24 Q F	LIME ROCK PARK SEPTEMBER 1 Q F	WATKINS GLEN SEPTEMBER 20 Q F	COLUMBUS GRAND PRIX OCTOBER 5 Q F	DAYTONA INT'L SPEEDWAY OCTOBER 26 Q F
1. Scott Pruett	196	1 30*	17 2	5 40*	6 5	1 7	19 1
2. Bruce Jenner	175	6 6	17 2	8 25*	6 5	8 38*	20 3
3. Jack Baldwin	159	4 23*	22 8*	1 1	4 3	4 30*	23 4
4. Dennis Aase	98	3 3	19 1	2 2	1 1	2 37*	24 16*
5. Willy T. Ribbs	92	2 1	20 13*	3 3	2 2	3 1	22 26*
6. Craig Carter	70	— —	— —	7 28*	5 4	6 3	27 23*
7. Chris Cord	60	5 2	18 7*	6 23*	12 36*	7 4	25 2
8. Chet Vincentz	59	— —	26 9*	19 6	10 6	11 9	— —
9. Tommy Riggins	57	— —	25 12*	7 28*	7 8	9 5	— —
10. Kikos Fonseca	46	— —	— —	— —	— —	— —	— —

Q = Qualifying
F = Finished
* = Not running at the finish

Results Charts

IMSA/CAMEL GTU

	DRIVER	POINTS	DAYTONA INT'L SPEEDWAY FEBRUARY 2		MIAMI GRAND PRIX MARCH 2		SEBRING INT'L RACEWAY MARCH 22		ROAD ATLANTA APRIL 5		RIVERSIDE INT'L RACEWAY APRIL 27		LAGUNA SECA RACEWAY MAY 4		CHARLOTTE MOTOR SPEEDWAY MAY 17		MID-OHIO SPORTS CAR COURSE JUNE 7		WEST PALM BEACH JUNE 22		WATKINS GLEN JULY 6		PORTLAND INT'L RACEWAY JULY 27	
			Q	F	Q	F	Q	F	Q	F	Q	F	Q	F	Q	F	Q	F	Q	F	Q	F	Q	F
1.	Tom Kendall	226	48	2	3	4	48	2	17	2	44	5	13	1	13	1	15	15*	3	2	41	2	20	2
2.	Roger Mandeville	219	45	6*	1	2	32	1	18	10	41	1	12	3	15	9*	13	2	1	1	39	1	16	9*
3.	Amos Johnson	155	49	1	5	3	55	12*	21	3	48	4	14	2	20	2	14	3	2	3	43	8	17	11*
4.	Bob Earl	118	—	—	4	1	—	—	16	1	35	8*	11	15*	8	11*	11	1	4	14*	37	7*	24	1
5.	Terry Visger	93	—	—	8	6	—	—	23	12	46	2	16	4	12	3	23	18*	7	18*	37	7*	19	13*
6.	Danny Smith	80	45	6*	—	—	32	1	—	—	41	1	—	—	—	—	—	—	—	—	39	1	—	—
7.	Al Bacon	75	51	4	7	10	53	7*	22	5	47	6	18	5	—	—	—	—	8	4	44	6	26	12*
8.	Bob Reed	73	48	2	2	25*	48	2	24	4	—	—	21	9	—	—	—	—	—	—	41	2	—	—
9.	Helmut Silberberger	52	—	—	—	—	—	—	30	7	—	—	—	—	26	4	20	5	—	—	49	4	—	—
10.	Dick Greer	39	—	—	16	11	—	—	34	14	—	—	—	—	30	6	28	11	17	7	47	3	—	—

Q = Qualifying
F = Finished
* = Not running at the finish

IMSA/CAMEL GTU

	DRIVER	POINTS	SEARS POINT INT'L RACEWAY AUGUST 3		ROAD AMERICA AUGUST 24		LIME ROCK PARK SEPTEMBER 1		WATKINS GLEN SEPTEMBER 20		COLUMBUS GRAND PRIX OCTOBER 5		DAYTONA INT'L SPEEDWAY OCTOBER 25	
			Q	F	Q	F	Q	F	Q	F	Q	F	Q	F
1.	Tom Kendall	226	11	7	51	2	11	1	13	2	—	—	—	—
2.	Roger Mandeville	219	14	19	46	1	13	3	16	1	14	1	2	1
3.	Amos Johnson	155	13	8	52	7	14	2	15	4	16	16	6	21*
4.	Bob Earl	118	10	10	47	8*	12	4	14	3	13	18*	3	18*
5.	Terry Visger	93	15	12	53	10*	22	5	17	16*	20	2	4	2
6.	Danny Smith	80	—	—	46	1	—	—	—	—	—	—	—	—
7.	Al Bacon	75	20	15	50	5	25	14*	21	15*	18	22*	5	4
8.	Bob Reed	73	—	—	50	5	—	—	—	—	—	—	—	—
9.	Helmut Silberberger	52	—	—	54	3	26	7	24	14*	28	7	—	—
10.	Dick Greer	39	—	—	56	4	—	—	29	8	34	10	8	13

Q = Qualifying
F = Finished
* = Not running at the finish

IMSA/CAMEL LIGHT

	DRIVER	POINTS	DAYTONA INT'L SPEEDWAY FEBRUARY 2		MIAMI GRAND PRIX FEBRUARY 23		SEBRING INT'L RACEWAY MARCH 22		ROAD ATLANTA APRIL 6		RIVERSIDE INT'L RACEWAY APRIL 27		LAGUNA SECA RACEWAY MAY 4		CHARLOTTE MOTOR SPEEDWAY MAY 18		LIME ROCK PARK MAY 26		MID-OHIO SPORTS CAR COURSE JUNE 8		WEST PALM BEACH JUNE 22		WATKINS GLEN JULY 6	
			Q	F	Q	F	Q	F	Q	F	Q	F	Q	F	Q	F	Q	F	Q	F	Q	F	Q	F
1.	Jim Downing	189	65	9*	3	3	18	2	17	1	28	1	14	2	12	9*	17	5	17	2	—	—	21	3
2.	Jim Rothbarth	131	31	5*	—	—	25	1	—	—	43	3	15	5	18	2	26	6	22	4	24	3	33	6
3.	Mike Meyer	127	31	5*	—	—	25	1	—	—	43	3	15	5	18	2	26	6	22	4	24	3	33	6
4.	John Maffucci	114	65	9*	—	—	18	2	17	1	28	1	—	—	—	—	—	—	17	2	—	—	21	3
5.	Bob Earl	100	—	—	—	—	—	—	15	7*	—	—	11	1	10	1	14	3	15	13*	13	5	—	—
6.	Howard Katz	85	—	—	—	—	35	4	—	—	—	—	—	—	20	3	22	4	23	5	—	—	29	4
7.	Jeff Kline	77	31	5*	—	—	25	1	—	—	20	5	18	6	22	4	20	9	21	7	18	2	25	11
8.	Don Bell	75	29	6*	2	1	—	—	19	3	22	11*	13	3	—	—	20	9	—	—	18	2	25	11
9.	Mike Brockman	70	26	10*	1	9*	—	—	20	2	25	8*	—	—	—	—	15	2	14	1	—	—	—	—
	Steve Durst	70	26	10*	—	—	—	—	20	2	25	8*	16	10*	—	—	15	2	14	1	16	10*	26	12*

Q = Qualifying
F = Finished
* = Not running at the finish

IMSA/CAMEL LIGHT

	DRIVER	POINTS	PORTLAND INT'L RACEWAY JULY 27		SEARS POINT INT'L RACEWAY AUGUST 3		ROAD AMERICA AUGUST 24		WATKINS GLEN SEPTEMBER 21		COLUMBUS GRAND PRIX OCTOBER 5		DAYTONA INT'L SPEEDWAY OCTOBER 26	
			Q	F	Q	F	Q	F	Q	F	Q	F	Q	F
1.	Jim Downing	189	19	1	17	1	32	4	18	4	32	10*	41	3
2.	Jim Rothbarth	131	21	3	21	3	40	18*	23	6	33	3	42	17*
3.	Mike Meyer	127	21	3	—	—	32	4	23	6	33	3	—	—
4.	John Maffucci	114	—	—	—	—	—	—	18	4	32	10*	41	3
5.	Bob Earl	100	18	4*	16	4	—	—	16	1	19	12*	35	11*
6.	Howard Katz	85	20	2	—	—	35	12*	—	—	33	1	—	—
7.	Jeff Kline	77	—	—	—	—	24	5	—	—	40	4	64	6
8.	Don Bell	75	—	—	—	—	24	5	—	—	26	11*	64	6
9.	Mike Brockman	70	—	—	—	—	31	15*	—	—	23	1	—	—
	Steve Durst	70	—	—	—	—	31	15*	20	16*	23	1	36	16*

Q = Qualifying
F = Finished
* = Not running at the finish

IMSA CHAMPION SPARK PLUG CHALLENGE

		ROAD ATLANTA APRIL 6		RIVERSIDE INT'L RACEWAY APRIL 27		LAGUNA SECA RACEWAY MAY 4		CHARLOTTE MOTOR SPEEDWAY MAY 18		LIME ROCK PARK MAY 26		MID-OHIO SPORTS CAR COURSE JUNE 8		WATKINS GLEN JULY 6		PORTLAND INT'L RACEWAY JULY 27		SEARS POINT INT'L RACEWAY AUGUST 3		ROAD AMERICA AUGUST 24		DAYTONA INT'L SPEEDWAY OCTOBER 26	
DRIVER	POINTS	Q	F	Q	F	Q	F	Q	F	Q	F	Q	F	Q	F	Q	F	Q	F	Q	F	Q	F
1. Doug Peterson	126	7	4	6	5	8	6	9	7	10	3	1	2	4	5	1	1	3	1	3	2	7	5
2. Kal Showket	112	1	1	2	30*	5	9	1	1	7	30*	5	4	5	4	2	26*	4	4	2	1	2	1
3. Tommy Archer	109	5	6	3	4	2	3	2	2	2	1	4	6	1	2	6	4	2	2	1	15	1	19
4. Bobby Archer	101	2	2	1	3	1	4	4	4	1	27*	—	—	2	1	18	31*	1	3	5	3	5	4
5. Amos Johnson	86	3	48*	4	1	6	5	5	43*	3	5	8	3	—	—	8	3	6	6	8	5	3	3
6. Dave Jolly	69	4	3	8	27*	4	1	3	9	8	2	7	5	3	3	7	27*	5	29	7	32*	14	22*
7. Dennis Shaw	62	6	17*	5	2	3	2	6	5	4	29*	6	1	7	7	5	29*	8	18	6	42*	8	46*
8. Phil Currin	61	—	—	—	—	—	—	—	—	5	4	11	8	9	6	4	2	7	9	4	4	6	2
9. Chuck Ulinski	30	18	14	11	32*	10	10	10	45*	6	6	3	7	8	8	9	28*	9	5	9	7	16	7
10. Joe Varde	27	8	5	—	—	7	8	20	3	30	7	15	12	—	—	—	—	—	—	—	—	—	—

Q = Qualifying
F = Finished
* = Not running at the finish

IMSA/KELLY AMERICAN CHALLENGE

		ROAD ATLANTA APRIL 6		CHARLOTTE MOTOR SPEEDWAY MAY 18		LIME ROCK PARK MAY 24		MID-OHIO SPORTS CAR COURSE JUNE 8		MEADOWLANDS GRAND PRIX CIRCUIT JUNE 28		PORTLAND INT'L RACEWAY JULY 26		SEARS POINT INT'L RACEWAY AUGUST 3		ROAD AMERICA AUGUST 23		WATKINS GLEN SEPTEMBER 21		COLUMBUS GRAND PRIX OCTOBER 4		DAYTONA INT'L SPEEDWAY OCTOBER 26	
DRIVER	POINTS	Q	F	Q	F	Q	F	Q	F	Q	F	Q	F	Q	F	Q	F	Q	F	Q	F	Q	F
1. Irv Hoerr	195	2	1	1	1	3	1	1	1	1	1	1	2	1	1	2	1	1	1	1	18*	1	1
2. Patty Moise	110	3	26*	3	2	5	2	2	2	4	4	3	1	4	12	6	2	5	4	6	14	4	4
3. Clay Young	93	5	22*	2	3	1	3	5	30*	2	21	6	4	3	3	3	28*	6	2	14	5	3	3
4. Dick Danielson	87	6	25*	4	6	10	18*	3	3	3	2	2	3	2	2	1	3	2	24*	2	22*	2	2
5. Jerry Thompson	60	7	17*	6	22*	4	5	4	4	5	16*	10	18*	7	5	11	5	8	5	4	3	6	6
6. Robin Dallenbach	41	—	—	14	12	17	11	10	31*	7	19*	8	5	6	19*	5	4	14	22*	3	2	7	5
Steve Clark	41	27	27*	5	4	15	10	9	5	—	—	5	16*	5	6	4	7	4	3	7	23*	5	26
8. Craig Tennant	32	8	4	8	7	8	7	8	7	8	5	4	17*	—	—	9	9	11	25*	—	—	—	—
9. Tommy Riggins	25	2	2	—	—	2	4	—	—	—	—	—	—	—	—	—	—	3	28*	—	—	—	—
10. Mike Ciasulli	23	19	8	9	21*	9	8	33	24	12	8	14	7	9	6	10	18	13	20	5	14	8	10

Q = Qualifying
F = Finished
* = Not running at the finish

SCCA BOSCH/VW SUPER VEE CHAMPIONSHIP

		LONG BEACH GRAND PRIX APRIL 12		INDIANAPOLIS RACEWAY PARK MAY 24		WISCONSIN STATE FAIR PARK JUNE 7		DETROIT GRAND PRIX JUNE 22		MEADOWLANDS GRAND PRIX CIRCUIT JUNE 28		BURKE LAKEFRONT AIRPORT JULY 5		ROAD AMERICA JULY 27		MID-OHIO SPORTS CAR COURSE AUGUST 31		ROAD AMERICA SEPTEMBER 21		LAGUNA SECA RACEWAY OCTOBER 12		PHOENIX INT'L RACEWAY OCTOBER 19		TAMIAMI PARK NOVEMBER 9		ST. PETERSBURG GRAND PRIX NOVEMBER 15	
DRIVER	POINTS	Q	F	Q	F	Q	F	Q	F	Q	F	Q	F	Q	F	Q	F	Q	F	Q	F	Q	F	Q	F	Q	F
1. Didier Theys	155	6	4	6	1	—	—	1	29*	1	1	1	1	3	13	2	8	22	2	1	2	2	23*	1	1	1	1
2. Mike Groff	153	4	2	1	3	4	1	5	8	4	3	3	26	7	29*	7	4	1	1	5	4	1	1	3	2	6	4
3. Steve Bren	132	1	1	2	6	1	2	2	30	3	21*	5	2	1	12	1	1	4	4	2	1	3	3	2	32*	7	16
4. Scott Atchison	122	9	23*	5	8	2	10	4	1	2	2	2	6	4	10	6	4	2	21	9	3	4	6	9	8	10	24*	5	7
5. Cary Bren	93	—	—	—	—	—	—	7	27*	7	24*	7	7	8	2	5	7	3	3	4	5	8	9	4	3	13	6
6. Dave Kudrave	87	11	6	3	20*	dnq	—	3	17*	6	4	4	3	5	3	3	3	2	5	9	27	7	4	7	27*	4	24*
7. Gary Rubio	86	25	27*	7	4	8	6	17	28*	10	14	12	11	4	4	10	6	6	21*	7	7	6	5	8	9	9	8
8. Thomas Knapp	80	15	18	8	7	9	9	9	3	—	—	—	—	2	1	8	24*	5	1	10	21	—	—	14	6	12	27*
9. Dennis Vitolo	77	10	5	10	9	7	7	—	—	13	25*	8	9	6	23*	9	5	8	6	8	5	4	16	9	12	10	9
10. Johnny O'Connell	68	16	30*	4	2	5	3	6	20*	5	20*	2	22*	11	5	6	26*	—	—	—	—	11	12	5	4	8	5

Q = Qualifying
F = Finished
* = Not running at the finish
dnq = Did not qualify
dns = Did not start
dnf = Did not finish

SCCA BENDIX BRAKES TRANS AM CHAMPIONSHIP

		RIVERSIDE INT'L RACEWAY MAY 18		SEARS POINT INT'L RACEWAY JUNE 1		PORTLAND INT'L RACEWAY JUNE 14		DETROIT GRAND PRIX JUNE 21		MID-OHIO SPORTS CAR COURSE JULY 14		BRAINERD INT'L RACEWAY JULY 20		ROAD AMERICA JULY 27		LIME ROCK PARK AUGUST 16		MOSPORT PARK SEPTEMBER 14		SEARS POINT INT'L RACEWAY SEPTEMBER 28		ROAD ATLANTA OCTOBER 12		TAMIAMI PARK NOVEMBER 8		ST. PETERSBURG GRAND PRIX NOVEMBER 15	
DRIVER	POINTS	Q	F	Q	F	Q	F	Q	F	Q	F	Q	F	Q	F	Q	F	Q	F	Q	F	Q	F	Q	F	Q	F
1. Wally Dallenbach, Jr.	166	1	38*	1	1	2	1	2	1	2	32*	4	4	1	2	2	28*	3	2	2	1	1	6	3	3	5	7
2. Pete Halsmer	119	6	2	7	3	1	34*	22	2	4	33*	3	2	4	1	1	23*	1	7	6	20	3	25*	1	25*	1	1
3. Chris Kneifel	112	2	3	5	2	4	3	4	20	7	18*	8	5	14	3	5	5	7	23*	7	19*	9	1	10	38*	4	4
4. Elliott Forbes-Robinson	109	8	35*	3	6	5	4	6	15	3	2	5	20*	5	10	6	2	6	25*	4	4	10	2	5	2	6	12
5. Mike Miller	103	—	—	12	7	15	10	10	6	11	4	11	11	15	5	10	6	12	6	17	26*	16	4	14	9	11	5
6. Greg Pickett	100	—	—	—	—	—	—	5	4	6	1	2	1	3	31*	—	—	—	—	3	2	6	8	8	7	9	15*
7. Les Lindley	97	7	4	8	4	11	5	9	5	23	7	9	6	6	9	9	7	10	14	13	21*	17	10	15	8	15	25
8. Scott Pruitt	94	31	1	2	26*	6	32*	—	—	1	22*	1	9*	—	—	3	3	2	1	1	3	2	28*	2	34*	3	3
9. Jim Miller	92	4	31*	4	5	3	2	3	3	5	34*	7	10	2	26*	4	24*	5	4	5	7	4	3	7	6	28	dns
10. Jim Derhaag	71	9	29*	10	10	8	6	7	22*	8	6	10	7	9	8	15	21	13	9	8	12	15	7	17	15	16	9

Q = Qualifying
F = Finished
* = Not running at the finish
dns = Did not start

AutoRacing/USA 269

Index

Aase, Dennis — 230, 235, 267
Adams, Bubba — 115, 116
Adams, Jim — 226, 227
Adams, Terry — 266
Adcox, Grant — 110, 112, 113
Akin, Bob — 211, 212, 267
Alderman, Darrell — 86, 266
Alexander, Mike — 102, 115
Allen, Bobby — 17, 20
Allen, Bruce — 80, 83, 91, 266
Allison, Bobby — 102, 128, 138, 140, 265
Allison, Davey — 110, 126
Amato, Joe — 68, 69, 266
Anderson, Dick — 114
Andretti, Jeff — 33, 50, 55
Andretti, John — 217, 222
Andretti, Mario — 36, 38, 43, 47, 50, 58, 59, 60, 61, 264
Andretti, Michael — 6, 36, 38, 39, 46, 47, 48, 50, 58, 59, 63, 264
Archer, Bobby — 200, 245
Archer, Tommy — 200, 245, 246
Arciero, Jr, Frank — 252
Armstrong, Dale — 64, 72, 75
Atchison, Scott — 28, 32, 269

Bacon, Al — 268
Baer, Roger — 146
Baker, Buddy — 143, 159
Baker, Kim — 200
Balch, Sherman — 250
Baldwin, Ivan — 161, 163
Baldwin, Jack — 230, 233, 235, 240, 267
Balough, Gary — 102, 109, 114
Barbazza, Fabrizio — 32, 34
Barilla, Paola — 211
Beadle, Raymond — 77, 266
Beck, Gary — 69, 71, 266
Behm, Les — 197, 199
Behm, Mark — 197, 199
Bell, Derek — 200, 208, 210, 211, 267
Bell, Don — 268
Benson, Gary — 197
Bernstein, Kenny — 64, 72, 73, 77, 88, 89, 266
Berrier, Ed — 125
Bettenhausen, Gary — 24
Beverly, Don — 86, 87, 266
Bierschwale, Eddie — 143
Bigley, Jr, Bill — 114
Bishop, John — 208
Blackstock, Roger — 112
Bleil, Larry — 200
Bodine, Brett — 110, 122, 124, 127, 264, 265
Bodine, Geoff — 131, 135, 140, 143, 151, 155, 156, 158, 265
Boesel, Raul — 50
Bonnett, Neil — 135, 140, 150, 155, 156
Bouchard, Ron — 151
Bowley, Ed — 97
Bowley, Tom — 97
Bown, Chuck — 122
Boyce, Walter — 257, 260
Bozony, Jake — 22
Brabham, Geoff — 38, 42, 47
Brandt, Jim — 260
Brassfield, Darin — 267
Bren, Cary — 31, 269

Bren, Steve — 28, 31, 33, 269
Brevak, Bob — 110
Brockman, Mike — 286
Bromme, Bruce — 22
Brooks, Dick — 150
Broomall, Jack — 200
Brown, Darrell — 114
Brunnhoelzl, Jr., George — 94
Buffum, John — 257, 258
Bundy, Doc — 211, 215, 221, 267
Burks, Kenny — 125
Busby, Jim — 226, 227
Butler, Steve — 22, 23

Calabrase, Jack — 26
Campanello, Don — 86, 266
Candies, Paul — 73, 77
Carey, John — 68
Carlye, Doug — 100
Carter, Craig — 267
Carter, Pancho — 50, 119, 121
Caudill, Larry — 117
Childress, Richard — 146, 155
Childs, John — 107
Christensen, Ron — 203, 204
Churchill, Jerry — 102, 105
Ciasulli, Mike — 269
Cicale, Tony — 43
Ciconni, Bob — 26
Clark, Steve — 241, 242, 244, 269
Clinton, Jerry — 186
Cobb, Price — 200, 216, 219, 267
Cogan, Kevin — 7, 38, 43, 52, 63, 120, 121, 264
Combs, Dean — 117
Coniam, Warren — 98
Cookman, Corky — 92
Coonce, Don — 80, 266
Cooper, Ed — 105, 108, 109
Cope, Derrike — 163, 164
Cord, Chris — 35, 267
Cotter, Craig — 234
Cotter, Dan — 63
Coville, C.D. — 101
Coyle, Jim — 110
Craw, Nick — 257
Crawford, John — 255, 257, 259
Curley, Tom — 114

D'Allesandro, Bruce — 94
Dallenbach, Robin — 241, 244, 269
Dallenbach, Wally — 121
Dallenbach, Jr., Wally — 6, 176, 177, 178, 180, 187, 190, 192, 269
Daly, Derek — 120, 121
Danielson, Dick — 241, 242, 243, 269
Davis, Steve — 22
Davis, Jr., Bobby — 17, 18, 20
Derhaag, Jim — 184, 196, 269
Deschner, Ric — 266
DiMarco, Chad — 257
Dilcher, Rick — 180
Dinkel, John — 200
Dobson, Dominic — 38
Dolan, Roger — 115
Donnelly, Glen — 100

Doran, Gregg — 200
Dotter, Bobby — 102, 106, 108
Doty, Brad — 17, 18, 20
Downing, Jim — 228, 229, 236, 268
Dunn, Mike — 266
Durst, Steve — 268
Dus, Peter — 186
Dykstra, Lee — 46, 63
Dyson, Rob — 214, 215, 219, 267

Earl, Bob — 228, 229, 236, 240, 268
Earnhardt, Dale — 6, 122, 128, 129, 130, 132, 133, 135, 136, 137, 138, 139, 140, 142, 143, 146, 147, 154, 155, 265
Eckman, Jerry — 266
Eddy, Mike — 102, 105
Elder, Ray — 161
Ellington, Hoss — 151
Elliott, Bill — 136, 139, 140, 143, 147, 156, 163, 166, 167, 235, 265
Elliott, Dan — 147
Elliott, Ernie — 146
Ellis, Tommy — 148, 149
Erb, Don — 245
Esquerra, Manny — 250, 252
Evans, Gary — 99
Evans, Tim — 200
Evans, Walker — 250
Ewing, Billy — 266

Fair, Harold — 102
Fennig, Jimmy — 107
Fernly, Bob — 51
Fish, Calvin — 170, 172
Fish, Sal — 249
Fittipaldi, Emerson — 47, 56, 59, 264
Fitzgerald, Jim — 184
Fonseca, Kikos — 267
Forbes-Robinson, Elliott — 185, 189, 193, 269
Force, John — 66
Forette, Maynard — 101
Fortner, Tim — 170
Fortune, Damon — 24
Foyt, A.J. — 50, 59, 215
Fuller, Jeff — 94

Galles, Rick — 51
Gant, Harry — 154, 155, 159, 166
Garcia, Ruben — 164
Gardner, Barney — 200
Gardner, Jack — 22
Garlits, Don — 4, 6, 65, 66, 70, 71, 84, 85, 266
Gartner, Jo — 211, 212
Garza, Josele — 38, 50, 51
Gee, Tim — 17, 20
Gelztoff, Vic — 105
Gibson, Gene Lee — 99
Gibson, Mark — 112, 113
Gibson, Todd — 98
Gioia, Steve — 97, 98
Glidden, Billy — 79
Glidden, Bob — 78, 79, 80, 86, 91, 266
Glidden, Rusty — 79

Goodyear, Scott — 170, 171
Gordon, Bob — 252
Gordon, Rob — 6, 252
Gosek, Joe — 97
Green, Barry — 36
Greer, Dick — 268
Gregg, Mike — 26
Grimshaw, Tom — 258
Grissom, Steve — 114
Groenvelt, Aat — 58
Groff, Mike — 28, 31, 33, 269
Grose, Tim — 73, 75, 266
Guerrero, Roberto — 36, 40, 41, 54, 59, 62, 63, 264
Gurney, Dan — 230
Gwynn, Darrell — 6, 64, 66, 67, 70, 71, 266

Haas, Jerry — 79
Hacker, Karl — 197, 248
Hacker, Paul — 197, 246
Hage, Ed — 110
Hagen, Billy — 151
Hagle, Rick — 252
Hall, Rod — 252
Halladay, Doc — 266
Halsmer, Peter — 176, 178, 179, 182, 184, 186, 187, 188, 190, 230, 269
Hannemann, Neil — 200
Hardy, Dempsey — 266
Harmon, Bob — 114
Harris, Trevor — 249
Harsch, Gene — 102
Haudenschild, Jac — 17, 19, 20
Haywood, Hurley — 166, 223, 267
Head, Jim — 266
Hearn, Brett — 100, 101
Hearst, Tom — 115
Heimrath, Jr., Ludwig — 184, 185, 187, 196
Hemmingson, Chuck — 197
Henderson, Bob — 203
Hendrick, Rick — 82, 143, 151
Hensley, Jimmy — 127, 264, 265
Heotzler, Jeff — 100
Heveron, Doug — 92
Hewitt, Jack — 24
Heywood, Jeff — 22
Hill, Roy — 82, 86, 266
Hillin, Jr., Bobby — 139, 140, 150, 265
Hitt, Kerry — 184
Hobbs, David — 218
Hoerr, Irv — 241, 242, 269
Hoffman, Doug — 100, 101
Holbert, Al — 200, 208, 209, 210, 212, 224
Honegger, Pierre — 228
Hood, Rick — 23
Hopkins, Lindsey — 7
Hoppen, Jo — 254
Horne, Steve — 36, 49, 59
Horning, Craig — 203, 204
Horton, Jimmy — 100
House, Tray — 23
Houston, Tommy — 122, 125, 264, 265
Hughes, Leonard — 73, 77
Hutchens, Dave — 266
Hyde, Harry — 143, 151

Iaconio, Frank — 87, 266
Ifft, David — 241
Illien, Mario — 38, 55
Ingersol, Bud — 266
Ingram, Jack — 122, 124, 125, 264, 265
Ingram, Robert — 59, 63, 125
Into, David — 115

Jacks, Bobby — 110, 113
Jarrett, Dale — 122, 264, 265
Jarzombek, Charlie — 92, 96
Jefferson, George — 163
Jefferson, Jerry — 77
Jenkins, Alan — 38
Jenner, Bruce — 230, 232, 267
Johnson, Amos — 236, 240, 246, 268
Johnson, Danny — 100
Johnson, Jack — 100, 101
Johnson, Junior — 135, 140, 147, 151, 152, 153, 155
Johnson, Ken — 28, 32
Johnson, Terry — 98
Johnson, Warren — 79, 80, 82, 86, 91, 266
Jolly, Dave — 246
Jones, Alan — 169
Jones, Alton — 114
Jones, Bubby — 22
Jones, Davy — 33, 217, 222
Jones, Johnny — 236
Jones, Max — 203
Jones, Ralph — 110, 112, 113
Jones, Tom — 102, 104
Judd, John — 63

Kalitta, Connie — 266
Karamesines, Chris — 64
Katz, Howard — 268
Kendall, Tom — 6, 203, 236, 237, 268
Kent, George — 92, 93, 96, 115, 116
Kenyon, Mel — 25
Keselowski, Bob — 113
Kielts, Eric — 207
King, Wayne — 151
Kinser, Bobby — 23
Kinser, Karl — 21
Kinser, Mark — 17, 19
Kinser, Sheldon — 23
Kinser, Steve — 7, 16, 17, 18, 20, 21
Kline, Jeff — 268
Knapp, Thomas — 31, 269
Kneifel, Chris — 178, 179, 180, 189, 190, 269
Knepper, Steve — 26
Kong, Ray — 197
Korman, Ray — 203
Kosiski, Joe — 115, 116
Kraines, Maurice — 36, 41
Kudrave, Dave — 31, 269
Kuhn, Jerry — 184
Kulwicki, Alan — 143

LaFrance, Marcel — 100, 101
LaHaie, Dick — 66, 67, 68, 266
LaHaie, Kim — 67, 68
Labonte, Terry — 128, 130, 134, 140, 148, 149, 151, 154
Ladyman, Alan — 230
Lane, Mal — 100
Lanier, Randy — 62, 63
Larrauri, Oscar — 226, 227
Leal, Butch — 79, 80, 90, 266
Ledel, Howie — 106
Lepone, Jr., Joe — 266
Leven, Bruce — 211, 221, 235
Lewis, Willy — 205, 207
Lindley, Les — 183, 187, 196, 269
Little, Chad — 161, 163, 164
Loring, David — 228
Lott, Walt — 249
Low, Spencer — 250
Luck, Charlie — 122, 127, 264, 265
Ludwig, Klaus — 166, 178, 193, 224
Luyendyk, Arie — 43, 215
Lyons, Kevin — 97

MacInnes, Bruce — 200
Maffucci, John — 229, 268
Mammolito, Joe — 96
Manchester, Ronny — 266
Mancinez, Felix — 233
Mandeville, Roger — 236, 238, 268
Mansell, Nigel — 169
Marcis, Dave — 140
Marlin, Sterling — 151
Martin, Mark — 102, 103, 107
Marvin, Dan — 170, 172
Mash, Richard — 117, 118
Mass, Jochen — 166, 218
Mathewson, Kurt — 197
Maxwell, Dick — 257
Maxwell, Scott — 200
McClain, Denny — 118
McClure, Allen — 94
McCoun, Doug — 115, 116
McCoy, Jack — 161
McCreadie, Bob — 100, 101
McCulloch, Ed — 73, 74, 75, 266
McDuffie, J.D. — 154
McEwen, Tom — 73, 77, 266
McFarlin, Rob — 7
McGinn, Carl — 203
McGriff, Doug — 161
McGriff, Jr., Hershel — 160, 161, 163
McIntosh, Paul — 200
McLaughlin, Mike — 92, 96
McLellan, Mack — 27
McMillin, Mark — 250, 253
Mears, Rick — 36, 38, 43, 45, 46, 47, 50, 54, 58, 59, 63, 120, 121, 166, 264
Mears, Roger — 250, 252
Meyer, Billy — 77, 81, 91, 266
Meyer, Mike — 229, 268
Millen, Rod — 257
Millen, Steve — 35, 249, 251
Miller, Butch — 102, 104, 122
Miller, Jerry — 196
Miller, Jim — 180, 183, 190, 230, 269
Miller, Mike — 182, 190, 269

Miller, Paul — 176
Minor, Larry — 71, 75, 266
Mitchell, Tom — 170
Mizell, Stan — 86
Mockler, Warren — 23, 27
Moise, Patty — 241, 242, 269
Mol, Greg — 107
Moore, Bud — 139, 146
Moore, Eric — 27
Moreno, Roberto — 46, 50
Morgan, Paul — 38
Moroso, Rob — 117, 118
Morrison, Buddy — 80
Morton, John — 214
Muldowney, Shirley — 64, 119, 266
Myhrie, Richard — 207

Nabors, Tim — 266
Nelson, Gary — 135, 144, 145
Newey, Adrian — 36, 46
Newman, Paul — 178, 186, 190, 193
Nierop, Kees — 200
Noffsinger, Brad — 22
Norman, John — 170

O'Brien, Pat — 100
O'Connell, Johnny — 28, 31, 269
O'Neill, Jere — 97, 98, 99
Oag, Alistair — 197, 199
Oatley, Neil — 169
Olson, Bob — 266
Olson, Drake — 200, 219
Ongais, Danny — 119
Ormsby, Gary — 68, 266
Oswald, Mark — 72, 73, 75, 266
Ottinger, L.D. — 122, 125, 127, 264, 265

Paine, Steve — 101
Park, Bob — 94
Parrot, Peter — 47
Parsons, Benny — 154
Parsons, Johnny — 26, 51, 54
Pasteryak, Carl — 94
Pastorini, Dan — 64, 69, 70, 266
Patrick, Pat — 38
Patterson, Jim — 7
Patterson, Kris — 113
Pauch, Bill — 101
Paul, John — 208
Paul, Jr., John — 208
Pawuk, Mark — 86
Pearson, David — 122, 139
Pearson, Larry — 6, 122, 123, 125, 264, 265
Pearson, Terry — 113
Peterson, Doug — 245, 246
Petris, Terry — 163
Petty, Kyle — 135, 138, 140, 150, 265
Petty, Richard — 128, 132, 133, 135, 139, 143
Phillips, Tom — 170
Pickett, Greg — 176, 191, 269
Pimm, Ed — 51
Pobst, Randy — 248

Pollard, Larry — 125, 126, 264, 265
Polverari, Bob — 94
Porter, Randy — 114
Powell, Doug — 21
Powell, Robert — 115, 116
Prappas, Ted — 32, 170, 172
Pressley, Ronnie — 122
Prost, Alain — 169
Provo, Geoff — 200
Prudhomme, Don — 71, 77
Pruett, Scott — 176, 178, 179, 188, 189, 222, 230, 231, 235, 267, 269
Pulde, Dale — 73, 75, 266

Quintanilla, Roberto — 170, 172

Radford, Bob — 257
Radisich, Paul — 28, 31
Ragland, Larry — 250
Rahal, Bobby — 36, 37, 38, 42, 43, 44, 46, 47, 49, 50, 54, 58, 59, 63, 166, 218, 264
Rammage, Don — 99
Ramsay, Jack — 249
Raymond, Lee — 110, 111, 112
Redican, John — 22
Redman, Brian — 120, 223
Reed, Bob — 268
Reese, Ginny — 259
Regester, Bobby — 255
Reher, David — 80
Ribbs, Willy T. — 176, 188, 194, 230, 233, 234, 235, 267
Richardson, Paul — 97
Richmond, Tim — 142, 143, 150, 151, 157, 158, 163, 265
Ridley, Jody — 114
Riggins, Tommy — 184, 195, 241, 242, 267, 269
Riley, Bob — 176, 188
Rivera, Gordie — 266
Robbins, Rex — 114
Robinson, Chip — 215, 221, 222, 267
Robinson, Jim — 160, 163
Roos, Bertil — 32
Roper, Dean — 113
Rose, Howard — 110
Ross, Brian — 92, 95
Rossi, Paul — 203
Rothbarth, Jim — 229, 268
Roush, Jack — 176, 179, 180
Rubio, Gary — 31, 269
Rudd, Ricky — 135, 139, 140, 235, 265
Rude, Kathy — 119, 120
Rudolph, Charlie — 100
Ruggiero, Reggie — 92, 95, 96
Ruth, Jim — 266
Rutherford, Johnny — 36, 42, 47
Ruttman, Joe — 135, 154, 155, 159

Sacks, Greg — 92, 96
Salerno, Al — 197, 198
Samples, Jr., Jesse — 117
Sanborn, Jim — 184
Santucci, D.A. — 266
Sawyer, Elton — 125
Schacht, Bob — 110, 113

AutoRacing/USA 271

Index

Schmitt, Bill — *162, 163*
Schneider, John — *189, 193*
Schroder, Dorsey — *203*
Schulz, Karen — *117*
Senna, Ayrton — *168*
Senneker, Bob — *102, 104*
Shaw, Dennis — *246*
Shea, Rick — *170*
Shepherd, Doug — *257, 259*
Shepherd, Morgan — *122, 140*
Shierson, Doug — *54*
Showket, Kal — *245, 246, 248*
Shullick, Dave — *99*
Shuman, Ron — *17, 18*
Silberberger, Helmut — *268*
Sills, Jimmy — *17, 19*
Silver, Ronnie — *122, 264, 265*
Simko, Dave — *113*
Smith, Clive — *257*
Smith, Danny — *268*
Smith, Paul — *73, 74, 266*
Smith, Rickie — *80, 82, 266*
Sneva, Tom — *42, 46, 50, 264*
Snow, Gene — *266*
Sosebee, David — *110*
Spencer, Jimmy — *92, 93, 94*
Sprague, Chuck — *39*
Sprow, Bob — *43*
St. Amant, Gary — *102*
St. James, Lynn — *215*
Stacy, J.D. — *241*
Stauffer, Kent — *102*
Stefanik, Mike — *94*
Steurer, Glen — *163*
Stewart, Ivan — *250, 251*
Stott, Ramo — *113*
Stovall, Jim — *113*
Stovall, Scott — *110, 113*
Strait, Bob — *110*
Stricklin, Hut — *117, 118*
Stuck, Hans — *166, 211, 212*
Sullivan, Danny — *36, 38, 39, 46, 47, 54, 58, 59, 215, 265*
Swain, Mike — *117, 118*
Sweeney, Mike — *22, 23*
Swindell, Jeff — *17, 19, 20*
Swindell, Sammy — *17, 19, 20, 59*

Teague, Brad — *127*
Tennant, Craig — *269*
Tetrick, Steve — *252*
Theys, Didier — *28, 29, 30, 269*
Thompson, Dave — *257*
Thompson, Jerry — *269*
Thompson, Mickey — *249*
Timbrook, Willy — *200*
Tomaino, Jamie — *92, 95*
Treichler, Roger — *94*
Tremont, Kenny — *100, 101*
Trickle, Dick — *102, 104, 105*
Trueman, Jim — *7, 35, 36, 42, 43, 49*
Tullius, Bob — *221, 222*
Tuttle — *266*

Ullom, Garth — *200*
Ulmann, Alec — *7*

Unser, Al — *36, 38, 49, 166*
Unser, Jr., Al — *6, 36, 38, 42, 50, 51, 58, 61, 63, 166, 167, 208, 210, 264*
Unser, Bobby — *207, 254*
Unser, Robby — *207*
Urlin, Russ — *102, 107*

Vahsholtz, Leonard — *255*
Van der Merwe, Sarel — *211, 215, 221, 267*
Venturini, Bill — *110, 111, 112, 113*
Villeneuve, Jacques — *59*
Vincentz, Chet — *267*
Visger, Terry — *236, 240, 268*
Vitolo, Dennis — *31, 269*
Vogler, Rich — *23, 25*

Wallace, Kenny — *102, 105, 107*
Wallace, Rusty — *102, 114, 140, 156, 265*
Waltrip, Darrell — *122, 128, 135, 136, 137, 138, 139, 140, 143, 146, 147, 151, 155, 163, 166, 265*
Waltrip, Mike — *117, 143*
Warren, Bentley — *97, 98*
Watson, John — *218*
West — *266*
Wetmore, Donnie — *100*
Wheeler, Humpy — *128*
White, Lee — *176*
Whittington, Bill — *208*
Whittington, Don — *208*
Wietzes, Eppie — *196*
Willingham, Haskell — *125*
Wilson, Rick — *143*
Wilson, Waddell — *151*
Wirth, Eddie — *22, 23*
Wolfgang, Doug — *17, 19, 20*
Wolin, Dave — *200*
Wollek, Bob — *211, 216, 222, 267*
Wood, Leonard — *150*
Woodner, Jon — *257*
Wright, Mitch — *200*

Yarborough, Cale — *128, 139, 166*
Young, Clay — *241, 242, 269*